D0782280

POLICING THE WORLD

POLICING THE WORLD

Interpol and the Politics of International Police Co-operation

MALCOLM ANDERSON

CLARENDON PRESS · OXFORD
1989

Oxford University Press, Walton Street, Oxford OX2 6DP
Oxford New York Toronto
Delhi Bombay Calcutta Madras Karachi
Petaling Jaya Singapore Hong Kong Tokyo
Nairobi Dar es Salaam Cape Town
Melbourne Auckland
and associated companies in
Berlin Ibadan

Oxford is a trade mark of Oxford University Press

Published in the United States
by Oxford University Press, New York

© Malcolm Anderson 1989

All rights reserved. No part of this publication may be reproduced,
stored in a retrieval system, or transmitted, in any form or by any means,
electronic, mechanical, photocopying, recording, or otherwise, without
the prior permission of Oxford University Press

British Library Cataloguing in Publication Data
Anderson, Malcolm
Policing the world: Interpol and the politics of
international police co-operation.
1. International Criminal Police Organisation
I. Title
364.1'35
ISBN 0–19–827597–8

Library of Congress Cataloging in Publication Data
Anderson, Malcolm.
Policing the world: Interpol and the politics of international
police co-operation / by Malcolm Anderson
Bibliography: p. Includes index.
1. International Criminal Police Organization. 2. Law
enforcement—International cooperation. 3. Law enforcement–
Political aspects. I. Title.
HV7240.I25A58 1989   363.2'06'01—dc20   89–3318
ISBN 0–19–827597–8

Typeset by Cambrian Typesetters, Frimley, Surrey

Printed in Great Britain by
Courier International Ltd.
Tiptree, Essex

HV
7240
.I25
A58
1989

OCT 1 2 1989

CONTENTS

LIST OF FIGURES

ACKNOWLEDGEMENTS

MY grateful thanks are due to the Trustees of the Nuffield Foundation for granting me a research fellowship, to the Woodrow Wilson International Center for Scholars, Washington, DC, for giving me, at very short notice, hospitality and support as a visiting scholar, to the Fondation Nationale des Sciences Politiques, Paris, for giving me the status of research associate and allowing me the use of the facilities of the Foundation. The research for this book could not have been completed without the generous support provided by these institutions.

I owe the most profound individual debt to Mr Raymond Kendall, Secretary General of Interpol, whose willingness to give time to an inquisitive scholar and to encourage other law-enforcement officers to do the same provided an indispensable basis for this book. I hope that his policy of increased openness in the affairs of Interpol will not lead others to strain the resources of the organization and the patience of its officials. Retired Secretaries General André Bossard and Jean Nepote, and Presidents of Interpol Carl Persson and John Simpson, have been generous with their time. A selection of present and retired directors of divisions and subdivisions within Interpol Headquarters have also patiently answered my questions. My thanks are also due to officials of eight National Central Bureaus of Interpol and of national police forces of Austria, France, the Netherlands, Spain, and Sweden, of the Saarland Police department and the German Federal Criminal Office, the regional directorate of the Police Judiciaire of Strasbourg, Scotland Yard, the US Departments of Justice and Commerce, US Customs, the Federal Bureau of Investigation, the Immigration and Naturalization Service, the Drug Enforcement Administration, the Secret Service, the European Community, and Council of Europe, the UN Division of Narcotic Drugs, and the UN Fund for Drug Abuse Control.

Many others have helped me with this study. In particular, I would like to thank Serge Hurtig and Pierre Birnbaum for their friendly and valued support, and my colleagues in the University of Edinburgh, Mary Buckley, Nigel Bowles, Richard Gunn, Desmond King, and Jeremy Waldron, for providing an environment of intellectual curiosity and stimulation. Also in the University of Edinburgh, Mona Bennett has been a model of patience and efficiency in typing the manuscripts.

Desmond King, Cyrille Fijnaut, and Neil Walker have read the whole manuscript; Mary Buckley and Neil MacCormick have read parts of the manuscript. They have saved me from many errors and infelicities. Those which remain are entirely my own responsibility.

M.A.

Edinburgh
September 1988

ABBREVIATIONS

ASEAN	Association of South East Asian Nations
BKA	Bundeskriminalamt
BVD	Binnelandse Veiligheids Dienst
CCC	Customs Co-operation Council
CIA	Central Intelligence Agency
CNIL	Commission Nationale de l'Informatique et des Libertés
COCOM	Co-ordinating Committee for Export Controls
DEA	Drug Enforcement Administration
DGSE	Direction Générale de la Securité Extérieure
DST	Direction de la Surveillance du Territoire
ECOSOC	Economic and Social Council of the United Nations
EPC	European Political Co-operation
EPIC	El Paso Information Center
FANC	Foreign Anti-Narcotics Community
FBI	Federal Bureau of Investigation
FLETC	Federal Law Enforcement Training Center
FOPAC	Financial Operations, Profits, and Assets of Crime
GAL	Grupo Anti-terroriste de Liberación
GAO	General Accounting Office
GIGN	Groupement d'Intervention de la Gendarmerie Nationale
G7	Group of Seven
HONLEA	Heads of Narcotic Law Enforcement Agencies
IATA	International Air Transport Association
ICAO	International Civil Aviation Organization
ICPC	International Criminal Police Commission
ICPO–Interpol	International Criminal Police Organization–Interpol
IDEC	International Drug Enforcement Conference
IIP	Institut International de Police
ILO	International Labour Office
INS	Immigration and Naturalization Service
MCRAP	Mouvement contre le Racisme et pour L'Amitié entre les Peuples

NCB	National Central Bureau
NCIC	National Crime Information Center
PACTE	Programmed Action Cocaine Traffic Europe
QUEST	*Quarterly Enforcement and Statistical Review*
RAID	Service de Recherche d'Assistance, d'Intervention et de Dissuasion
RCMP	Royal Canadian Mounted Police
RG	Renseignements Généraux
RUC	Royal Ulster Constabulary
SEPAT	Stupéfiants Europe Plan d'Action à Terme
SFIP	Special Field Intelligence Programs
SIS	Strategic Intelligence System
STCIP	Service Technique de Coopération Internationale de Police
SWAP	South West Asia Programme
TCCE	Technical Committee for Co-operation
TECS	Treasury Enforcement Computer System
UCLAT	Unité de Coordination pour la Lutte Anti-Terroriste
UNDND	United Nations Division of Narcotic Drugs
UNFDAC	United Nations Fund for Drug Abuse Control

Introduction

IT has become a commonplace that state boundaries do not delimit autonomous independent societies. Activities on the territories of states are increasingly open to external influences, and even to external control, and many agencies of government cannot perform their functions adequately without close international co-operation. But the police function has different implications from, for example, economic management: police and crime control have appeared the expression of state sovereignty in its pure form. To what extent does this remain true?

In the last two decades, awareness that the issues of policing and of crime control are international, as well as national and local, has increased as a result of the impact of international terrorism, drug trafficking, and the internationalization of social and economic activities. The implications of the international component of policing are far-reaching; they are not widely understood because of the complexity of the issues relating to them. These issues are briefly mentioned in this introduction: proliferation of different forms of co-operation, uncertainty about the limits of state sovereignty, varying influences of police training, different understandings of police functions, the shadowy role of the security services, and divergent expectations about the outcomes of international police co-operation. Aspects of these issues are discussed further in Chapter 1; they often affect the relatively humdrum detail of international police co-operation and have to be borne in mind when considering the more specific matters discussed in Chapters 2 to 8 of this book.

Police co-operation has a variety of forms—the exchange of intelligence about crimes and criminals, joint or co-ordinated surveillance of suspects, investigation of crimes, as well as provision of training facilities and exchange of information about police techniques. These activities take place on a multilateral and bilateral basis and at the global, regional, and local levels.

The International Criminal Police Organization–Interpol (ICPO–Interpol) is the oldest in existence and the most important instrument of multilateral police co-operation and, with (in 1988) 146 countries participating, it has almost universal membership. Interpol's present Statutes date from 1956, although its predecessor organization, the International Criminal Police Commission (ICPC), was established in Vienna in 1923. Interpol has many of the same features as other international organizations. It has a President—a senior law-enforcement official in his own country, who does not always have time to play an active role in the organization—and three Vice-Presidents, who help the President by chairing various committees of Interpol. They are all elected for four-year terms of office by an annual General Assembly in which each member country has one vote. They are assisted in the running of the organization by a broadly based Executive Committee. The Secretary General, the exective head of Interpol, is also elected by the General Assembly; he heads an international General Secretariat, which is based at Saint-Cloud just outside Paris but which is due to move to Lyons in 1989. The main function of the General Secretariat is to manage a global telecommunication system for conveying information about suspects, criminals, and criminal activity. This information comes from National Central Bureau (NCBs), established in each member country for this purpose: the organization of the NCBs varies considerably and is entirely a matter for the countries concerned. Although most of Interpol's activities are matters of routine, the organization has been adapting rapidly to new circumstances in the 1980s.

The United Nations, which has an even wider membership than Interpol, has interests in law enforcement and crime prevention. It has been particularly active in efforts to control traffic in narcotic and psychotropic drugs. The United Nations Commission on Narcotic Drugs, established in 1946, has considered the changing nature of these problems and, under the direction of the Economic and Social Council (ECOSOC), has promoted international agreements for control of drug trafficking; the United Nations Division of Narcotic Drugs (UNDND) acts as a permanent secretariat but also promotes studies and research, and sponsors meetings such as that of the Heads of Narcotic Law Enforcement Agencies (HONLEA). Several other UN agencies in various fields such as human rights, health, treatment of prisoners, and migrant workers have tangential interests in law enforcement. The UN family of institutions are mainly forum organizations for debate, exchange of information, and the preparation of international treaties, but some deliver services: none of the service-delivery UN institutions is directly involved in police operations.

At the regional level, the Council of Europe sponsors meetings similar to those of the United Nations on crime problems and crime prevention. The European Group to Combat Drug Abuse and Illicit Traffic in Drugs, usually known as the Pompidou Group because founded on the proposal of the former French President, is one such forum. This is a consultative group which attempts to establish common approaches to problems through meetings of ministers and officials, rather than of law-enforcement officers. The Pompidou Group has been overshadowed by an important development in the European Community: at a European ministerial meeting in 1975, James Callaghan, the British Foreign Secretary, proposed setting up a loose inter-governmental structure (called the Trevi Group after the famous fountain in Rome) to co-ordinate the fight against terrorism. This group meets under the auspices of European Political Co-operation (EPC) at the ministerial and official level. As in the European Community Council of Ministers, the chair rotates every six months; the inconvenience of this arrangement is mitigated by the 'troika' of the past, present, and future occupants of the chair co-operating to arrange the business of the Group and, at a Brussels meeting of the Trevi Group in 1987, a proposal was accepted to establish a light administrative structure to assist continuity in the handling of business. The Trevi Group succeeded, slowly and with some difficulty, in establishing a secure communications system for sensitive information about terrorism between the governments of the member states. The Group extended its interests, and the committee dealing with terrorism became known as Trevi 1, whilst Trevi 2 was concerned with the exchange of information about police methods and techniques, and Trevi 3 was concerned with serious crime other than terrorism. The Trevi Group has the potential to develop into a comprehensive European police co-ordinating mechanism, which may become necessary after the abolishing of frontier controls within the European Community in 1922. Whether either the former or the latter occurs, remain open questions.

Regional organizations in other parts of the world, such as the Association of South East Asian Nations (ASEAN), co-operate in law enforcement but the most intensive form of co-operation on case-related matters takes place at the bilateral level. There has been an enormous increase in international crime and this has stimulated direct police-force-to-police-force contacts. The United States has taken the lead in this sort of co-operation and federal law-enforcement agencies such as the Federal Bureau of Investigation (FBI), the Drug Enforcement Administration (DEA), and US Customs now maintain permanent representatives in many countries. Canada and Japan have also adopted the practice of posting police officers as embassy attachés. The main European countries do not generally use diplomatic representation in this way but France, the United Kingdom, West Germany, and Italy are now sending police officers abroad on a regular basis, usually as liaison officers to counter drug trafficking. Terrorism and other forms of serious crime also encourage this trend. There is no general international agreement regulating the posting of police officers in other countries; it is based on a variety of formal treaties or treaty-like agreements and informal arrangements.

Contact between police forces of different states is always a delicate matter because it touches on sensitivities concerning sovereignty and the territorial principle. Indeed, the police and criminal justice may be regarded as the last bastion of the doctrine of sovereignty—the absolute control by the state in its territory, untrammelled by external agencies, except for reasons of self-interest. But there are signs that the first breaches in this bastion are appearing because of increasing economic interdependence and the internationalization of society. Important forms of crime cannot be controlled within state boundaries. Nevertheless, very different views of police functions and of the role which the police perform in society remain, despite the awareness in a wide range of countries of shared problems. In addition, the connection between social conditions, patterns of criminality, and the evolution of official and public attitudes towards crime are matters of vigorous dispute and involve issues about which there are no well-established truths. This means that there are inevitably opposing views on how and why police should co-operate across international frontiers. Strongly held opinions in government and public opinion about both the causes and the relative importance of certain types of crime influence police behaviour, even though the police often have, in professional matters, considerable independence from direct political control. These opinions affect international police co-operation because public and governmental pressure has encouraged development of co-operation on certain issues, such as drugs and terrorism, and not on others, such as environmental policing and traffic in women.

A powerful influence on police co-operation is the effect of the growing internationalization of society on police education and training. All professions have been increasingly exposed to the international environment in recent years and, to varying degrees, have taken this into account in their training programmes; the police are no exception. In addition, the former imperial powers Britain and France and, since its emergence as a superpower, the United States have played important roles in training police of other countries. West Germany also provides assistance in training and aims at setting up an international police academy. The Spanish police academy at Avila is now attracting more international interest, particularly from Latin America, after the 1986 reforms of the Policia Nacional. Interpol has pioneered genuinely international police training courses and some of its NCBs are making national police forces aware, through lectures and videos, of the international dimension of policing. These and similar activities will almost certainly expand in future because an increased educational effort is necessary to ensure good international co-operation. The way in which the police are educated affects the tone and quality of co-operation.

The implications of international police co-operation are not always understood in identical ways because there is no general agreement between countries about the boundary between police and administrative functions: the police are defined differently in different countries. For example, in some countries, the customs service is regarded as a police function and in others as an administrative function. The most difficult borderline case is state security, because of the various forms of organization of security services. Agencies with police powers are always involved, to some degree, in internal security, almost never with intelligence work and operations abroad. The classic example of a police agency with responsibility for counter-espionage is the US FBI; another is the Direction de la Surveillance du Territoire (DST) in the French Police Nationale. In Britain and West Germany, responsibility for internal security is divided between a security service and the police.

A serious analysis of the various roles of the security services is difficult in a study of this sort. Some of the agencies involved in state security live in a highly charged political atmosphere. On the one hand, their role, utility, and very existence are questioned by civil libertarians and by various sceptics. On the other, they are highly valued by governments when there are overt threats to state security, either from foreign powers or from internal subversion. There is a considerable volume of literature on them, responding to a public appetite for accounts of spying and treason; most of it is of dubious quality and difficult to assess.[1] Their connections with other forms of policing have been tenuous, sporadic, and often antagonistic. They can, however, contribute to the souring of international relations, sometimes in a slightly ludicrous way, as, for example, when the French security services placed a bomb in the gardens of the French embassy during a visit of President Mitterrand to London in order to 'test' the efficiency of British security. Relatively little attention is given to the security police and security services in this study because the focus of the book is on co-operation for criminal investigation purposes resulting in prosecution before the courts: the vast majority of such cases have little or no security implications. But the security services, directly and indirectly, have a pivotal role in police relations and it is impossible to draw a clear line between issues of criminality and state security. A fully comprehensive treatment of police co-operation would have to include a careful analysis of co-operation between security services, but the unreliability of current information makes this impractical.

Defining the police is also made difficult by the sometimes hazy borderline between military and police forces. Generalizations in this area are hazardous but Italy with the Carabinieri, Spain with the Guardia Civil, France with the Gendarmerie Nationale, and West Germany with the Border Police all have militarized police forces. These have no direct parallels in the Anglo-American tradition, although the Royal Ulster Constabulary in the United Kingdom and the National Guard in the United States share some common features with them. Militarized police forces, because of their roles in ordinary policing and, more particularly, in counter-terrorism, are associated with international co-operation but are usually not directly involved in the regular channels of co-operation such as Interpol, generally regarded as a civil police preserve. Even more troublesome in the quest for a universal definition of the police are the states with a *Polizeistaat* tradition, such as Germany and Austria, where the notion of police is intertwined with all acts of administrative authority by the state. The differences in definitions of the police and in police organization reflect the diversity of state traditions which have

---

[1] Only the CIA is well documented, partly as a result of the 1976 US Senate Hearings (the Church committee); the vast amount of information available is put to good use in J. Ranelagh, *The Agency: The Rise and Decline of the CIA* (London, 1986).

created a variety of expectations about the exercise of public authority in general and of police authority in particular.

The definition of the police adopted in this book is too narrow to accommodate the *Polizeistaat* tradition and too broad for most countries in the English-speaking world. This definition is—all those civilian agencies possessing powers of arrest, charged with protecting the constitutionally established authorities, maintaining public order, and investigating criminal offences. This definition excludes those civilian security services responsible for counter-espionage and investigating internal subversion which do not possess powers of arrest; for example, in the United Kingdom MI5 cannot make arrests and the Special Branch has to be called in when a case becomes a matter for the courts. This is not a wholly defensible boundary for the subject because a particular issue which involves agencies such as MI5—international terrorism—has been a crucial factor in putting international police co-operation on the political agenda. Also the largest intelligence agency in the non-communist world, the Central Intelligence Agency (CIA), was instructed by President Reagan to use its resources to combat drug trafficking, the other great stimulus to international police co-operation.

International co-operation, for the police forces involved in it, is essentially about practical matters—how to conduct investigations and to make arrests in societies which are increasingly penetrated from the outside and open to international influences. In the middle ground, governments are faced by pressures, sometimes conflicting, from the law-enforcement community over ways to adopt to changing circumstances, and from public opinion outraged, often for relatively short periods, by terrorist actions or the prevalence of crime related to drug abuse. These pressures impose difficult policy choices on governments concerning the kind of international agreements to be sought and the institutions of co-operation to be supported or created. The policy-makers have to take account of the practical law-enforcement issues as well as the general expectations of citizens about the purposes and functions of the state. Both the issues and the expectations vary from country to country, although there is emerging an ever greater agreement about them in the highly industrialized democracies.

These highly industrialized democracies—the countries of the European Community, the United States, Canada, Japan, and the Scandinavian countries—have most influence on the evolving system of police co-operation. Public and official opinion in these countries is deeply concerned about crime; they also have strong police and criminal justice systems. The USSR and the majority of East European countries are not members of Interpol and are rarely involved in co-operation; drug trafficking and the theft of religious art is, however, drawing them more into the system. Developing countries, especially those whose territories are used for the growing, manufacture, or transit of drugs, are heavily involved in the system. Their governments and law-enforcement agencies often have views on the way co-operation should develop but they do not carry great weight because of lack of political influence and professional expertise.

The field of international police co-operation is one in which few can make a claim to genuine competence and authority. Very little has been written about it. Tribute must be paid to a recent book, part polemic and part history, by Laurent Greilsamer on Interpol. It is a useful introduction to the subject by a journalist on *Le Monde*.[2] The work of Professor Fijnaut, particularly his paper on the internationalization of investigation in western Europe, is important because he identifies the tendencies towards operational co-operation which go beyond the circulation of police information.[3] Claude Valleix has published a rigorous analysis of the juridical basis of Interpol.[4] There is an American legal literature relating to cases which have come before US courts involving Interpol.[5] Otherwise, publications are scant, consisting of lectures, articles in the Press and the police journals, and popular books on Interpol. The majority of them have little to offer the scholar or policy-maker.[6]

[2] L. Greilsamer, *Interpol: Le Siège du soupçon* (Paris, 1986).

[3] C. Fijnaut, 'The Internationalization of Criminal Investigation in Europe', in C. Fijnaut and R. H. Hermans (eds.), *Police Cooperation in Europe* (Lochem, 1987).

[4] C. Valleix, 'Interpol', *Revue générale de droit international public*, 3 (1984) repr. in *International Criminal Police Review* (Apr. 1985), 90–107.

[5] See A. Ellis and R. L. Pisani, 'The United States Treaties on Mutual Assistance in Criminal Matters: A Comparative Analysis', *International Lawyer*, 19/1 (1985), 189–223; W. S. Kenney, 'Structures and Methods of International and Regional Cooperation in Penal Matters', *New York Law School Law Review*, 29/1 (1984), 39–99; L. Paikin, 'Problems of Obtaining Evidence in Foreign States for Use in Federal Criminal Prosecutions', *Columbia Journal of Transnational Law*, 3/2 (1984), 233–71; W. R. Slomanson, 'Civil Actions against Interpol—A Field Compass', *Temple Law Quarterly*, 57/3 (1984), 553–600.

[6] The most useful are two books hostile to Interpol and apparently influenced by the Church of Scientology (subsequently the Church of the New Comprehension) led by Ron Hubbard: O. G. Garrison, *The Secret World of Interpol*, (New York and London, 1976); T. Meldal-Johnsen and V. Young, *The Interpol Connection:*

Almost all of the people who are well informed about the subject work in the international law-enforcement community or are closely connected with it. This book is mainly based on interviews with practitioners in law-enforcement agencies in nine European and North American countries, in Interpol, and in other international institutions. I have found those I interviewed accessible and willing to discuss various social and political factors openly, although, for reasons relating to rules and conventions concerning confidentiality, they must remain anonymous. In many cases, information and impressions given by informants cannot be attributed and there is no direct quotation from the interviews. These interviews were informal and no attempt was made to use standardized interview techniques. Some academic critics may find fault with this use of interviews but it is necessary in this type of enquiry. Inevitably, the law-enforcement officers interviewed are committed to certain institutions and practices; they have priorities which are determined by practical problems in a rapidly changing environment. None of them will agree with everything in this book, but it could not have been written without them.

The subject is a wide-ranging one and difficult to pin down. Chapter 1 attempts to do so by describing the background to the agenda of issues of the last decade. In this chapter the significance of current developments and the connections between police co-operation and evolving social and political conditions are outlined. The lowering of frontiers as barriers to the movement of people and goods has a direct impact on policing, providing a striking example of the influence of political and economic change on international police co-operation. Police interaction across the international boundary varies according to the police function in question and to the geographical location of the police force involved. Evaluations of the desirability and effectiveness of this interaction vary considerably. Different assumptions about the state and about the function of the police lead to radically different appraisals of Interpol and other arrangements for international

An Enquiry into the International Criminal Police Organisation (New York, 1979). A useful short account of the history and organization of Interpol may be found in P. Wilkinson, 'European Police Cooperation' in J. Roach and J. Thomaneck (eds.), *Police and Public Order in Europe* (Beckenham, 1985), 273–87. A survey sympathetic to Interpol is provided by M. Fooner, *Interpol: The Inside Story of the International Crime Fighting Organisation* (Chicago, 1973). Interpol is mentioned in textbooks on the police but without any evaluation of its role; see, for example, J. Aubert and R. Petit, *La Police en France* (Paris, 1981), 201–5.

police co-operation. Changes in public mood and in moral values also affect attitudes towards policing and police co-operation: for example, prevalent attitudes towards prostitution, pornography, and drug taking have all shifted over the last twenty-five years. These large and important topics form a necessary background to any serious discussion of police co-operation.

Three chapters are then devoted to the ICPC, which became ICPO–Interpol in 1956. These chapters support arguments for the necessity and the legitimacy of Interpol's functions; this is not a position to which everyone would subscribe and some basis for other views is provided in subsequent chapters, particularly Chapter 8 on models of international police co-operation. Interpol is shown as an intrinsically interesting institution because it developed from an informal association of police forces to a full-fledged international organization without the benefit of an international treaty or convention. It has enjoyed a mythical reputation, based largely on radio and television series, as a global police force sending agents to investigate international crime wherever it occurs. This glamorous or sinister reputation is far removed from mundane reality. But the reason for devoting three chapters to it is neither to analyse an interesting institutional development nor to dispose of an erroneous reputation, but to explain its pioneering role, and to identify its present position and the major policy issues this raises.

Interpol cannot be understood without considering certain contextual matters. The pressures created by drug trafficking and terrorism are essential to any analysis of recent developments and Chapters 5 and 6 are devoted to them. They are complex phenomena and the police problems they pose are intractable. Faced by an apparent lack of progress towards repressing them, governments and politicians are tempted to search for new ways of tackling the problems; this can pose a threat to the position and development of Interpol. Some officials and ministers see a way forward in strengthening existing arrangements or creating new bilateral ones: the establishment of operational systems, the posting of police liaison officers abroad, direct police-force-to-police-force communications, and the like. Chapter 7 is devoted to this untidy world of special bilateral relations. Consideration of both multilateral and bilateral relations as well as the awesome problems of the apparently inexorable rise of international crime raises the question—is there a better way? Chapter 8 on models of international police co-operation is a contribution to the consideration of this question. Two matters, the legal instruments of co-operation and the practical difficulties of investigatory techniques such as 'controlled delivery' of drugs, are mentioned but are not treated in the detailed manner which the practitioner requires. Other publications should fill this gap.

In conclusion, a survey of the arguments about co-operation is presented and the main lines of development of the system are reviewed. During periods of governmental and public indifference to certain forms of crime these may be temporarily forgotten, but when the issues come to the forefront again the arguments will be much the same. These arguments raise the question of how far police co-operation should be allowed to go. There is a limit to how far it can go without a harmonization of criminal law procedures. There has been some progress in Europe in the perennially troublesome area of extradition and more ambitious schemes have been mooted in discussion of the notion of an 'espace judiciaire européen'. Some progress has, for example, been made in harmonizing the legislation on drug trafficking between the United Kingdom and the United States. The practical problems of law enforcement will almost certainly race ahead of developments in these fields. The pressures towards police co-operation are inexorable and there will be increasing communication between forces whether or not there is harmonization of law and legal procedures. The questions are how is this to be organized, and how should it be supervised and controlled?

1. The Background

IN the three decades following the Second World War international police co-operation was regarded by all but a tiny minority of people as a low-level technical–administrative exercise which raised few, if any, general political questions. Since the middle of the 1970s an agenda of issues and controversies has been established; some of these have become matters which are of direct interest to governments and to well-informed members of the public. The aim of this chapter is to set out the fundamental themes which underlie this agenda.

Certain basic factors create barriers to international police co-operation: varying state traditions, different levels of economic and social development, ideological and foreign-policy conflicts. There are political, legal, and psychological barriers to the development of improved co-operation. But there are also factors tending to break down barriers, such as the convergence of methods of policing in the highly industrialized democracies and a growing awareness of common problems of crime control; these influences are reinforced by a process of learning from the experience of other countries in the field of law enforcement. The development of co-operative attitudes and practices depends on the seriousness with which particular forms of criminality are regarded. But governments do not always give effective support to police co-operation. Although, in principle, they strongly support crime control and crime prevention, they often do not seriously press for the abolition of the thicket of legal rules and administrative procedures which slow down the investigation and prosecution of offences with international dimensions. At worst, governments sometimes appear to collude in crime, as, for example, in cases where intelligence services, particularly the CIA, have co-operative associations with drug dealers.[1] Considerations of political advantage as well as the pressure of powerful economic interests often work against the effective suppression of drug

[1] See A. W. McCoy, *The Politics of Heroin in Southeast Asia* (New York, 1972). In 1988 the CIA has been linked with drug trafficking in Central America, particularly through close association with General Noriega of Panama; there are also allegations that China and Warsaw Pact countries have promoted drug trafficking; see J. Ranelagh, *The Agency: The Rise and Decline of the CIA* (London, 1986), 691 n.

trafficking and other types of serious crime. Pressure on governments for more effective crime control is, however, becoming
stronger; even tacit government tolerance of criminal activity
causes scandal in public opinion in the highly industrialized
democracies.

In this chapter four assumptions are made about the current
state of international police co-operation: first, it is going through
a period of rapid and significant change; second, these changes are
symptomatic of important developments in the international
system and the states which make up that system; third, forms of
international co-operation raise fundamental questions about the
nature of policing; fourth, although police functions have become
highly controversial within the highly industrialized democracies,
there is now more agreement about the issues involved in
international police co-operation than at any time in the recent
past.

This chapter deals in turn with the context of police co-
operation, with special reference to the doctrine of sovereignty,
the historical development of police forces, and how theories of
the state may contribute to the understanding of current changes;
the characteristics of contemporary police co-operation, relating,
in particular, to different types of crime, to frontier controls, and
to relations between the police and judicial authorities; the
changing pattern of international crime, and the evolution of
public and official attitudes; and, finally, the limits, both practical
and desirable, of international police co-operation. These are
large and complex subjects which deserve more extensive treatment than is possible here. They form, however, an essential
background to the difficulties which police co-operation encounters
and which limit its further development.

The historical and theoretical context

The assertion that something is changing immediately raises the
question of exactly what is changing. The answer may be
expressed simply: contact between police forces of sovereign and
independent states has been intensifying to the point where there
is a qualitative shift in its nature. It has become routinized, and
some senior policemen are participating in an international
professional community on a regular and systematic basis.

The contact provokes sensitivities and suspicions precisely
because it touches the core of state sovereignty; foreign police

intrusion or direct influence on state territory are usually regarded
as blatant infringements of sovereignty. There is a reluctance to
use the word sovereignty in contemporary political analysis
because any definition includes the notion that the state is the final
and absolute authority within a given territory.[2] The nineteenth-
century claim, never fully realized, of the state as 'the sole,
exclusive fount of all powers and prerogatives of rule'[3] is no longer
an axiom of political life. Since 1945 military, political, and
economic changes have ensured that all major policy decisions
made within states must take very careful account of the external
environment. However, the principle of sovereignty still has
relevance in policing and criminal justice because all agencies with
authority to investigate criminal offences are state agencies and all
criminal laws applied to individuals are national laws.

In police matters, the degree of sensitivity about sovereignty
depends on the kind of international co-operation which takes
place. The issues are different if it is between police responsible
for state security, criminal investigation, frontier control, or
customs law enforcement. The very diversity of police functions,
as well as the sensitivities associated with international co-
operation, raise the fundamental question: what are the police
for?

In the advanced industrial democracies, the police are widely
accepted as an essential arm of the state to protect the constitutionally established public authorities and as necessary for the
protection of the liberties, rights, and property of individuals and
associations. These roles are, in the absence of revolutionary
change, unlikely to alter fundamentally.[4] Although the police
function is very old, the origins of the police forces of the advanced
industrialized democracies are relatively recent: the professional
police forces covering the whole of the state territory had their
beginnings in eighteenth- and early nineteenth-century Europe.
These police forces were often used to further personal and
domestic ambitions, but justifications for establishing them were
to enforce the law, to protect citizens against criminals, calamities,
and public disturbances, and to secure the institutions of the state.
Behind these justifications lay the belief that the legitimacy of

---

[2] For a recent discussion, see S. D. Krasner, 'Sovereignty: An Institutional
Perspective', *Comparative Political Studies*, 21/1 (1988), 66–94.

[3] G. Poggi, *The Development of the Modern State* (Stanford, 1978), 92.

[4] For a discussion of this point, see D. H. Bayley, *Patterns of Policing: A
Comparative International Analysis* (New Brunswick, 1985), ch. 9, 'The Future of
Policing'.

state authority rested in part on the ability of the state to protect the life and property of its citizens.

The fear felt in most countries of an over-mighty police institution, especially in centralized state systems in the Napoleonic tradition, usually ensured that these tasks were divided between several authorities and a bewildering variety of forms of police organization came into being. Some forms of policing were claimed to be completely different from others. The most remarkable of these was the British tradition of regarding the police as the servants and protectors of society, politically independent, because deriving their powers from the common law and not statute, and therefore not subject to government control in the performance of their professional duties. Another was the American pattern, where law enforcement commenced as a state and local responsibility, with the federal authorities slowly setting up a large number of independent agencies with powers of enforcing specifically federal laws. The police systems which developed in continental European countries were regarded in Britain and the United States as being the harbingers of tyranny. In the European countries, scepticism has often been expressed as to the possibility that police activities can be properly co-ordinated and controlled in systems with a large number of police authorities. These attitudes have by no means disappeared, and there is little prospect that the fragmented and decentralized law-enforcement agencies of the United States and the United Kingdom will be replaced by unified national police forces on the lines of the national police of France, Spain, or Italy, despite recent trends in the United Kingdom towards increased centralization.

Because the police, in normal circumstances, have the monopoly of the use of force[5] in the highly industrialized democracies, police functions cannot be defined without reference to the most fundamental political questions concerning the purpose of public authority and the ends of the state. These questions are the perennial topics of political philosophy: the nature and justification of the state, the meaning of sovereignty, the notion of an international society, and, for individuals, the problem of the nature of our duties beyond the boundaries of the states of which we are citizens. In these areas there are no certainties except in the minds of uncritical ideologues. Marxist scholars have helped to

---

[5] This view is sometimes contested by feminists who argue that men use violence against women and this is regarded as legitimate by large sections of society.

revive an interest in the theory of the state in recent years. Scholars influenced by Marxism have also written on the police, both in the tradition of radical pamphleteering, splendidly exemplified by Edward Thompson, and in the sober academic work of Tony Bunyan and of Michael Brogden.[6] Representing the police as an instrument of class oppression may serve some political interests in certain circumstances, and, indeed, in some countries at some times, it is almost certainly true. But Marx and his followers have been consistently criticized for what Anthony Giddens calls 'class reductionism', in other words, seeking to explain too many of the characteristics of modern societies in terms of class domination and class struggle. This seriously undermines the usefulness of Marxist theory in analysing the police. A similar criticism can be made of structuralist interpretations of penal policy, advanced in recent years by Michel Foucault and Michael Ignatieff. Both these authors have interpreted the establishment of modern prisons and police forces as the structural necessity of industrializing societies to discipline the working class. This approach to the changing forms of policing is altogether too deterministic.[7]

Other contending theories of the state—pluralist, élitist, corporatist, statistic, social democratic, new right—although frequently admitting the importance of the police, have little specific to say about policing.[8] Different analyses of police roles and functions and, by extension, the nature of international police co-operation can be based on these theories. Some modern sociological accounts, developing the thought of Max Weber, greatly assist the study of the professionalization and bureaucratization of the police in the nineteenth and twentieth centuries. A contemporary political sociologist, Pierre Birnbaum, has, in an incisive way which could be further developed, shown the link between the organization of the police and the forms of state which emerged in

[6] E. P. Thompson, *Writing by Candlelight* (London, 1980), 91–256; T. Bunyan, *The History and Practice of the Political Police in Britain* (London, 1976); M. Brogden, *The Police: Autonomy and Consent* (London, 1982).

[7] A. Giddens, *The Nation State and Violence* (Cambridge, 1985), 143. M. Foucault, *Discipline and Punish* (London, 1977); M. Ignatieff, *A Just Measure of Pain* (London, 1979); both authors sought to escape the charge of determinism; for a criticism of their position, see C. Emsley, *Policing in its Context, 1750–1870* (London, 1983).

[8] For a recent review, see P. Dunleavy and B. O'Leary, *Theories of the State* (London, 1987); R. R. Alford and R. Friedland, *Powers of Theory: Capitalism, the State and Democracy* (Cambridge, 1985); M. Carnoy, *The State and Political Theory* (Princeton, 1984).

Europe in the late Middle Ages.[9] The contribution of other scholars to the debate on the state and the links between theories of the state and the police cannot be examined here, but the starting-point of any examination of policing must be clearly set out.

This study is based firmly in a sceptical liberal tradition. States are assumed to be the result of a process of historical development in which economic structures played a role, but not always the decisive role, in the crucial political and military struggles which formed these states. Marxist and some modern conservative views about the overriding importance of economic forces or of the market are rejected. States in which representative institutions and an independent judiciary have developed were based or have come to be based on a large measure of consent among their citizens. This consent may in some cases be based on ignorance of alternatives, but it plays a significant part in determining the form and the nature of policing in these states. Privilege and exploitation exist in liberal democracies, but the social organization within them cannot simply be reduced to conflict between antagonistic social classes; class consciousness plays a varying, but never a dominant, role. The relations between states and their citizens, and states with one another, is in a constant process of change; critical reflection on problems and political action are necessary to adapt to change. This process of adaptation, essentially the political process, is necessary to secure the legitimacy of state authority.

The police can be regarded as the most basic and essential of government institutions because, apart from the occasions (exceptional in the highly industrialized democracies) when the army is used to maintain order, the police have the monopoly of the legitimate use of force against citizens within the territory of the state. Governments, therefore, have powerful instruments, in the form of police forces, at their disposal with which to enforce their will, but, for technical and political reasons, governments are seldom in complete control of them. Many government agencies may, indeed, be granted limited legal autonomy to perform certain tasks and this is frequently the case of the police. However, police organizations cannot be understood only in terms of legal

---

[9] P. Birnbaum, *La Logique de l'État* (Paris, 1982), 134 ff. The contemporary writing which can be classed as neo-Weberian (see G. Poggi, *Development*, and T. R. Gurr and D. S. King, *The State and the City* (London, 1987)) is closest to the general view presented in this chapter.

authority or the functions they are required to fulfil; the professional and individual interests of policemen play a role in moulding police institutions and in directing their activities.

The police have a symbolic role as the representatives of authority, stability, and order as well as a functional role of performing certain essential tasks and duties. This combination makes them feared and suspected by dissident groups, by those concerned about the rights of individuals, and by members of governments. It has been relatively easy to create anti-police feeling by representing the police as instruments of oppression. These representations, whether Marxist or not, are at best gross simplifications. The way in which the police are involved in society and in the governmental structure varies a great deal because in all societies the police are only one of several forms of social control.

It follows from this very general starting-point that the position and significance of the police vary according to time and place. Police functions and operations are not, for example, the same in the less developed countries as they are in the highly industrialized democracies. Events occur in the one category of countries which are inconceivable in the other. Incidents in Senegal in April 1987, for example, could have no parallel in the highly industrialized democracies. Following the sentence of two policemen to terms of two years' imprisonment for torturing to death a suspect whom they had arrested, there were serious police riots—whereupon the government suspended, and then sacked, the whole national police force. Senegal had, of course, adopted the model of an advanced country—France—and therefore had a substitute for the police in the form of the *gendarmerie*. Without the *gendarmerie* this action would have been impossible, but such an action would not be feasible in France unless the French state itself was on the brink of disintegration.

There is a dearth of comparative studies of the police: as a distinguished contributor to this field writes, 'By and large, the police have not been subjected to comparative analysis. Until very recently neither historians nor social scientists appeared to recognise that police existed, let alone that they played an important part in social life.'[10] This situation is changing, although it is still the case that most in-depth studies concern police within individual states. More research is necessary to analyse developments in highly industrialized democracies, such as the profession-

---

[10] Bayley, *Patterns of Policing*, 3.

alization of the police, the creation of specialized police forces, and the acquisition by the police of some autonomy and independence from governmental control, as well as the growth of discretionary police practices which are to a degree outside the law. Similarities have become much more marked in recent years because in the police, as in virtually all other domains, a process of learning from the experience of others has got under way.

Changes in police institutions are frequently influenced by the practices and by the experience of other countries. When police reforms are envisaged, foreign examples are examined. Some convergences have even taken place in legal systems, still remarkable for their diversity. International harmonization of criminal law is of fundamental importance because police practices are greatly influenced, where they are not directly controlled, by the judicial authorities. The examining magistrate (the *juge d'instruction*) and the public prosecutor, or the absence of one or both, can have a profound effect on police organization and behaviour. Equally important, the police, whatever claims British police constables make to complete independence, are *in the last resort* always subject to governmental supervision and control. Police autonomy in areas where professional judgement is required depends, even in the United Kingdom, on the restraint of the government and the legislature. It is not part of a natural or necessary order.

These simple propositions about the subordination of the police to the courts and to the government have to be elaborated in great detail to convey a true impression of how this subordination is manifest in different contexts. Also, examples can be readily found in every major country of the police apparently escaping the control of either the government or the courts or both. Having final authority over the police and actually exercising it as a matter of routine are two very different things. But these propositions illustrate the limits of international police co-operation. The extent of this co-operation is severely limited by political and legal constraints. On the other hand, the degree of autonomy over professional matters, which all police forces enjoy, has assisted international co-operation. As in domestic policing, the rigidities of legal constraints are made more tolerable by the existence of informal arrangements which, although not authoritatively sanctioned, gain acceptance. Allowing the growth of informal practices is more congenial to some national traditions than to others; it has advantages and drawbacks.

Characteristics of contemporary police co-operation

Particular attention is paid in this study to international criminal investigation co-operation—the communication of information on request and the co-ordination of police operations on criminal matters—because interesting developments have taken place in this area and because it goes to the very heart of the difficulties posed by co-operation. The factors generating this co-operation have been present since the nineteenth century: urbanization, the development of rapid transportation systems, large numbers of people crossing international boundaries, almost instantaneous communications after the development of the telegraph, great increases in the volume of financial and commercial transactions, and the development of large international markets. Virtually all those factors which have contributed to the increasing wealth of the highly industrialized countries have facilitated the growth of international criminality. In addition, certain factors—tastes in the rich countries for narcotic and psychotropic drugs, and the necessity of exporting the profits of crime to escape legal and fiscal controls—have drawn groups in less developed societies into international criminal networks.

Multilateral police co-operation through Interpol has some similarities with a modern military alliance. Both are based on an understanding of mutual interests and of the nature of the enemy to be combated. They are characterized by permanent secretariats, systems of communication, and some pooling of resources. Within a multilateral alliance, and in police co-operation, close bilateral arrangements may exist between certain members. Leading members of an alliance and an international police organization may enjoy somewhat greater freedom of action than the smaller and weaker states, but it is difficult to modify the basic understandings of the alliance without provoking major upheaval. However, international police co-operation is a much more untidy system of relationships than a military alliance. NATO, the Warsaw Pact, and other military alliances are based on a specific security threat and an agreement, both in military and political terms, about how that threat should be countered. A single treaty covers most forms of military collaboration among the allies, although important practical matters such as arms procurement may be left out.

In the field of crime, there is no specific enemy, since criminals can only be identified after crimes have been committed. There are also a large number of specialized international agreements intended to contribute to the suppression of specific forms of crime—narcotics, prostitution, counterfeiting, fraud, traffic in stolen goods—but very few have any provision for operational co-operation in policing. The UN single convention on narcotic and psychotropic drugs which is currently being negotiated has such provisions, but these are highly controversial. In bilateral agreements, discussed in Chapter 7, arrangements are sometimes envisaged which come near to operational collaboration, but in multilateral understandings the closest approach to this collaboration is the regular exchange of information and co-ordination of some police strategies. Treaty obligations usually commence after legal processes have started, not at the stage of criminal investigation by the police. Even in those regions where bilateral police agreements between states are the rule, as between West Germany and its non-Communist neighbours, the treaties usually envisage voluntary co-operation. They legitimize direct police-to-police contacts but, like the 1960 German–Belgian agreement and the 1977 German–French agreement, they do not impose obligations on states to co-operate. These agreements often seem designed to limit rather than extend police contacts. In practice, however, there are often close, informal bilateral relations based on direct personal contact.

Some important police functions—public order, welfare, and environmental policing—involve little international co-operation because it is not thought to be either practical or desirable or necessary. Nevertheless, some police co-ordination takes place in these fields. The transfrontier demonstrations against the siting of power stations along the German, French, and Swiss frontiers in the 1970s and 1980s stimulated some co-ordination of policing the demonstrators. Similarly, the movement of football supporters from one country to another has resulted in contact between police forces for public-order purposes. In September 1987 representatives of the relevant ministries and police authorities of the European Community countries met in London to co-ordinate the strategy on football hooliganism and appointed contact officers in each country who would be directly in touch with one another to deal with transfrontier problems. Police officers in the host country of a major international match sometimes travel to the guest country for briefing. In 1988 the Spanish government requested the sending of UK police officers to Spain to assist in controlling rowdy UK holiday-makers. But public-order problems are posed overwhelmingly within the borders of states and, when political groups have on the odd occasion 'invaded' a foreign country, such as Northern Ireland Democratic Unionists in 1986 led by Mr Peter Robinson into the Republic of Ireland, they are easily contained by the local police force.

Similarly, the functions of promoting social welfare and protecting vulnerable groups within society—the young, the old, the mentally ill, and religious and racial minorities—generally have few international policing implications, although they may be a complicating factor in the problems posed by international migrations. The one very important exception to this is traffic in women. Early in the twentieth century there was American pressure to establish international co-operation on this issue,[11] in the inter-war period it was a matter taken very seriously by the ICPC. It remains a problem, even in Europe, and international rings have recently been exposed by joint police action.[12] However, as a result of changing public attitudes towards prostitution and widespread decriminalization of prostitution, it has become increasingly difficult to take effective police action against the traffic. Consequently, Interpol is less used as a facility to combat the traffic in women than it was in the past.[13]

Despite the growing number of international agreements in environmental protection, co-ordination of enforcement of environmental rules is still in its infancy except in the rare examples of transfrontier natural parks. Economic and political interests continue to prevent this form of police co-ordination coming on to the agenda, even though it is widely recognized that some of the most troublesome pollution problems, such as poisonous effluent in the Rhine and the Mediterranean, and atmospheric pollution, are international in character. Interpol itself has tried to make police opinion more sensitive to environmental issues by publishing a number of reports.[14]

---

[11] The international conventions on traffic in women and children of 18 May 1904, 4 May 1920, and 30 September 1920 were negotiated largely as a result of American pressure.

[12] In March 1987 the Police Judiciaire of Metz uncovered, with the help of the Portuguese, Luxemburg, and Dutch police, a ring which forced young Portuguese women into prostitution in northern Europe.

[13] Information supplied by the General Secretariat of Interpol.

[14] 'Police Intervention and Co-operation in the Traffic in Wild Animals', Report to the General Assembly, Accra, 1976; 'Role of the Police in the Protection of the Environment', Report to the General Assembly, Nairobi, 1979; 'Role of the Police

Athough welfare and environmental policing are still regarded as local matters, there is much international discussion, and several international treaties and conventions on these matters have been negotiated. Police officers are sometimes involved in these discussions, although they are always a small minority of the participants, and they are occasionally consulted when international conventions are being negotiated. The United Nations has regular meetings on traffic in persons, on combating drugs, and on crime prevention. Similar meetings take place under the aegis of the Council of Europe and a small number of police officers participate in most of them. Interpol has held seminars on crime prevention and circulates information about crime prevention. Police officers responsible for airport security, such as the North West European Association of Air and Seaport Police, have international meetings, and study how incidents have been handled in other countries; the international contact officers (appointed in every major airport, after the Montreal Convention 1972) who can be telephoned or telexed whenever necessary, participate in such meetings. In one area in civil policing, traffic control, foreign systems are frequently studied and international seminars held. This is also true of the most prominent kind of public-order policing, crowd control. International contacts and meetings therefore abound.

A relatively free flow of information about police matters is channelled either through forum organizations or via nationally or internationally sponsored training programmes. Police training services such as the UK Police College at Bramshill, the French Service Technique de Coopération Internationale de Police (STCIP), the French National Police College at Sens, and the FBI College at Quantico receive visits of foreign police personnel and have students from other countries on courses. This activity results in the dissemination of information about all aspects of policing. In Trevi 2, there is an exchange of information about the technical aspects of policing—police methods, training, and equipment. Developments of this kind have contributed to the widening of police horizons.

Regular police contacts on operational matters are intensifying quickly. Frontier police and customs services must routinely co-operate with their counterparts on the other side of land frontiers and in certain regions very high levels of co-operation are

in the Protection of the Environment', Report to the General Assembly, Manila, 1980.

achieved, exemplified by the joint controls at the Franco-German border. This co-operation is to be further enhanced by the Schengen agreement of 14 June 1985, which, in three stages, will establish a common police and frontier control at ports of entry to Benelux, France, and Germany: at the internal frontiers of this geographical bloc individuals and goods will not be regularly controlled, and this has important police implications.

Immigration and customs co-operation, to a greater extent than mutual assistance in criminal matters, is a trade in services and based on considerations of mutual advantage. The nature of customs business falls into three categories and the forms of international co-operation are somewhat different in each. The first is preventing tax evasion and fraud; the second is repression of the traffic in prohibited goods such as narcotics and child pornography; the third is serving national strategic or foreign-policy objectives such as preventing the export of so-called 'critical' technology to the Soviet bloc countries.

In the first area there is a high degree of co-operation through customs agreements, in multilateral discussion and exchange of information through the Customs Co-operation Council (CCC; established in 1953), and informal co-operation between customs officers, sometimes of an unorthodox kind. But no country yet accepts the responsibility of enforcing the fiscal legislation of another state. In the second, customs officers are often acting in concert with other police agencies and intelligence sources outside the customs services. The drugs problem gave a considerable impetus to customs co-operation, as to police co-operation, and was the most important factor leading to the 1977 negotiation of an ambitious international agreement, the Nairobi Convention.[15] The CCC has been adopting a more activist role in recent years with the establishment in 1984 of its enforcement committee, an enforcement division within the secretariat, and the regular circulation of information through its enforcement bulletin.[16] In terms of seizures of prohibited goods, customs services apparently have a good record compared with other police agencies, but real

---

[15] CCC, *Introducing the Nairobi Convention on Mutual Administrative Assistance for the Prevention, Investigation and Repression of Customs Offences* (Brussels, n.d.); G. D. Gotschlick 'Action by the Customs Cooperation Council to Combat Illicit Drug-Trafficking', *Bulletin on Narcotics*, 35 (Oct.–Dec. 1983, 77–81.

[16] G. R. Dickerson, 'The Customs Cooperation Council and International Customs Enforcement', *Police Chief* (Feb. 1985), 16–18. CCC, *The Customs Cooperation Council: Its Role in International Customs Enforcement* (Brussels, n.d.).

effectiveness could only be measured by comparing seizures with an unknown quantity—the volume of smuggled goods. In combating drugs traffic, joint police–customs co-operation is now regarded as essential both nationally, as in the Organized Crime Drug Enforcement Program in the United States, and internationally, in the growing links between Interpol and the CCC.

In the case of the third type of activity the *sine qua non* of success is the co-operation of the non-Communist advanced countries. Without this, the re-export of 'critical' technology would be very easy. A committee composed mainly of NATO countries and Japan, the Co-ordinating Committee for Export Controls (COCOM), established in 1949 with a headquarters in Paris, is charged with drawing up a list of goods which should not be exported to the eastern bloc and with co-ordinating customs co-operation to enforce this prohibition. The Japanese firm Toshiba, and the Norwegian firm Konigsberg Vaapenfabrikk, have breached COCOM rules and, in 1987, have suffered serious penalties.[17] In all these categories the same basic methods are used: a professional knowledge of ingenious systems of evading customs controls, intelligence work, well-informed sources, and random checks. Customs and immigration administrations both face enormous problems posed by huge movements of persons: even a relatively small country like Yugoslavia has over 100 million entries per year; the United States has 300 million; West Germany a staggering 900 million. These massive movements of population have completely changed the basic issues of frontier control and have implications for all kinds of policing.

Co-operation between customs and immigration authorities is often defined as mutual administrative assistance and this presents fewer difficulties than mutual assistance in criminal matters. When criminal offences and courts of law are involved, the transaction of business becomes more complicated for reasons related to sovereignty, discussed earlier in this chapter. Co-operation between court systems in different countries has been established through treaties of mutual legal assistance, but arrangements are often slow and unsatisfactory. This has particularly been true of extradition where states jealously guarded their prerogatives. The United Kingdom and the Republic of Ireland have not yet ratified the European Conventions on Extradition (1957) and Mutual Assistance in Criminal Matters (1962), although the United

---

[17] *Financial Times*, 27 Oct. 1987.

Kingdom has declared an intention to sign in 1989. Even the commitment in the European Convention on Terrorism either to extradite or to try persons accused of terrorist offences has met with reservations by certain states: France did not ratify until 1987 because of fears of infringing rights to political asylum. Moreover, this Convention, although important because it seeks to criminalize terrorist offences, does not touch the procedural difficulties of extraditing from one jurisdiction to another.

An additional complication for international relations is the constant tension in certain states between the courts and the police over international relations—in some jurisidictions virtually all matters concerned with criminal charges are controlled by either the courts or other legal authorities such as public prosecutors. This leaves virtually no autonomy for the police criminal investigation departments and therefore no space for international police co-operation as an activity with some independence from the legal authorities. Once the legal process has commenced, international co-operation usually proceeds via Ministries of Justice and diplomatic channels and these are very slow. Occasionally, however, a French *juge d'instruction*, holding out against this tendency, will order an enquiry to be made via Interpol.

All police officers agree with the proposition that effective criminal law enforcement requires rapid action and therefore international circulation of information by the police. This circulation has developed informally through the ICPC from 1923 and then through ICPO–Interpol: attempts to stop it by legal action have failed. In the absence of a treaty basis (supported by enabling legislation making treaty obligations binding on domestic courts) for the communication of police information, there will doubtless be further attempts at legal action in those countries where it is still possible. The present informal system, with no international treaty and a low level of direct government involvement, has certain clear advantages but legal and political difficulties could call it into question. The low juridical, governmental, and public profile of Interpol has been a strength but it is also an Achilles heel.

The changing pattern of international crime

International crime is something of a misnomer. Except for 'crimes against humanity' and war crimes, which are not the objects of international police co-operation, there are no international crimes. The states define crimes through the criminal law; state officials are responsible for prosecuting criminals and for the administration of justice. International co-operation is therefore directed towards mutual aid in enforcing the laws of sovereign states. Despite the highly specific nature of each state's criminal law and the very wide range of acts defined as crimes, there is very broad agreement across the world about what constitutes serious crime—murder, kidnapping, traffic in human beings, traffic in drugs, theft, and fraud. This agreement depends, to a large degree, on the dominance of western liberal values: as William Seagle has noted, 'while heresy and treason are the great crimes of theocratic and absolute societies, murder and theft are the great crimes of democratic, secular and individualistic societies'.[18] However, a consequence of this agreement has been a large number of international conventions and treaties for mutual aid in the suppression of these crimes.

Serious crime is the main subject of international police co-operation and when such crime has transfrontier implications it is often called international crime. However, the areas of criminal activity which are the subject of international co-operation change over time and with the state of public opinion. Petty crime is usually a very minor element in police co-operation, but there are exceptions. In the inter-war period the public anxiety about the petty criminality of itinerant gypsies caused the old ICPC to take notice of it. In the 1970s international gangs of shoplifters operating in London and other major European cities attracted similar attention. Car theft, even on the massive scale experienced in the United States, is regarded as a local problem, but this is not the case in West Germany, where a high proportion of luxury cars stolen are exported. In all such instances, crime ceases to be treated as petty when it becomes both widespread and organized.

Changes in government policy can affect the pattern of international crime. The abolition of exchange controls facilitates the transfer from one country to another of ill-gotten gains as well as certain forms of international fraud. Tightening up regulations for the registration of credit transfers and of tax laws can, as American experience has shown, make organized crime more difficult. Since the early 1970s two forms of crime—armed political violence, usually called terrorism, and drug trafficking—have brought the problems of international police co-operation to the

---

[18] W. Seagle, *The History of Law* (New York, 1946).

attention of governments. Terrorism came as a direct challenge to state authority which found the advanced industrialized democracies almost totally unprepared. The drugs traffic, on the other hand, is a profit-seeking operation based on a market created by the criminalization of the non-medical use of narcotic and psychotropic drugs. There are some tenuous similarities between the two—both have an important international dimension and both are deeply rooted in some societies. Connections between the two, mainly in the less developed countries, have been found in so-called 'narco-terrorism' (the financing of terrorism by drug trafficking) and in the use of drugs as an alternative currency for the illegal purchase of weapons. Both pose intractable problems of public policy and of policing. Political action as well as police action is necessary to make an impact on them.

There are historical precedents for the wave of terrorism which has affected many countries in the last two decades. The anarchist bomb outrages and the assassinations of the last two decades of the nineteenth century made a similar impact on European governments and public opinion. In 1897, on the initiative of the Italian government, a secret conference was convened in Rome, at which Ministries of the Interior and police were represented, with the object of co-ordinating anti-anarchist measures and circulating information about anarchists. Similar initiatives took place in the 1970s with the establishment of the Club of Berne and the Club of Vienna to co-ordinate anti-terrorist measures among adjacent countries. The Trevi Group is significant because it is a more systematic form of co-operation. It established a secure communications network for anti-terrorist intelligence messages and has attempted to extend its scope into other forms of police co-operation. Interpol was not directly used for terrorist crimes until the 1980s because of a restrictive interpretation of its statutes which forbid involvement in political, religious, or racial cases. At the Luxemburg General Assembly of 1984 this interpretation was modified and the Interpol network has been extensively used since that time for crimes connected with terrorism offences.

The problem posed by narcotic and psychotropic drugs has created pressures for even more sustained and routinized police co-operation than the problem of terrorism. In the early 1960s drug abuse was still regarded as a mainly American problem, but this attitude rapidly disappeared, especially after 1970, when drugs became an obvious problem for all highly industrialized democracies and some developing countries. The nature of the trade in drugs makes international co-operation among police and customs authorities essential if any impact is to be made on it. The objective sought, first by the Americans and now by most European countries, is a common strategy by producer, transit, and consumer countries to repress the traffic. Political, economic, and technical difficulties stand in the way of achieving this. There are sharp differences of view between producer and consumer countries about where the major responsibility lies. The producer countries in the third world, which face intractable problems, often naturally take the view that the root cause is the insatiable market for drugs in the rich countries. Part of the huge profits derived from these markets is used to corrupt officials in poor countries which are sometimes heavily dependent on revenues from drug cultivation. Even when the governments of these countries are resolved to co-operate in drug law enforcement, their police forces are not sufficiently well trained and equipped to be a match for the drug traffickers. The Americans, in particular, have sometimes taken the view that, if supplies could be cut off, the drugs problem would be solved.

Drug trafficking is the one area in which there has been significant operational activity by police agencies outside national territories. All major European countries now have drug liaison officers posted abroad, but the United States leads the way with over sixty overseas offices of the DEA in forty-three countries. DEA action has reached the level of military operations in Columbia and Bolivia. The successes claimed for these operations raise the question of whether extraterritorial operational activity, with the consent and collaboration of the relevant governments, is a pattern for future activity or whether, for technical, legal, and political reasons, it is likely to be confined to special situations in the drugs field. One of the main reasons why special bilateral arrangements have proliferated in the drugs field is that the co-operation provided through Interpol channels was too slow and joint operations could not be organized through them. The two forms of co-operation—bilateral and multilateral—are now widely seen as complementary.

Terrorism and narcotics are two pressing issues which have compelled a greater degree of governmental attention to the issues of international police co-operation in the highly industrialized democracies. But a third reason why this co-operation is on the agenda is probably even more compelling in the long run. It is posed with considerable urgency in western Europe. Within the

European Community, a target of a single market has been set for 1992. This means a common external frontier for Europe and the virtual abolition of all frontier controls between the states of the Community. Frontier controls have, in the past, been a crucially important barrier to the movement of suspect persons and goods. During the German Presidency of the European Community in 1988, Chancellor Kohl proposed at a summit meeting of heads of government a European bureau of investigation along the lines of the FBI. This proposal encountered scepticism, particularly from Prime Minister Thatcher, but increased police co-operation is necessary if frontier controls are dismantled. Outside the Community, frontier controls have to be simplified and streamlined in order to cope with ever-increasing volumes of traffic, so similar problems are faced. The ever closer integration of the highly industrialized economies and the main financial markets will further break down the barriers represented by international frontiers. Police surveillance and control will have to be adapted to prevent international criminals taking advantage of the new situation. The development of a strengthened system of police co-operation, in Europe or elsewhere, must be carefully scrutinized in order to prevent the emergence of a 'secret society' of international police officers and to protect individual liberties.

The limits of international police co-operation

The difficulties posed by co-operation in criminal matters across different systems of law have already been mentioned. The current practical problems are extradition, rules of evidence, data protection, differences in police powers, misunderstandings of law-enforcement problems in other countries, and communications difficulties. The problem of extradition is a very old one and remains an obstacle to the administration of justice. Despite the proliferation of extradition treaties, these have to respect the procedural rules of natural legal systems. The Interpol 'red notice' is a request for arrest of a suspect with the assurance that an extradition request will follow. For some countries in the English common-law tradition, this assurance has been regarded as insufficient and evidence against a suspect must be presented, although US courts now issue arrest warrants almost automatically on request of an Interpol red notice. All western European countries, except the United Kingdom and the Republic of Ireland until they sign the European Convention on Extradition, regard the red notice as an international arrest warrant. The evidence required by British courts, and by the Irish courts where practice in this derives from the doctrines of English common law, to allow extradition is more stringent; this may involve the physical presence of witnesses to establish whether there is a case to answer. Again, rogatory commissions to establish evidence for foreign courts are not a traditional part of British judicial procedure and they have been accepted only with reluctance by American courts in criminal cases.

There is no universally accepted definition of letters rogatory and rogatory commissions. Letters rogatory are usually regarded as a form of introduction from a competent legal authority to an investigator seeking assistance in gathering evidence in a foreign jurisdiction. A rogatory commission is a vehicle by which the results of a foreign enquiry can be brought home by the requesting state and used as evidence in its courts. A rogatory commission facilitates the presentation of the evidence of witnesses unable or unwilling to attend the court in the requesting country. Until recently, in the British legal practice, the first were not needed and the second were not recognized. The US courts were also unwilling to use these instruments until the 1960s.[19] In general, until the relatively recent past, the US courts have shown a marked reluctance to grant judicial assistance in criminal matters. Change was stimulated in the United States as well as in Europe by the 1962 European Convention of Mutual Assistance in Criminal Matters. A number of mutual assistance treaties between the United States and other countries were negotiated and the US courts came to recognize, as a matter of routine, the letters rogatory issued by foreign courts in criminal cases. There is now an evident desire in the United States, as in the other highly industrialized democracies, to press forward with mutual assistance whilst preserving due process guarantees and ensuring that rights recognized in domestic law are not undermined by the execution of treaties. However, what the courts recognize as evidence is an important constraint on police work.

What happens when criminal charges are brought and cases come before the courts is beyond the scope of this book. But the

---

[19] L. Paikin, 'Problems of Obtaining Evidence in Foreign States for use in Federal Criminal Prosecutions', *Columbia Journal of Transnational Law*, 3/2 (1984), 233–71; A. Ellis and R. L. Pisani, 'The United States Treaties on Mutual Assistance in Criminal Matters: A Comparative Analysis', *International Lawyer*, 19/1 (1985), 189–223; 'Transnational Aspects of Criminal Procedure', *Michigan Yearbook of International Legal Studies 1983* (New York, 1983).

nature of legal systems must always be kept in mind when
considering the practice of international police co-operation. One
illustration is that, in most highly industrialized democracies, the
request for information or the circulation of information must
have a legal basis. This requirement has frequently become much
more stringent in recent years with the passage of data protection
legislation. The problem is scarcely posed in Britain, where police
information is excluded from data protection legislation and where
the courts have been reluctant to intervene in the procedures of
criminal investigation. Until recently the police in England and
Wales (but not in Scotland) were allowed to collect and disseminate
information at their discretion. The international circulation of
police information can be made secure against national data
protection legislation and the intervention of national courts by
two methods. Either legal immunity can be granted to the
authority which engages in this activity—the *de facto* situation in
the United Kingdom and the formal situation in the United States
after the presidential order of 1983 giving legal immunity to
Interpol; or treaties or treaty-like agreements (either ratified by
parliaments or enabling legislation enacted) can be reached with
agencies to whom the information is circulated, which is the
solution favoured in West Germany. There is a third possibility
but this was available in a unique situation. During the negotiation,
discussed in Chapter 3, for the second Headquarters Agreement
with Interpol, the organization accepted data protection rules
close enough to French practice to avoid any legal challenge in
French courts.

There may be broad international agreement on what constitutes
serious crime, but the criminal law which police forces enforce
varies from country to country. There are also variations in the
penalties for serious crimes, as well as the rigour with which the
law is enforced. These differences are sometimes dealt with in
relatively straightforward ways: countries where the death penalty
has been abolished refuse to extradite if a suspect runs the risk of
the death penalty or extradite only on the condition that the death
penalty is not imposed. But, at the level of police co-operation, the
issues are more complex and are often blurred. The law on drugs
and proxenetism may vary between two neighbouring countries
and the rigour with which the law is enforced may also vary. Both
may make the police unwilling to pass on information. In the latter
case, if there is any suspicion that the police are corrupt, the
reluctance may become total. In all cases, mutual trust and a

common approach to problems form the effective basis for co-operation. Whether or not the trust and common approach exist depends to a degree on the nature and the operation of the legal system. There is, for example, a better police understanding between those European countries with a codified law tradition, on the one hand, and between those European and non-European countries with a common law tradition, on the other. This relates also to cultural and linguistic factors, but the legal tradition is, none the less, important.

In the long run, there will be pressures to harmonize criminal justice systems and serious proposals to do so go back to the series of international conferences, held between the two world wars, on the unification of criminal law. The idea of an 'espace judiciaire européen' was first floated by President Giscard d'Estaing as a way of combating terrorism, and it has been enthusiastically taken up by others, such as Prime Minister Felipe Gonzales of Spain. The proposal is that a uniform law should be administered throughout the European Community on a particular type of crime and that there could be a European prison for those convicted of the crime. If harmonization takes place, it is likely to be a very slow process, even in Europe. Without harmonization of criminal law and judicial procedures there are strict limits to police co-operation in criminal matters. Many would argue that, in principle, these strict limits are desirable, because legislative power in the area of criminal law should be kept as close to local communities as possible. Legal sanctions may become less effective the more remote the sanctioning authority becomes. Police accountability should similarly be kept close to the people. The authority of the rules of criminal law and public co-operation with the police in criminal investigation are better preserved if there is clear public support for them. International courts and international police have their place, but it remains a limited one until the cultural and political bonds created by the nation-state have been loosened and replaced by a greater sense of international community.

At the present time, police co-operation occupies a relatively small space both in the huge volume of official exchanges between states and in the collaborative activity of states in international organizations. It is a rather untidy mix of global, regional, and bilateral arrangements, established without a great deal of thought given to the overall pattern. Some serious consideration of the pattern has started in policy-making circles, because of the growing volume of business; and, if present trends continue, this business will expand rapidly. An overall review is necessary, although it will not necessarily happen, because there are potential conflicts between the forms of co-operation which already exist. Unless some general understandings are reached, the proliferation of special *ad hoc* arrangements could cause considerable confusion.

2. The Discreet History of Interpol

LAURENT GREILSAMER exaggerates when he writes that Interpol is an international institution 'for which the cultivation of secrecy is a religion',[1] but there are, none the less, difficulties in writing a history of Interpol and its predecessor, the ICPC. In the case of the latter most of its archives were destroyed in Berlin during the Second World War and in the case of the former its archives are not yet available to scholars. There has been some attempt to create an aura of conspiracy about the disappearance of the ICPC archives, because of potentially embarrassing material in them, but there is no credible evidence to support this.[2] The reasons why the affairs of both the ICPC and Interpol have seldom entered the public domain are much more mundane than those preferred by the connoisseurs of scandal. Their activities have, for the most part, been matters of routine circulation of information, and the men in charge have not sought publicity. There is, therefore, little published information emanating either from the organization itself or from official publications of member countries, or in the Press. This has been changing in the last six years and more information about Interpol is now available, although it is still small by the standards of major international organizations.[3]

A detailed history of the organization must await the opening of all relevant archives, but the general features of this history are clear and are outlined in the first section of this chapter. This is followed by a discussion of four particular aspects of the history: the peculiar origins of the ICPC in 1923 and its revival in 1946; the rare intrusion of political discord within Interpol; the impact of changes in membership, and the low public profile in the media of the organization throughout most of its history.

[1] L. Greilsamer, *Interpol: Le Siège du soupçon* (Paris, 1986), 10.
[2] For an account of efforts of the first post-war President of the ICPC, Florent Louwage, to find the archives, see *International Criminal Police Review*, 1 (Sept. 1946). The matter is fully discussed in Greilsamer, Interpol, ch. 7, 80–1, 'Les Archives disparues'.
[3] The organization publishes, *inter alia*, the *International Criminal Police Review* in four languages and, although semi-confidential, it may be consulted in major libraries. It also provides on request a useful brochure: *Interpol—Purpose, Structure, Activities*.

The general features of the history

The origins of the ICPC and its history in the inter-war period show how co-operation became well established without an inter-governmental agreement. However, the international political environment of police co-operation was very different in the inter-war period from the one which emerged after the Second World War. The pre-1939 ICPC was as different from the post-war ICPC as the League of Nations is from the United Nations and, therefore, little attention is given to it in this book, except to describe the origins of the Commission. Since 1946 there have been considerable changes and the post-war period can be divided roughly into four phases: 1946–56, from the re-establishment of the ICPC until the adoption of the Statutes of ICPO–Interpol; 1956–72, which was marked by the establishment of the physical independence of Interpol, the rapid expansion of membership, and the first Headquarters Agreement; 1972–84, which saw the first serious challenges to the operation of Interpol, the inter-nationalization of the Headquarters staff and the second Head-quarters Agreement; 1984 to the present, which has been a period of turbulence and change.

The first three phases were not radically different in character and do not mark any important changes in the policy of leading members of the organization—there was a steady expansion of activities from modest beginnings. Governments did not take any great interest in the organization and did not, for the most part, have policies about international arrangements for crime control and crime prevention: government positions were modified from time to time by public concern over certain types of law-breaking and the rise in the overall crime rate. Until the growth of US interest in Interpol in this decade, explicit national policies have not had a major impact on the general direction taken by the organization. In the last two decades, discussion in policy-making circles of alternative forms of international police co-operation has compelled Interpol to take greater account of the development of policy in its major member countries.

The period from 1946 to 1956 was one of austerity, with the Headquarters of the organization dependent on French goodwill, and the membership of the organization affected by withdrawal of East European countries during the Cold War. The second period from 1956 to 1972, was characterized by the adoption of a new constitution, the acquisition of a purpose-built Headquarters, and the quest for both financial independence and greater international recognition. In the third period, problems emerged which were partly generated by the achievements of the second—the organization's international standing required an internationalization of Headquarters' personnel, a new legal basis for the operation of the Headquarters, the framing of data protection procedures for information about individuals passing through the Interpol communications system, and the introduction of new technologies. The period since 1984 has been marked by the maturing of Interpol as an international organization with the coming into force of the second Headquarters Agreement, the preparation of a personnel statute, the election of the first non-French Secretary General, the assertion of a role for Interpol in anti-terrorist activity, and the building of a new headquarters in Lyons, due to be occupied in 1989.

The history of the organization is characterized by several general features. The quality and intensity of co-operation has varied over time and between different regions of the world, depending on influential opinion concerning certain forms of criminality, general political conditions, and technical factors such as communications. Governments have played a minor or low-key role in the development of police co-operation through the ICPC and then through Interpol. It is possible that governments have informally used criminal police networks to further political ends; since all governments have political police and security services at their disposal, this is unlikely. However, in some countries, the distinction between security services and criminal police is not clearly defined.

The level of financial resources devoted to international co-operation in this domain has been and remains small. Partly as a result, there has been a relative isolation of criminal police co-operation from the great conflicts in international affairs and Interpol itself has attracted little public attention. This lack of publicity has allowed suspicions and misunderstandings about its nature to flourish. There are a number of old stories concerning involvement in the persecution of gypsies and Jews, and Nazi penetration of the organization after the Second World War; they are reviewed in a lively way by Laurent Greilsamer. There is little remarkable in these incidents, although they amply illustrate that police forces were deeply affected by the prevailing sentiments, prejudices, and crises of the period. They also illustrate that police action regarded as perfectly proper at one time may be regarded as suspect at another: Paul Marabuto in his study of police co-operation published in the 1930s regarded ICPC help in police action against gypsies as one of its noteworthy achievements.[4] The main effect of lack of publicity has been the undervaluing of Interpol within national law-enforcement communities and this undervaluation is only now being corrected.

The origins of the ICPC

The original initiative for systematic international police co-operation in the area of ordinary criminality came not from governments but from police officials and criminal lawyers, although it could not have occurred without behind-the-scenes encouragement from governments. This took the form of the first International Police Conference held in 1914 under the patronage of Prince Albert of Monaco.[5] The conference was organized by lawyers and chaired by a distinguished academic lawyer, but with wide representation of relevant professional groups—judges, magistrates, criminologists, academics, members of learned societies, members of parliaments, civil servants from Ministries of Justice, Interior, and Foreign Affairs, as well as the police.[6] Delegates came from seventeen predominantly European countries—the exceptions were four Latin American countries and one Asian country (Persia/Iran). The conference was well prepared, with a carefully drafted set of rules to regulate the conduct of business. Most of the proposals made have become commonplaces of international police co-operation. One of the few which has not been revived was the enthusiastic plea by Leon Mouquin, an honorary director of the Paris Prefecture of Police, for the use of Esperanto as a medium of communication. His suggestion underlined a problem—the difficulty of finding a satisfactory language policy for multilateral police co-operation.

The conference passed a number of resolutions expressing the wish to improve direct police-to-police co-operation and, in

[4] P. Marabuto, *La Collaboration policière internationale* (Nice, 1935).

[5] Although it has been argued that the secret conference held in Rome in 1898 to co-ordinate international action against anarchist bomb outrages was the forerunner of Interpol, the Rome conference was more like the anti-terrorist action co-ordinated by the Trevi group established in 1977; see R. B. Jenson, 'The International Anti-Anarchist Conference of 1898 and the Origins of Interpol', *Journal of Contemporary History*, 16 (1987), 323–47.

[6] F. Larnaude and J.-A. Roux (eds.), *Premier Congrès de Police Judiciaire Internationale (Monaco 1914)—Actes du Congrès* (Paris, 1926).

general, give it a more systematic and official character. These included resolutions for the establishment of centralized international criminal records, of a kind which have not yet been agreed, and a standardized extradition procedure which has also eluded the efforts of governments. A significant move was the adoption of French as the official language. As French was the major language of diplomacy before 1914, this was not surprising, but it highlighted the very weak representation of the English-speaking world. The British were represented by two solicitors and a magistrate and there is no record of American participation. Countries having land frontiers with other countries, and an important amount of traffic across them, were more interested in police co-operation than the British on their island and the Americans with half a continent practically to themselves.

The atmosphere of international goodwill which characterized this conference was shattered by the First World War. The need for police co-operation, however, remained, and in central Europe, because of the establishment of new states, it became more pressing. The police chief of Vienna and future Chancellor of the Austrian Republic, Johann Schober, took the initiative in 1923 and invited police forces to send representatives to an International Police Conference.[7] Again the participation was overwhelmingly continental European, but, on this occasion, the United States was represented. Two suggestions were made at this conference which have subsequently been revived in different forms: the first was that an international police organization should be attached to the secretariat of the League of Nations; the second was that there should be police attachés posted to embassies. The first was not achieved, although co-operative relations have been established between Interpol and the United Nations; the second was started by the United States after the Second World War and has become a rapidly developing practice in the 1970s and 1980s. The delegates to the 1923 Conference followed Schober's lead and decided that diplomatic channels should be avoided in favour of direct police-to-police contact. It was immediately pointed out by *The Times* that this informal method of proceeding had disadvantages and nothing binding could be achieved without the intervention of governments. The relations between governments and the ICPC and subsequently ICPO–Interpol remained unresolved. This, in part, reflected the

[7] M. Sicot, *A la Barre de l'Interpol* (Paris, 1961), 21.

very different, and sometimes uncertain, relations between police and government in the member countries. It may also have related to unspoken motives of some participants for whom the 'enemies of society' were not only common-law criminals but a variety of political subversives who might engage in illegal acts. Fears about the political stability of central Europe and the threat of Communist revolution were inevitably part of the concerns of senior officials of the Austrian police. The old habits of the Habsburg police of maintaining international contacts to keep track of political radicals and subversives probably survived.

Whatever their hidden motives, Johann Schober and his associates pressed ahead in setting up an international bureau based in Vienna charged with collecting and holding information about persons and crimes. The bureau for Long Distance Identification (the fingerprint department) was located in Copenhagen. The ICPC also published a journal and held annual conferences. Harry Soderman, a regular participant in the conferences, described them as valuable because they created personal links between police chiefs which were useful in dealing with specific criminal cases. These links could be useful for political purposes, but Soderman justified them by saying that requests for arrests made directly from one police force to another could be acted on immediately.[8] By contrast, requests for extradition had to go by diplomatic channels and orders for extradition had to be granted by the appropriate courts and these processes took a long time. The usefulness of immediate arrest, of course, depended on arrangements for extradition, the length of time suspects could be held, the granting of police bail, and other legal conditions.

The activities of the ICPC were more intensive in central Europe than elsewhere, as a consequence of the break-up of the Austro-Hungarian Empire. The Vienna police records were the most extensive to be found anywhere in Europe and the police forces of the successor states wanted access to them. The intermingling of the peoples of the former Habsburg territories and the social dislocation resulting from the First World War facilitated the migration of criminals and encouraged the development of transfrontier crime. The strong *Polizeistaat* tradition in Austria and the successor states encouraged the belief that police co-operation had a role in maintaining political stability in central

---

[8] H. Soderman, *A Policeman's Lot* (New York, 1956).

Europe.[9] The United States law-enforcement community was also taking some interest in international co-operation. The United States was experiencing, with Prohibition, an unprecedented increase in organized crime involving men who had, and frequently made use of, European connections. A Belgian police officer had been present at a conference held in New York in 1920 of the Association of Chiefs of Police and helped to promote awareness of the necessity of international co-operation. US police structure made international co-operation difficult because police authorities were state and local: there was scarcely any federal law-enforcement capability at this time—the FBI was established only in 1919. At the 1923 Vienna Conference which established the ICPC the United States was represented by the Chief of Police of New York, R. E. Enright. Difficulties about who should represent the United States recurred after the Second World War, partly because of the fragmentation of federal law enforcement into a number of agencies. As for the United Kingdom, despite its position at the centre of a world empire, it was not an active force behind increased co-operation—the absence of a national police force, the firmly established belief that the British police were very different from other police forces, and the island location of the United Kingdom contributed to this lack of interest.

The first ICPC was taken over by the Nazis in 1938 after the takeover of Austria by the Third Reich. The Headquarters of the ICPC was removed to Berlin after the outbreak of war. Implausible claims about continuing Nazi influence within Interpol after the Second World War are based on this catastrophic episode. These claims were made long after the event, when the role of Interpol became controversial in the 1970s; the election to the Presidency of Interpol in 1968 of Paul Dickkopf, a former member of the SS who defected to Switzerland in the later stages of the Second World War, gave the charges a certain plausibility. The main burden of the claims is that most of the policemen who reconstituted the ICPC in 1946 were tainted by association with Nazism.[10] There is no direct evidence for this.[11] The Nazis could

---

[9] For a review of the attitudes of participants in the ICPC, see C. Fijnaut, *Opdat de macht een toevlacht zig? Een historische studie van het politieapparat als een politieke instelling* (Antwerp, 1979), i. 396–408.

[10] These charges were first made, in very vague terms, in *Le Quotidien*, 13 Feb. 1972. The charge that Interpol had received, after 1945, files on Jews compiled by the Nazis was revived by the Mouvement contre le Racisme et pour l'Amitié entre les Peuples (MCRAP) in 1981 but was rebutted by Interpol; see *Le Monde*, 9 May, 11 Oct. 1981.

[11] T. Meldal-Johnsen and V. Young, *The Interpol Connection: An Enquiry into*

not, in any case, have derived much benefit from their possession of the ICPC files. The religion of wanted persons was recorded on ICPC notices, so the Nazis could identify Jewish criminals. However, access to national police files in occupied Europe was of much greater value to the Nazis than the probably very limited amount of information in the ICPC files.

The political and social conditions of post-1945 Europe were radically different from those which prevailed before 1939, and the revived ICPC, had, therefore, a different character. The conditions immediately following the war—with many displaced persons and a flourishing black market—made international police co-operation an urgent matter. The initiative was taken by Florent Louwage, Inspector General of the Belgian Police Nationale and a member of the Executive Committee of the pre-war ICPC, who invited police forces to a conference in Brussels. Although the Netherlands offered to provide a location for the central services of the revived ICPC, it was decided by the inaugural General Assembly held in Brussels in September 1946 that the Headquarters should be in France. There is no suggestion that the French lobbied for this outcome, but the French government was subsequently helpful to the Commission, placing premises and police officers at its disposal. The Statutes adopted by the Brussels meeting also stipulated that the Secretary General should generally be a citizen of the country in which the Headquarters was located. The practices and character of the revived ICPC were therefore strongly influenced by the French police tradition. The first Secretary General, Louis Ducloux, was a senior and widely respected policeman who had a notable resistance record and was, at the time of his appointment, director general of the Sûreté Nationale. The first four Secretaries General were French police officers.

The description of the ICPC–ICPO as 'a policeman's club' was an oversimplification but none the less appropriate for the first twenty-five years after the Second World War. It provided a meeting place for senior police officers and a means of establishing

the International Criminal Police Organization (New York, 1979), ch. 5; the authors try to demonstrate the reality of the Nazi connection but produce no convincing evidence. O. G. Garrison, *The Secret World of Interpol* (New York and London, 1976), 66: 'Several of the committee which reconstituted the ICPC in 1946 had worked with the Nazis. Four out of seven of Interpol's presidents since the restructuring in 1946 may reasonably be considered carriers of the police state germ'; no supporting evidence is given.

mutual confidence among them; as such its function was political and social. Fourteen of the seventeen participants in the Brussels meeting in 1946 were European and the organization was largely influenced by its European founders, although, in terms of numbers, the Europeans quickly became a minority. There was rapid growth of membership as a result of decolonization in the late 1950s and 1960s but this does not seem to have radically altered the club-like atmosphere of the organization. In police matters, the newly independent countries were content, for the most part, to accept European leadership. Although behind-the-scenes lobbying was a feature of some appointments and elections, the public impression was one of harmonious co-operation among colleagues, in which the French played a leading role. The Secretaries General were appointed by an informal process in which the role of the French government was openly acknowledged. There is no instance of a Secretary General being imposed on a reluctant organization. The new Statutes approved in 1956 (which changed the name from the International Criminal Police Commission to the International Criminal Police Organization–Interpol) also had some of the characteristics found in clubs rather than in international organizations (see Chapter 3).

The relations with the host government were not regulated by any legal document until the first Headquarters Agreement of 1972. This is testimony to the lack of conflict between the host government and the organization, and the acknowledged dependence of the Headquarters of the ICPC–ICPO on the goodwill of the French government. According to a US House of Representatives Judiciary Committee Report of April 1959, the French government provided three-quarters of Interpol Headquarters finance. The premises of the General Secretariat were either provided by or rented from the French government until the purpose-built and independently financed building in Saint-Cloud was ready for occupation in 1967. Even in this case the French government guaranteed the necessary loan. The permanent staff, predominantly French, was small in numbers and had, according to its former members, a family atmosphere.[12] Most of the work was of a routine and non-controversial kind—although some of the cases which passed through the Interpol communications network were fascinating, as Marcel Sicot abundantly illustrates in his

---

[12] Interviews with former Secretaries General Jean Nepote, 9 Dec. 1986, and André Bossard, 18 Nov. 1986.

memoires.[13] Every effort seems to have been made to make the annual General Assemblies agreeable, informative, and conflict-free occasions. But policemen are not diplomats and occasionally some very blunt things were said about the ineffectiveness of some countries' law-enforcement procedures, although these were soon glossed over. Publicity was not actively sought—the Press was excluded from the annual General Assemblies—and not much was given to the affairs of Interpol. The intention was to keep intrusive publicity and 'politics' out of police work as far as possible.

The Cold War, however, had certain effects, in particular the withdrawal of members. The General Assembly 6–10 September 1948 took place in Prague just before the Communist takeover. Czechoslovakia and the other East European countries withdrew as they came under Soviet domination. Only Hungary and Romania have rejoined—the first because the Austrians wanted the Hungarians in: the second as one of many gestures of independence from the USSR. This helped to keep the politics of the Cold War out of the internal politics of the ICPC–ICPO, although the absence of the East Europeans was officially regretted. The Cold War also indirectly caused the departure of the FBI from the organization in 1950 over disagreement about the handling of a hijacking incident. The FBI had joined in 1946 and J. Edgar Hoover had immediately been made a vice-president but, despite this honour, the American departure was regarded by some as an act of personal pique by Hoover.[14] The ostensible grounds were that Interpol was involving itself in political matters by issuing wanted notices, at Czechoslovak request, for the hijackers of three aircraft from Prague to West Germany. For the Interpol General Secretariat this was a case of air piracy but for Hoover it was a case of refugees from a Communist regime using a legitimate means of escape. The significance of the FBI's departure was played down at the Lisbon General Assembly of 1951 and the US Department of the Treasury was present at the Stockholm General Assembly in 1952; from 1958 the United States resumed full participation in General Assemblies, although there was no operational Washington NCB until 1969.[15]

[13] Sicot, *A la Barre, passim.*

[14] Interpretations of Hoover's behaviour vary: arising from strong anti-Communist convictions; personal offence at not being made President of Interpol; wishing to establish a strong overseas network of FBI agents using the argument that no other effective channel of communication existed.

[15] US GAO, *United States Participation in Interpol—The International Criminal Police Organization* (27 Dec. 1976).

The intrusion of political issues

In 1959 the organization survived two potentially disruptive internal crises. The first occurred because, at the 1958 General Assembly, after complaints that General Assemblies always took place in European cities, the Pakistan delegates offered Lahore as a venue for 1959. The established practice for summoning General Assemblies was that the Secretary General circulated details of the meeting to members but that the formal invitations were sent through diplomatic channels by the host country. In May 1959 the Pakistan NCB informed the Secretary General that invitations had been sent to all countries but Israel. The Executive Committee of Interpol immediately came to the conclusion that it was unacceptable that any member country should be excluded. The Secretary General received a visit from a senior Pakistani police official in June 1959 who understood the difficulty faced by the Executive Committee, but the Goverment of Pakistan maintained its position.[16] The General Assembly was cancelled and a special General Assembly was convened in Paris in December 1959. As a gesture of support to the Pakistan police, a specialized conference on drug trafficking in Asia was held in Pakistan. At the Paris extraordinary General Assembly the attitude taken by the Executive Committee was approved, despite the reservations of Muslim countries, and a motion was accepted that any delegation inviting the General Assembly would have to give a written undertaking on behalf of its government that all delegations would be admitted, without exception and without reservation.[17] The success of this policy was demonstrated when both sides continued to send delegates to General Assemblies during the two subsequent Arab–Israeli wars without any major difficulties occurring. Similarly, since 1981 Iran and Iraq have participated in the Assemblies during the Gulf War.

The difficult question posed at the extraoradinary General Assembly of 1959 was the request made by the police of the new Cuban regime that Interpol should assist in the search for former police officials of the Battista regime. The grounds for this were that the Battista policemen should be regarded as the worst sort of criminals who had violated the human rights which Interpol was committed to upholding. This was overwhelmingly rejected, on

[16] Sicot, *A la Barre*, p. 219.
[17] Report of General Assembly, *International Criminal Police Review*, Jan. 1960.

the grounds that searching out officials of fallen regimes would involve the organization in political matters, forbidden by its constitution. The refusal of Interpol to engage in the pursuit of Nazi war criminals was based on the same considerations. Practical difficulties also strengthened the organization's resolve. The United States was unlikely to grant extradition to Cuba; the two countries most active in tracking down war criminals, Israel and West Germany, had no extradition treaties with the countries where former Nazis were most likely to be found. The 1959 decision resulted in the departure of Cuba from Interpol; in 1986 Cuban delegates reappeared for the first time as observers at a General Assembly. The policy on war criminals was eventually reversed: on 3 April 1985 an Interpol red notice was issued for Dr Joseph Mengele, the Auschwitz concentration camp doctor, after it had become certain that he was in Latin America. This decision was based on a rereading of the UN Convention on Prevention and Punishment of the Crime of Genocide of 1948 and was due to the influence of Raymond Kendall, the acting Secretary General.

Political considerations have only recently become involved in the consideration of applications to join the organization. Until 1984 applications for membership were approved by the quasi-unanimous votes of the General Assembly. The approval of the membership of the People's Republic of China in 1984 was an exception because it involved the exclusion of Taiwan. The application to join had been negotiated by the Secretary General André Bossard, and some members, particularly the Americans, did not approve of the way in which it had been done. Two votes were required to reach the necessary two-thirds majority, and a good deal of behind-the-scenes arm-twisting took place. The *Financial Times* (15 September 1984) reported that this was a difficult meeting. China was suspected of a simple political motive—the replacing of Taiwan in as many international organizations as possible. An additional difficulty was that the importance of Taiwan in Far East regional police co-operation was generally recognized. But the People's Republic of China was one of the two remaining great powers outside the organization (the other was the USSR) and bringing China in was an important step towards universal membership. This consideration outweighed the disadvantages of the exclusion of Taiwan.

Although there was, and remains, in Interpol a desire to avoid the intrusion of the ideological divisions, the foreign-policy considerations, and the diplomatic conflicts which characterize the life of most international organizations, this does not mean that there are no sharp divisions of opinion on particular matters. Indeed there are broad and persistent cleavages within the organization. One example of the former concerned the proposal by the American delegates at the 1968 General Assembly for a change in the system of controlling the accounts. The Americans thought that it was desirable to follow the practice common to other international organizations to have specialists from outside the organization to audit the accounts. This, they argued, would remove Congressional difficulties which could call into question future US participation. Others vigorously opposed the American arguments on the grounds that the existing arrangements gave full satisfaction and that they should not be changed for more expansive ones, giving outsiders the opportunity of examining the affairs of the organization. A compromise was reached by which an outside firm and two persons elected by the General Assembly would audit the accounts. Persistent tension has remained between the United States, which wanted modern accounting and budgetary planning techniques, as well as transparency in financial affairs, and those who thought that in a small club-like organization these were of little importance or relevance. The US position eventually triumphed (see Chapter 5), although there are still no published accounts.

The question of financial management was one issue which divided the 'traditionalists' from the 'modernizers' in Interpol. From the early 1970s there were tensions between those who wished to preserve Interpol as a small and discreet organization—these characteristics were necessary, in their view, for its effective operation—and those who wanted to increase the resources, improve the facilities, and gain greater public recognition for Interpol. The split was not a clear-cut one because individuals took different sides depending on the issue in question. But Carl Persson of Sweden was definitely in the category of the modernizers and some of the French permanent officials among the traditionalists. The division between traditionalists and modernizers does not correspond with the cleavage between the rich and the developing countries because modernizers in the rich countries sometimes found allies among less developed countries seeking assistance for their own purposes.[18] But differences in approach between the rich and poor countries emerged in many ways. There

[18] Richard Stiener, chief of the Washington NCB, made this point; interview, 13 Feb. 1987.

have been few signs of third world militancy within Interpol, but, given the diversity of the membership, there are different expectations about the management and administration of the organization. The reports of Secretaries General have, for example, remarked that most NCBs do not provide reports on activity—and the worst offenders are the poor countries. Poor countries often fail to report statistics of drug seizures or answer questionnaires sent out by Headquarters;[19] this reflects a general problem of poor record-keeping of police information. Persistent complaints are made that the studies prepared by the General Secretariat do not get circulated by some of the NCBs to the relevant police authorities within their countries. The General Secretariat has been keenly aware, since the late 1950s, of the desirability of technical aid in police matters to the less developed countries, and several initiatives have been taken in the fields of advisory services, training, and equipment. The different levels of resources and professionalism of the police forces of rich and poor countries can be a real source of tension when direct co-operation between them is necessary.

Securing international recognition of Interpol was a pre-occupation of Louis Ducloux and Marcel Sicot, the first two Secretaries General. Nepote, the third Secretary General, proposed the idea of an international convention to the Executive Committee to secure this end.[20] There was no political impetus behind the suggestion and it came to nothing. The desire to keep the organization apolitical and unpublicized always tended to run counter to the drive to secure greater international recognition. Moves were made by Ducloux in the late 1940s and, in the early 1960s, by Marcel Sicot, to draw closer to the United Nations, possibly indicating a wish to join the UN family of institutions. Both Secretaries General were seeking to enhance the reputation of the ICPC–ICPO to minimize competition from other forms of international police co-ordination; the ICPC–ICPO, because of the discreet nature of its everyday activities and general lack of publicity surrounding it, could be forgotten. For example, at the seventh session of the Narcotics Commission of the UN (1955), a proposal was made by Egypt, France, Mexico, and the United States for direct permanent contacts between national police forces reponsible for combating drug trafficking: the Interpol

---

[19] Only 26 NCBs returned their activity reports in 1986; see report of Belgrade General Assembly, *International Criminal Police Review*, Dec. 1986.

[20] Interview with Jean Nepote, 9 Dec. 1986.

representative supported this but pointed out that permanent direct contacts already existed between police forces in the form of the Interpol NCBs and these could be used for the purpose envisaged.

In the early 1960s a serious move was made for practical co-operation with the United Nations. On 16 February 1962 the Secretary General of Interpol sent a letter to the UN Secretary General asking three main questions: whether the United Nations could finance a programme of technical assistance in police matters and use Interpol as an agent to execute this programme; whether an international organization such as Interpol could offer a plan of measures of technical assistance to the United Nations; whether the United Nations itself could provide technical assistance in police matters, for example, in the field of training and equipment for purposes other than combating drug trafficking. The answer from the United Nations on 14 May 1962 was no to all three questions.[21] Despite this apparent setback, relations with the United Nations were subsequently given prominence in the Secretary General's annual report of the activity. In 1963, for example, the UN Secretary General was reported as being impressed by the speed with which Interpol had responded to a request to provide a list of investigators who could undertake a criminal enquiry on behalf of the United Nations in the Congo.[22] In the same report mention was made of Interpol participation in the work of the United Nations Commission on Narcotic Drugs, in a UN seminar on juvenile delinquency in Rome, and in a seminar on human rights in Australia.

Until the second Headquarters Agreement of 1982, the status of Interpol as an international organization rested in large part on the recognition accorded by the United Nations. But Interpol also had contact with other inter-governmental and non-governmental international organizations. In terms of international recognition, co-operation with the Council of Europe was the most important of these contacts; the role of Interpol is recognized in the Council of Europe's conventions on Extradition and Mutual Assistance in Criminal Matters.[23] However, the CCC and Interpol have closer practical interests and have collaborated more effectively in recent years. Interpol has maintained longstanding contact with the International Air Transport Association (IATA) because of a

[21] *International Criminal Police Review*, Dec. 1962.   [22] Ibid.
[23] See below, ch. 3, for the nature of the recognition of Interpol by the Council of Europe and the United Nations.

common interest in the security of civil aircraft. Banking, legal, and criminological associations have also had links with Interpol, although the tendency in recent years has been to restrict relations to international associations having significant common interests with Interpol. Relations with international organizations have, on the whole, been harmonious; there is no case of a dispute about Interpol's status in its relations with other organizations, whether inter-governmental or non-governmental.

The impact of changes in membership

Interpol's own character as an international organization has changed with the growing number of its members. The increased membership in the 1950s and 1960s changed it from a Europe-centred organization into a global one. Broad, although not necessarily conflicting, divisions emerged between the first world (members of which have strong police and legal traditions), the second world (weakly represented by Hungary, Romania and the Republic of China), the newly industrialized countries (all of which are present with the exception of Taiwan), and the developing countries.

The absence of the Soviet bloc countries may be temporary. During the period when Andropov was Secretary General of the CPSU, a certain Soviet interest in Interpol was manifest. A visit of Soviet journalists to Saint-Cloud was interpreted as a preliminary move towards Soviet membership; during the first half of 1988 Soviet diplomatic contact with Interpol was established by three visits from officials of the Paris embassy.[24] Rare requests for information from Interpol to the Soviet Union have been efficiently answered by the Moscow procurator general's office. The USSR is increasingly aware of the problems of international drug trafficking since Afghanistan is a major source of raw opium and some other territories adjacent to the USSR's southern borders are involved in poppy growing. This has led to some co-operation with western countries; for example, in 1988 co-operation between the United Kingdom and the USSR traced the route used by smugglers of Afghan opium, leading to its eventual seizure. The distrust of the Soviet Union in the police services of western countries suggests a Soviet application for membership

[24] Interview with Raymond Kendall, 22 Aug. 1988.

would not be universally welcomed, but the present Secretary General has publicly expressed optimism about eventual membership of the USSR.[25]

The growth in membership has led to a modest degree of regionalization in the organization. The issue was publicly raised by Mr M. Nuamah of Ghana in 1960 at the Paris extraordinary General Assembly. The Secretary General, Marcel Sicot, responded positively, saying that regional meetings with the participation of the General Secretariat were desirable, although there could be no question of dividing Interpol into regional groupings. In May 1962 the first African Conference was held in Monrovia to discuss the form which police co-operation could take in the African context (Britain, France, and Spain who continued to have colonial responsibilities in Africa, were among the thirty-two countries attending). The second African Conference was held in 1965, the year in which the first European Conference took place. American and Asian Conferences followed. Meetings of the continental groups frequently take place at the annual General Assemblies. There has been no attempt to duplicate at the regional level the central institutions of President, Executive Committee, and General Assembly or to set up regional communications networks (apart from the regional relay stations), distinct from the global system. Since NCBs can communicate directly to one another, these latter would be redundant unless there was the intention to communicate about matters outside the competence of Interpol. The issue of regionalization is discussed below in Chapter 7.

Regional meetings are only one type of specialized meeting which developed within Interpol after 1960. There were a range of others: seven colloquia of directors of police academies have been held and there have been seminars on the use of electronic devices by the police, crime prevention, co-ordination with customs authorities, drug trafficking, and telecommunications services. Like the continental meetings, meetings of groups on these topics take place at the annual General Assemblies. The NCBs of the advanced industrial democracies consider that Interpol plays a useful educational role by holding these meetings.

Internationalization of the Headquarters staff of the organization became a topic seriously discussed in the 1960s, particularly after the Lebanon submitted a sharply critical report to the General

[25] Raymond Kendall, in a speech delivered in Glasgow, *Sunday Times*, 6 Apr. 1986.

Assembly in 1969. Interpol, like many other international organizations, is, however, relatively slow to change and it was only in the
1980s that a reasonable degree of internationalization was achieved.
Internationalization of the personnel was also one of the main
objectives of the Secretary General Jean Nepote and, from the
middle 1960s, pressed for by leading individuals such as Carl
Persson.[26] The goodwill of the richer members of the organization
was essential because this policy could only be implemented by the
secondment of officers from national police forces. The number of
nationalities reported as represented at Saint-Cloud gradually
increased to the point where efficiency might suffer if the process
were to be taken further; for example, in 1987 the Drugs Subdivision
had eighteen nationalities in a staff of about thirty.[27] The important
landmarks in the internationalization process in the 1980s are the
arrival of the representatives of the most prestigious US law-
enforcement agencies—the FBI, the DEA, Customs, Secret
Service, Alcohol Firearms and Tobacco; the appointment of a
British Secretary General in 1985; and the appointment, in the same
year, of a Japanese, Akira Kawada, as head of the Police Division.

The internationalization of the personnel of the Headquarters
was symptomatic of a desire to develop the organization. At the
end of the 1970s the pace of change was too slow for some
members. The prestige of Jean Nepote remained high, but by the
time he retired in 1978 there was dissatisfaction concerning the
apparent slowness of the operation of the communications
network, inadequate participation of countries in the telecommunications system, irritation at the lack of progress on computer-
ization, and a belief that the Headquarters staff was unenthusiastic
about promoting necessary reforms. Interpol had (and still has in
some quarters) a poor reputation among professional police
officers in the highly industrialized democracies. Among government policy-makers its reputation was vague and imprecise
because of lack of information.

The history of Interpol was tranquil from 1946 to the middle
1970s because it was a small, little known, and undemanding
organization. Apart from the incidents involving Cuba, Pakistan,
and the Republic of China there were no difficulties in relations
between Interpol and governments. In particular, the relations
with the host government were conflict free; there was virtually
nothing which could be described as a French government policy

[26] Interview with Carl Persson, 2 June 1987.
[27] Interview with head of Interpol Drugs Subdivision, 28 Aug. 1987.

towards Interpol. The attitude of the French delegate, Hacq, to the 1965 General Assembly encapsulates the French attitude. In a debate on a new system of calculating members' subscriptions, he recalled the special nature of the French contribution, particularly in providing personnel, but he argued that Interpol should pursue a policy of independence *vis-à-vis* the host government. Within the French Ministry of the Interior some officials viewed Interpol as a predominantly French organization, but no incidents have come to light which suggest a direct manipulation of Interpol policy. Until the 1970s no legally recognized group contested the validity of the aims and activities of Interpol. The low profile of Interpol helps to account for this. Government ministers, members of parliaments, and senior officials in the leading member countries probably had only a vague awareness of the organization's existence.

Interpol and the media

The name 'Interpol', invented in the early 1950s, has been the organization's major public relations success.[28] This name, first intended as an abbreviated telegraphic address, caught the imagination of journalists. It was soon used by a popular television series, screened in the late 1950s and early 1960s, called 'The Man from Interpol' in the United States and 'Interpol Calling' in other English-speaking countries. In a press conference in Washington in 1960, the Secretary General, Marcel Sicot, deplored this programme in rather starchy terms: 'I state unhesitatingly that it gives an entirely false idea about our organization . . . I deplore that the authors have abused the title of a serious organization which increasingly has the character of a great international public service. We must pursue proper measures to safeguard its spirit and its name.'[29] A radio broadcast in the 1960s and 1970s on Europe No. 1 for French-speaking audiences—'Dossiers de l'Interpol'—enjoyed great success and was subsequently published as a series of paperback books. Like 'Interpol Calling', this series gave the impression that the employees of the organization had power to make investigations in the member states. The problem for Interpol was that virtually nothing about the organization was known by the general public apart from its name and the misleading publicity given by such programmes.

[28] The invention of the term 'Interpol' is attributed to Dr Giuseppe Dossi, the head of the Rome NCB.   [29] Sicot, *A la Barre*, p. 14.

Serious press coverage of Interpol before 1985 was very thin. There were three categories of press article: first, background articles published as space fillers or because editors considered that an informative piece about a little known organization would serve a useful purpose and capture the attention of readers; second, rare accounts of Interpol activities; third, muck-raking attempts to discover improprieties or scandals. Background articles have appeared in the Press of many countries at rather infrequent intervals. They were usually written after a briefing received from the Headquarters staff of Interpol and they follow a rather similar pattern. Articles written in the last four decades illustrate the formula: Eugene Mannoni, 'L'Interpol intensifie la lutte contre "l'internationale du crime" ', *Le Monde*, 12 August 1955; Norman Fowler, 'Interpol's Strengths and Weaknesses', *The Times*, 15 November 1969; Joseph Fichett, 'Interpol begins to grow into its image', *Herald Tribune*, 21 October 1978; David Marsh, 'Interpol takes a step out of the shadows', *Financial Times*, 15 July 1986. Although the last mentioned took an important step towards more genuine news reporting, the formula normally adopted is reference to recent cases in which Interpol has been involved, a short historical sketch of the organization, the limitations imposed on it by the requirement to respect national sovereignty, the world-wide reach and the increasing problem posed by international crime, and the necessity of strengthening Interpol. Nothing in these articles gives the impression of personal investigation or observation by the authors, except for the occasional pen-portrait of the Secretary General or the President of the organization. Since 1984 this has begun to change, particularly in the articles by Danielle Rouard and Laurent Greilsamer in *Le Monde*.[30]

The second category of articles is restricted almost entirely to the reporting of General Assemblies. *Le Monde* is the only newspaper to carry regular articles on the Assemblies. The reports in the newspapers of other countries are sporadic, with special attention being paid only by the Press of the country in which the Assembly takes place. This has partly been due to journalists' lack of access to discussions. The organization has taken the view that the presence of journalists would create a tendency on the part of some delegates to address their remarks to the Press rather than to their colleagues and thus politicize the debates. There is almost

[30] See particularly two long background articles by Danielle Rouard, *Le Monde*, 21, 22 Nov. 1984.

certainly some basis for this view, although it appeals neither to the Press nor to supporters of freedom of information. The present Secretary General, however, used the Belgrade General Assembly as an occasion for making favourable publicity about the organization, and is prepared to talk to the left-wing Press.[31] But the availability of the senior officials of the organization to the Press has been limited. Journalists have always been received by the organization when they have requested a visit, but it is only through greater transparency in its affairs that journalists will consider Interpol as an important news source.

The third type of article has been remarkably rare, given that the Headquarters of Interpol is in France, a country where there have been many scandals involving the police. Attempts to build news stories about allegations of Nazi penetration of Interpol and secret agents at Interpol Headquarters failed for lack of adequate supporting evidence. Allegations of misuse of the Interpol communications system produced nothing more than small news items. In 1975 the International League against Anti-Semitism accused Interpol of infringing its statutes when the German police asked the French police via Interpol for information about rabbi Daniel Farhi, who had demonstrated in front of the Berlin house of Kurt Lischka, former head of the Gestapo in Paris. An enquiry by the French Commission Nationale de l'Informatique et des Libertés (CNIL) found no Interpol involvement. The Belgian leftist weekly *Pour* (21 February 1980) similarly accused Interpol–Wiesbaden of making politically motivated enquiries about German citizens to the Belgian NCB, but it was established that this was a bilateral enquiry with no involvement of Interpol Headquarters. Abuses of the Interpol system have not been proven. The Press has made very little of the internal management difficulties of Interpol in the 1980s because individual grievances have not revealed any general abuses.

Interpol faces similar difficulties in relation to the media to those encountered by other police organizations in the highly industrialized democracies. Members of the public are inclined to suspect the integrity of the police. This is based less on a belief that the police are particularly prone to corruption than on the conditions under which they work—low visibility when conducting investigations, proximity to criminals, and police officers' inevitable cynicism about human nature. A degree of confidentiality of police information is a basic requirement for the success of

[31] *Libération*, 14 Oct. 1986.

criminal investigations, but there is also a need for the police to maintain legitimacy in public opinion in order to acquire vital popular support for their activities. Publicity is an essential requirement for legitimacy. Interpol has increasing need for the media because other means of establishing its legitimacy are difficult to use. Its generally low profile, its attenuated form of accountability, and the absence of strong support from national law-enforcement communities create pressures to use the media more effectively. Police organizations require considerable subtlety in dealing with the media—journalists can neither be ignored nor taken wholly into police confidence. Interpol is no exception.

3. The Legal Basis of Interpol

THE greatest legal obstacle to international police co-operation— the chaotic and unsatisfactory arrangements for extradition which reduce police access to suspects and to witnesses—has no direct relationship to Interpol. The legal basis of Interpol as an organization is, none the less, of importance for two reasons. First, information is transmitted by a standardized system of notices through the Interpol communications system; this is intended to contribute to solving crimes and to lead to the successful prosecution of individuals for criminal activity.[1] It is essential that procedures for communicating information do not provide grounds for allegations of infringements of legal rights. In most countries and in most cases this problem does not arise because the gathering and dissemination of police information is covered by legal immunities. The introduction of data-protection legislation, however, has complicated the situation. Second, the legal basis of an organization gives an indication of the political importance attributed to it. An international treaty in which signatory states accept obligations to an organization ususally gives it more status than tacit acceptance by governments of co-operative arrangements.

In terms of juridical origins, the case of Interpol is extremely rare among international inter-governmental organizations.[2] Neither Interpol nor its predecessor the ICPC, was set up by an explicit agreement between states. Interpol's position as an international inter-governmental organization has been established over time. International police co-operation has grown from an unofficial meeting of representatives of police forces into an inter-governmental organization recognized explicitly by the United

---

[1] Interpol notices are usually issued by NCBs and routed through Interpol Headquarters to other NCBs. There are seven categories of notice: (1) red notice— request for arrest with a view to extradition; (2) blue notice—request for information about individuals; (3) green notice—circulation of information about individuals who have committed or are likely to commit offences; (4) black notice—information about corpses; (5) yellow notice—missing persons; (6) stolen property notice; (7) *modus operandi* notice—notification of criminals' methods of operating and possible hiding places.

[2] Other examples exist: for example, the Pan American Union founded in 1890 had no treaty basis until 1948.

Nations, the Council of Europe, France, Thailand, and the United States. For example, in 1983 the President of the United States described Interpol as a public international organization.[3] The inter-governmental character of Interpol was dubious until the 1970s, but it is now unlikely to be contested by any member country.

The pre-1938 ICPC did not claim to be an inter-governmental organization. Its Headquarters was staffed by members of the Vienna police department, employed and paid for by the Austrian government. It has none the less some standing in international law: in the multilateral convention of 17 April 1929 on the suppression of counterfeit currency, the ICPC was described as the international central office for this task. This did not, however, help to clarify its position in relation to governments. The legal position of the revived ICPC after the Second World War remained much the same as it had been prior to 1938. The Statutes adopted in 1946 were vague about exactly who was a member of the ICPC, although they specified that members were designated by governments. The Statutes of 1956 were even less specific and avoided mentioning states and governments.

This chapter commences with an analysis of the Statutes adopted by the 1956 General Assembly of the ICPC, which provided ICPO–Interpol with its present constitution. The second section assesses the Headquarters Agreements of 1972 and 1982, which have furnished the organization with a secure legal basis in France. The controversial topic in the negotiations leading up to the second Headquarters Agreement, the data protection problem, is treated separately. The other sources of legal recognition for Interpol are then discussed as a preliminary to the important question of whether it is possible to negotiate an international treaty or convention for Interpol.

The 1956 Statutes

Article 4 of the Statutes adopted in 1956 states that 'any country may delegate as a member of the organization any official body whose functions come within the framework of the activities of the organization'.[4] It was left entirely to the 'countries' how this

---

[3] In the Executive Order granting legal immunity to Interpol; Executive Order 12, 425, 48 Fed. Reg. 28069 (1983), issued under the authority of the International Organizations Act (1945).

[4] *ICPO–Interpol Constitution and General Regulations*, published by ICPO–Interpol.

process of delegation was to take place.[5] This had the advantage of permitting police forces to act on their own initiative in those countries where this was possible, and in the 1950s this still seemed to be the majority. A strict interpretation of Article 4 suggests that police forces and not countries are members. A broader and more practical interpretation is that the countries are members and this is a view taken by governments on the rare occasions when it has become an issue; the US Department of Justice advised Congress that 'Interpol members are nations'.[6] In effect, states are *de facto* members, despite membership in the past of some non-states such as Saarland and certain colonial territories. Article 4 recognizes the 'official' nature of membership and the same article also makes allusion to governmental authority: 'The request for membership shall be submitted to the Secretary General by the appropriate governmental authority of that country.' On a closely related matter, the Statutes are also enigmatic—they give some advice but no mandatory instructions about the composition of General Assembly delegations: they should preferably include high officials of departments dealing with police matters, officials whose normal duties are connected with the activities of the organization, and specialists in the subjects on the agenda.

The General Assembly is designated as the supreme authority of the organization in Article 6. Its powers, enumerated in Article 8, are to determine the principles and lay down the general measures suitable for attaining the objectives of the organization, to examine the programme of activity, to examine any necessary regulations, to elect office holders, to determine financial policy, and to approve agreements made with other organizations; it should meet once a year in ordinary session (Article 8). Although its decisions are not binding on members, Article 9 stipulates that members should do all in their power to carry out the decisions. The General Secretariat works under the authority of the General Assembly but the 1956 Statutes, like those of 1946, are studiously vague about the constitutional position of the Secretary General and his staff. The duties of the General Secretariat are (Article 26) to serve as an international centre in the fight against 'ordinary' crime, to serve as a technical and information centre, to ensure the

---

[5] This was *less* specific than the 1923 Statutes of the ICPC—Article 3 stated that members were delegated by their governments.

[6] *Hearings on HR 4641 before Subcommittee on Immigration, Citizenship and International Law of the House Committee on the Judiciary*, 95th Congress 1st Session, App. 2 107.

efficient administration of the organization, to maintain contact with the national and international authorities, to produce any publications which may be considered useful, to propose a programme of activities, and to maintain, as far as possible, constant contact with the President of the organization. The Secretary General is elected by the General Assembly for five years and, in exceptional circumstances, may be removed by it. The Secretary General is responsible to the Executive Committee and the General Assembly. In Articles 29 and 30 the independence of the Secretary General from particular influences is laid down: he should represent the organization, not any particular country, and therefore should neither solicit nor accept instructions from any government or authority outside the organization; and he should abstain from any action which might be prejudicial to his international role. Each member of the organization undertakes to respect the exclusively international character of the duties of the General Secretariat and to abstain from any action undermining this character.

The General Secretariat is statutorily a subordinate administrative authority, not an autonomous legal actor. This latter status was, however, established by custom and practice, and eventually recognized in the Headquarters Agreements with the French government. The business of appointing and paying staff and of administering property and funds has given the Secretary General a legal personality. Article 30, which states that all members shall do everything possible to make available to the General Secretariat all the facilities necessary for the fulfilment of its functions, has never caused difficulty and provides the basis for an argument that states have recognized Interpol as a public international organization. The Secretary General has also been regarded as the chief spokesman of the organization and chief negotiator. Limitations on his independence in these areas remain, but the Statutes of 1956 no longer correspond to day-to-day practice.

There are other respects in which the Statutes do not correspond to contemporary realities. The modest degree of regionalization which has taken place within the organization is not sanctioned by the Statutes. The Supervisory Board, set up according to the terms of the Headquarters Agreement of 1982 with the French government to ensure that the rights of individuals are not infringed, is not mentioned in them. The Statutes also suffer from technical defects, such as the non-correspondence of the English and the French texts. An up-dating of the Statutes is therefore desirable, but an out-of-date constitution does not seem to have any major implications for the day-to-day running of the organization.

The vagueness of the Statutes was deliberate and partly due to the influence of Sir Harold Jackson, the UK member of the Executive Committee and subsequently President of Interpol. He argued for informality as a way to avoid governmental or political interference and to retain the character of the organization as an association of policemen. This argument has become part of received wisdom for the majority of members; recent attempts to revise the Statutes have been resisted because of the possibility of introducing greater governmental representation in the General Assembly. Amendments must be approved by two-thirds of the whole membership and an attempt to change this to a two-thirds majority of those present and voting at a General Assembly has been successfully opposed on the grounds that this would change the balance and character of the organization.[7] Since about 20 per cent of countries do not turn up for General Assemblies and those participating are sometimes absent when voting takes place, it is immensely difficult to introduce changes.

Constitutional revision was written into the 1986–7 programme of the organization, but the Executive Committee of Interpol is concentrating its efforts on a modification of the two-thirds rule rather than on a comprehensive constitutional review.

Constitutional conservatism has become embedded in the mores of the organization. This *immobilisme* is supported by an unwillingness to reopen the traditional divisions of opinion about the desirability of governmental representation in the organization. The Statutes are one indication, the most public and obvious, of the desire to keep Interpol as an instrument of international co-operation between police and not a form of co-operation between governments about police matters.

The Headquarters Agreements

Until the 1972 Headquarters Agreement, the organization was not even officially recognized by the government of the country in which it had established its Headquarters for over twenty-five

[7] This provision was initiated by Jean Nepote, who subsequently regretted it because he had not envisaged the number of micro-states resulting from decolonization: these states are more likely to absent themselves from General Assemblies: interview with Jean Nepote, 29 Jan. 1987.

years.[8] This first Headquarters Agreement resulted from the rapid growth in the size of the membership and the potential problems created by foreign policemen residing in France. The *rapporteur* for the Foreign Affairs Committee of the National Assembly, which reviewed the agreement, rightly emphasized its restrictive nature. In the exchange of letters between the French Ministry of Foreign Affairs and the President of Interpol, the French government recognized the right to the organization to engage in property and financial transactions; exempted the goods and property of the organization from seizure or confiscation; exempted the organization from foreign exchange controls, from all direct taxation, and from customs duties on goods necessary for the operation of the organization; established the freedom of entry and residence in France of persons officially connected with the organization, and granted certain limited customs privileges to foreign permanent employees of Interpol. The premises, property, and personnel of the organization, however, remained subject to French law. This agreement was a tidying-up operation which aroused minimal interest in the French Press and in the French parliament, where the Foreign Affairs Committee report was not even debated.

Changed circumstances in the late 1970s led the organization to seek a new Headquarters Agreement. According to Secretary General André Bossard, who took office in 1978, there were three new issues arising: the lack of legal immunity from court actions, the 1978 French legislation on freedom of information, and the inappropriateness of French labour law for the personnel of an international organization.[9] The Church of Scientology took full advantage of the lack of legal immunity by using the opportunity to challenge the right of Interpol to hold and to disseminate information on members of the Church. Suits were filed in Sweden, Denmark, Holland, Canada, the United States, and the United Kingdom. None of these cases was decided against Interpol, but they caused embarrassment.

Between 1978 and 1981 four federal court cases were initiated in the United States which called into question the conduct of

---

[8] 'Échange de lettres constituant un Accord entre le Gouvernement de la République française et l'Organisation internationale de la police criminelle relatif au siège d'Interpol et a ses privilèges et immunités sur le territoire français signé à Paris le 12 mai 1972.' Rapport de Claude Roux, Commission des Affaires Etrangères, *Journal Officiel*, Annexe no. 2730, 6 décembre 1972; *Assemblée Nationale—Débats*, 12 décembre 1972, 6075–6.

[9] Interview with André Bossard, 18 Nov. 1986.

officials of Interpol Headquarters in Saint-Cloud and of Washington NCB, and the relations between Interpol and other federal agencies.[10] Two of these cases were raised by the Church of Scientology and two by private individuals. As in the 1976 Congressional Hearings on Interpol, an attempt was made to argue that the NCB was the agent of Interpol Headquarters—in other words, to represent Interpol as a kind of world police. This is mythology which appeals to imaginations prone to conspiracy theories, but court cases and Congressional disquiet represented a serious threat to US participation in Interpol. The courts decided that they had jurisdiction in two out of the four cases: *Steinberg* v. *International Criminal Police Organization* (1981) and *Sami* v. *United States* (1979). In the former, the plaintiff sued for defamation on the grounds that, as a result of mistaken identity, he had been represented as a criminal in a 'wanted' notice disseminated by Interpol. In the latter, the plaintiff alleged that the transmission of erroneous information through Interpol resulted in his wrongful arrest in Frankfurt and the violation of his constitutional rights.[11] Following these suits the Department of Justice made representations to President Reagan, who, in 1983, issued an order granting immunity to Interpol under the International Organizations Act (1945). This immunity can be withdrawn for reasons of abuse; it is limited to public acts and excludes commercial acts. Unlike other police agencies, Interpol imposes charges and this could provide a loophole for suits on a contractual basis.

A serious threat from disruptive court action also existed in France because the Headquarters of Interpol did not enjoy the legal immunities of a French police authority. Following the 1978 French data-protection legislation, Interpol files could be treated in the same way as any other files containing personal information. The first solution which occurred to Secretary General Jean Nepote was that diplomatic status should be acquired for the Secretary General. However, the possible consequences of the 1978 French legislation on data protection and freedom of information legislation required a broader solution. Interpol officials considered that allegations and evidence of criminal activity held on Interpol files should not be available to the

[10] W. R. Slomanson, 'Civil Actions against Interpol—A Field Compass', *Temple Law Review*, 57/3 (1984), 567–99.
[11] A. E. Evans, 'Judicial Decisions', *Americal Journal of International Law*, 7/74 (1980), 949–52.

individuals concerned. There were three ways of gaining exemption: an amendment to the 1978 legislation specifically excluding Interpol; legislation to establish Interpol as a French police authority; or formal recognition of Interpol as an international organization. The first two solutions would have called into question the international character of the organization—and the second, in particular, would have been obnoxious to many members of Interpol. The third solution was adopted by the signing of the second Headquarters Agreement in 1982.[12]

The immunities granted by the second Headquarters Agreement make it virtually impossible for criminal conspiracies to bring cases before the courts contesting the legality of the activity of Interpol's Headquarters. Article 18 grants 'immunity from legal process to members of the organization's staff, even after they have ceased to serve the organization, in respect of all actions performed by them in connection with their official duties and strictly within the limits of their official capacities'. Article 5 grants legal immunity to the organization itself, with the exception of certain civil suits. The files of the organization are explicitly protected under Article 7: 'The archives of the organization and, in general, all documents belonging to or held by it, in whatever form, shall be inviolable, wherever they are located.' Article 9 states: 'The inviolability of the organization's official correspondence shall be guaranteed. Its official communications shall not be subject to censorship and it may make use of codes.' This agreement does not, however, confer like immunities in countries other than France. When Interpol wished to set up a regional bureau in Bangkok, it had to begin the laborious process of negotiating a headquarters agreement with Thailand which was finally signed in 1987, after the bureau had been in operation for over a decade.

Problems of negotiations

The negotiations over the second Headquarters Agreement were long and there were some difficult moments.[13] The most serious issue was the form of control of information on file about individuals. The French authorities acknowledged that the law of 6 January 1978 ought not to be applicable to Interpol, but they could not accept a complete absence of accountability of the organization

[12] This became *Loi du 2 décembre 1983*, no. 83–103.
[13] Interview with André Lewin, minister plenipotentiary, who negotiated on behalf of the French government, 29 Sept. 1986.

in its information-gathering activities. Traces of doubt survived from the court cases brought by the Church of Scientology. The general French mistrust of the police, particularly on the left, also meant that some safeguards would be required. The left-wing victory in the 1981 Presidential and parliamentary elections in France led to a hardening in the French government's negotiating stance.

The French government proposed an external commission with power to examine the files of Interpol and to receive complaints from individuals. Some members of Interpol objected to control of police information other than by judicial authorities. There were also objections by some members to the imposition by one member country of a control of Interpol files. The President of Interpol, Carl Persson, suggested that his country, Sweden, would refuse to communicate information to Interpol in these circumstances.[14] He even hinted that Interpol might move its Headquarters to another country. Although this latter threat was not taken seriously by the French negotiators, an informal approach had been made by Carl Persson to Chancellor Kreisky of Austria.

Members of Interpol were not, however, united on this issue. The Germans were at one end of the spectrum in favour of an external commission. Data-protection law is particularly stringent in the Federal Republic and the general rule that there must be a legal basis for the communication of any information about individuals has been applied by the Constitutional Court to the Wiesbaden NCB. The Japanese, at the other end of the spectrum, were hostile to any form of control. There were arguments in favour of each position. An external commission could enhance the credibility of Interpol, at least in the eyes of informed publics in the highly industrialized democracies. It could help to ward off legal difficulties posed in some member countries by new data-protection legislation. The main counter-argument was that, since national authorities decide whether to communicate or to withhold information from Interpol, supervisory arrangements for the control of information should remain at the national level.

Interpol made a counter-proposal for an internal control commission and a compromise was reached. A supervisory board with a mixed membership was agreed in the exchange of letters which form an appendix to the second Headquarters Agreement

---

[14] Interview with André Lewin, 29 Aug. 1986; interview with Carl Persson, 2 June 1987.

between the French government and Interpol. The Board had a composition of five persons of different nationalities: three were to be appointed on the basis of their impartiality or because of their competence in matters related to data protection or because of their experience in high judicial posts—one to be nominated by the French government, one by Interpol, and the third, who was to have senior judicial experience and to serve as chairman of the Board, jointly by the first two appointed; the fourth member was a member of the Executive Committee of Interpol, and the fifth an electronic data-processing expert appointed by the chairman of the Board from a list of five submitted by the organization. Article 1 of the French government's letter states: 'For the internal control of its archives, the organization shall set up a Supervisory Board . . .'. Its tasks were laid down in Article 5—to verify that personal information contained in the archives was handled in a way which accorded with the Constitution of the organization, that it was recorded for specific purposes, that it was accurate, and that it was kept only for a limited period of time. Both in the composition of the Board and in its terms of reference, the compromise seemed to lean towards the Interpol rather than the French government's position.

The supervisory Board was relatively slow to get to work because of delay in choosing the chairman—the name eventually agreed was Robert Biever, a public prosecutor from Luxemburg. The French government appointed Jacques Fauvet, the former editor of *Le Monde*, and president of the CNIL (set up by the 1978 French data-protection law); Interpol appointed a Swiss public prosecutor Marcus Peter; the fourth member was Robert Van Hove, a member of the Executive Committee of Interpol from the Belgian Police Judiciaire; the fifth, the data expert, was Georg Wiesel from West Germany. The first meeting of the Board was 20–1 January 1986 and it was immediately called upon to consider a request from an individual to verify the information held on him. It is too early to make any judgement on the effect of the Board but its very existence will tighten up Interpol's internal procedures for collection and dissemination of information.

The other difficulties encountered in the negotiations were of a housekeeping nature. The Interpol negotiating team was naturally seeking the best arrangement possible in practical matters. Other headquarters agreements signed by France with international organizations were carefully scrutinized and the most favourable articles became the basis of Interpol's negotiating position. The

French tax and customs administrations were anxious to avoid the loss of revenue and their hesitations led to delay. A semi-public incident about the delay took place between an official of the Ministry of the Interior and Mr André Lewin, the minister plenipotentiary of the Ministry of Foreign Affairs who was in change of the negotiations.[15] The Ministry of the Interior charged the Ministry of Foreign Affairs with lack of a sense of urgency. The latter replied that, if ministers could be persuaded to speed up the necessary consultations, then there could be a rapid conclusion. After this both the Minister of the Interior and the Prime Minister's office became involved in facilitating the negotiations.

The final agreement was, in the event, reasonably generous to Interpol officials on tax and customs matters. Problems such as staff representation and the issue of trade-union rights were not directly tackled by the Headquarters Agreement, which stated that French law applied in the Headquarters unless exceptions were specifically made in the Agreement. But the Agreement stimulated an effort to formalize the rights of staff. A system of staff representation not based on trade unions (which would have difficulty in organizing a multinational staff) and a final right of appeal to the International Labour Office (ILO) in case of an unresolved grievance was implemented in July 1988.

With this Headquarters Agreement, Interpol acquired the independence, autonomy, and legal personality characteristic of inter-governmental organizations in general. It possessed some of these characteristics before the Agreement. It already had a permanent structure—General Assembly, Executive Committee, specialist advisers, and a secretariat, with a professional staff which had acquired a substantial and continuing role. It had an independent budget based on a regular system of subscriptions from member countries. It maintained a global communications network, published a review, disseminated studies, and processed information on serious crime with international ramifications. Most of these activities were of long standing and were more than a pooling of activities by member countries. The ICPC and ICPO–Interpol had also been mentioned in international agreements. These characteristics, even in the absence of a Headquarters Agreement, made it difficult to withhold recognition of Interpol as a public international organization.

---

[15] A sanitized account of the incident is given by André Lewin, *International Criminal Police Review* (Apr. 1985), 110.

The other bases of legal recognition

The first trace of the ICPC in international law was the reference to it in the 1929 multilateral convention on the suppression of counterfeit money. After the Second World War, ICPC then Interpol (as it was empowered to do by Articles 12 and 46 of the 1956 Statutes and Article 57 of its General Regulations) became more involved in arrangements established by multilateral conventions, especially those negotiated under the auspices of the Council of Europe. These are: European Convention on Extradition (Article 16); European Convention on Mutual Assistance in Criminal Matters (Article 15/5); European Convention on the International Validity of Criminal Judgements (Article 15); European Convention on the Repatriation of Minors (Article 21); European Convention on the Transfer of Proceedings in Criminal Matters (Article 13/2); European Convention on the Supervision of Conditionally Sentenced or Conditionally Released Offenders (Article 27/3); European Convention on the Acquisition and possession of Firearms by Individuals (Article 9/2).[16]

In February 1960 the Council of Europe and Interpol came to an agreement in an exchange of letters between the Secretary General of the Council of Europe, Lodovico Benvenuti, and the Secretary General of Interpol, Marcel Sicot.[17] Benvenuti wrote that a duty was imposed upon the Council of Europe to co-ordinate with other international organizations and the statutes of the two organizations showed that they had common aims— Article I of the statutes of the Council of Europe (to achieve a greater unity among its members for the purpose of safeguarding and fulfilling the ideals and principles which are their common heritage and facilitating their economic and social progress) and Article 2 of the Statutes of Interpol (to ensure and promote the widest possible mutual assistance between all police authorities within the limits of the laws existing in the different countries and in the spirit of the Universal Declaration of Human Rights; and to establish and develop all institutions likely to contribute effectively to the prevention and suppression of ordinary law crimes). The co-

---

[16] Listed in C. Valleix, 'Interpol', *Revue générale de droit international public*, 3 (1984), repr. in International Criminal Police Review (Apr. 1985), 90–107, and Council of Europe, Committee on Crime Problems, *Activities in the Field of Crime Problems, 1956–1976* (Strasburg, 1977).

[17] Council of Europe, *Exchange of Letters between Mr L. Benvenuti and Mr M. Sicot (February 1960)*, Document TN 142/KO.WM.

operation envisaged included exchange of documents likely to be of common interest, joint consultations when necessary, and the attendance of observers at meetings of either organization when matters of mutual interest were discussed. The Council of Europe holds statistical and legal information of value to Interpol and participation in the European Committee on Crime Problems of the Council gives Interpol access to discussions on law enforcement at the political level. For its part, Interpol offers its European telecommunications network to the member states of the Council of Europe for the transmission of urgent judicial information. These were modest services, from which only small benefits could be expected, but contact has been regularly maintained between the two organizations. The only hint of discord has been the suspicion that Interpol may be moving into a Council of Europe area by proposing a draft international convention on tracing the assets of crime.[18]

Recognition by the United Nations was more important to Interpol because of the greater political influence and the global membership of the UN. In 1947 Interpol applied for recognition as a non-governmental organization to the UN Economic and Social Council (ECOSOC). This was at first refused because UN officials could not see how an officially tolerated international police organization could be regarded as non-governmental—in most countries, the police are regarded as an essential arm of the state and are firmly integrated in the state administration. However, the Belgian President of Interpol Florent Louwage, with the encouragement and assistance of the Belgian Foreign Minister Paul-Henri Spaak, returned to the attack and the status of a non-governmental organization was granted.[19] The opportunity for recognition as an inter-governmental organization was not grasped. It would probably have been possible in the immediate post-war period to negotiate an international convention on police co-operation, but the opportunity to test these waters was also allowed to pass.

The position of the ICPC–ICPO as a non-governmental consultant to ECOSOC was always equivocal. The 1955 UN resolution on narcotics referred to the ICPC as the international agency for the circulation of information about drug trafficking—an anomalous status for a non-governmental organization. In addition, continuous membership of the UN Commission on Narcotic Drugs gave the ICPC–ICPO an unusual standing. In the early 1960s Jean

---

[18] Interview with Dr. jur. Ekkehart Müller-Rappard, 18 Mar. 1987.
[19] Interview with Jean Nepote, 29 Jan. 1987.

Nepote protested at being placed with the non-governmental organizations and was seated with the delegations of the inter-governmental organizations. Nepote was always striving to raise the status of the organization and he had the sympathy of some UN officials. The position of Interpol as a non-governmental organization was examined in 1954 and again in 1969. A 1971 report[20] of the UN Secretary General to ECOSOC on the inter-governmental organizations outside the UN family of institutions referred to '. . . Interpol, formerly a non-governmental organization in consultative status with the Council and now to be regarded as an inter-governmental organization'. This was followed by a resolution of ECOSOC which approved broad-ranging co-operation between the United Nations and Interpol for the purpose of contributing to the prevention and repression of commonly recognized crimes. In addition to the exchange of information, documentation, and observers at meetings, the agreement also envisages collaboration in the study of questions of common interest and collaboration in practical projects (Article 3 of the special arrangements); limited co-operation in the field of assistance in police training has taken place. Recently, the United Nations agreed to fund an Interpol telecommunications network in the Caribbean which is due to be operational in 1988. The resolution approved by ECOSOC in 1971 can be regarded as a treaty between the two organizations. An opinion submitted by a distinguished international lawyer, Paul Reuter, to Interpol supported this view; it is also subscribed to by Charles Valleix, a member of the French government's negotiating team for the second Headquarters Agreement.[21]

The relations with the United Nations and with the Council of Europe are the most important in securing Interpol a position within the network of international institutions, but co-operation with the CCC and the International Civil Aviation Organization (ICAO) has more practical benefits in case-related work. Police–customs co-operation, although often of poor quality at the national level, is crucial in combating drug trafficking; the joint police–customs conferences sponsored by the two organizations on controlled delivery, the diversion of controlled substances, and regional police–customs meetings such as those for Europe and for the Mediterranean area have this as a primary aim. The problems posed by hijacking brought contact between Interpol and the

---

[20] ECOSOC 1971, E/4945, paras. 6–14; followed by resolution of ECOSOC E/RES/1579 (L), 3 June 1971.   [21] Valleix, 'Interpol'.

ICAO and IATA in order to study methods of improving the security of civil aircraft. A number of other international organizations have had contacts or observer status at the General Assemblies of Interpol. Many of these have been formal courtesy relations or public relations exercises to make known the role and activities of the organization. Since Raymond Kendall took over as Secretary General in 1985 there has been some tightening up of practice regarding observer status at General Assemblies and limiting it to organizations whose role is directly related to the work of Interpol. On the other hand, the ILO, which has no obvious overlap with Interpol's activities, now has a practical connection—in the statute for the personnel of Interpol.

Is a convention possible?

Interpol is therefore formally recognized as an international inter-governmental organization by three states and two international organizations. It is tacitly recognized as such by the member countries and by a range of international organizations. It has a constitution which for certain purposes can be recognized in international law and a Headquarters with a history of activity conducted independently of the member states. The only obvious lacuna in the legal basis of Interpol is the lack of an international convention. The possibility of such a convention was raised on two occasions by Jean Nepote with the Executive Committee of Interpol. The minister plenipotentiary who represented France in the negotiations for the 1982 Headquarters Agreement raised it again.[22] The former President of Interpol, Carl Persson, has been strongly in favour of it.[23] There are no legal obstacles and it would have certain advantages. Obligations could be placed on governments, such as a requirement for NCBs to report all contacts with other NCBs to Headquarters, to submit annual reports of activities, and to pay subscriptions at a certain rate. It could stimulate long-awaited changes like the adoption of standard practices in extradition—as was proposed by the first International Police Conference in 1914; but progress since then has been slow. A convention would also require a revision of the 1956 Statutes of Interpol because many of the same topics would be covered in both. Above all, a convention would increase the prestige and strengthen the position of Interpol in the international system.

[22] Interview with André Lewin, 29 Sept. 1986.
[23] Interview with Carl Persson, 2 June 1987.

Governments would formally recognize that the Interpol function is essential in the contemporary world; this could be the basis for increasing its resources and extending its activities.

The practical obstacles to a convention are formidable. Member states are unlikely to agree a text within a reasonable period of time and to ratify would take even longer—the fate of the 1977 Nairobi Convention on Customs Co-operation is instructive in this regard.[24] This is one reason why the Interpol negotiators declined Mr Lewin's offer to consider a multilateral convention during the negotiations for the second Headquarters Agreement. An inconvenient and untidy situation would result if part of the membership agreed to a convention and another part would co-operate only on the basis of pre-existing arrangements. The contents of any proposed convention would be controversial because the obligations envisaged would be inadequate for some countries and excessive for others. There are many matters which would have to be addressed, such as the degree of regionalization of the organization, the basis of calculating financial contributions, the method of appointing the Secretary General, and the relationship with other forms of international co-operation in criminal matters. These, many would argue, are better left to a process of incremental change, rather than enshrined in a convention. A convention would almost certainly introduce into the organization greater governmental, that is non-police, representation and influence. This runs counter to the practice, tradition, and mores of Interpol. The criminal police are mainly interested in speedy circulation of information and informal consultation; many of the influential past and current members consider that the introduction of a 'political' element would be detrimental to these objectives. Even in the absence of this view, defining the relationship between member states and the organization would present major difficulties.

A convention is unlikely to be negotiated in the near future because of the lack of political interest in pressing the matter. Moreover, in the major areas of concern—narcotics and terrorism—there is some doubt in national law-enforcement and political circles whether Interpol can be developed into a more effective instrument. There are also suspicions that, as well as

---

[24] Ten years later only twenty-three countries had ratified the Convention; the CCC issued a brochure pointing out the advantages of ratification, particularly in the field of drug trafficking; interview with W. Thomson, chief of law-enforcement division of the CCC, 30 Apr. 1987.

imposing legal obligations on states, a convention would bring with it additional financial obligations. Interpol would probably become a more elaborate, bureaucratic, and expensive organization which, in the climate of the 1980s, would be most unwelcome. But, sooner or later, the nettle will have to be grasped because of the ever-increasing importance of the international dimension of criminal activity. Since a government is unlikely to take the initiative, it will probably require action by the President and the Secretary General of Interpol. For example, an eminent international lawyer from a neutral state might be commissioned to prepare a draft; such a draft could then be discussed informally with the Ministers of the Interior and of Justice of the leading states. If a group of the leading states could be persuaded to sponsor a draft, the battle would almost be won.

4. Changes in Interpol

THE activities and functions of international organizations evolve constantly—changes in membership, in the balance of forces within the institution, in policy priorities of members, and in general developments in international relations affect the rise and decline of their fortunes. Their capacity or lack of capacity to adapt is revealed by unexpected events and altered circumstances. From 1946 to 1972 the ICPC–ICPO was hardly exposed to external challenge but, since 1972, pressures from the environment have been mounting. Although Interpol has made remarkable progress in certain areas, there remain potential weaknesses in its capacity for further adaptation.

In this chapter an assessment is made of the role of the Secretaries General, concentrating on the last three holders of the office. The characteristics of a selection of NCBs are described because the NCBs have a decisive influence over the efficient operation of the Interpol system. The influence of leading members of Interpol on the policy of the organization is then assessed; the active support of Interpol by these members is necessary to avoid a situation in which other international institutions develop functions overlapping those of Interpol, resulting in boundary problems. The internal policy issues of Interpol are then briefly described, and, finally, the determining influence of the general international political context of Interpol is emphasized.

The role of the Secretaries General

The constant thread running through the four periods discussed in Chapter 2 is the crucial role played by the Secretary General in initiating policy and steering the ICPC–ICPO through organizational and political difficulties.[1] The Secretary General's managerial and representational roles are central to the effectiveness of the organization.

The first two Secretaries General—Louis Ducloux and Marcel

[1] This section is largely based on interviews with the present Secretary General Raymond Kendall, two previous Secretaries General, Jean Nepote and André Bossard, the present President of Interpol, John Simpson, and the former President, Carl Persson.

Sicot—were part-time; they also held senior positions in the French police. Ducloux was director of the Police Judiciaire (criminal investigation department) in the Ministry of the Interior; Sicot was the head of the inspectorate of the Police Nationale until his retirement in 1958, although he remained Secretary General of Interpol until 1963. Both were successful in maintaining conflict-free relations with the French Ministry of the Interior. All testimony suggests, however, that Jean Nepote, who was recruited to the organization in 1946 and who served as a loyal deputy to the first two Secretaries General, played a major role in day-to-day administration and in the development of policy. He was a man of remarkable personal qualities whose prestige and personal standing gave him great authority over the Headquarters staff, Executive Committees, and General Assemblies. With the exception of Carl Persson (1976–80), who came into office at a time when questions were being raised about some of the established practices of Interpol, the Presidents of Interpol were content to let Nepote run the organization.

Jean Nepote's programme was to establish the status of the ICPC as a universally recognized international organization with its own Statutes, its own resources, and its own building.[2] These objectives were achieved by the successful implementation of the Statutes of 1956, transforming the ICPC into ICPO–Interpol, the new purpose-built Headquarters at Saint-Cloud in 1964, and, with the occupation of this new building, a move away from dependence on the goodwill of the French government. But the achievements were by no means complete: the international status of the organization was not secure until the second Headquarters Agreement (1982) and still needs further strengthening; the Saint-Cloud Headquarters building was obviously inadequate by the time Nepote left office; the financial viability of the organization continued to depend on governments paying the salaries of seconded police officers. None the less the implementation of the Nepote programme laid a solid basis for further development. He also pursued subsidiary aims, such as the broadly successful internationalization of the personnel of Saint-Cloud. But one important aspiration—the establishment, which he first proposed to the 1972 General Assembly of Interpol, of an international data bank on crimes and criminals to which national police would have direct on-line access—has remained a pipe-dream.

[2] L. Greilsamer, *Interpol: Le Siège du soupçon* (Paris, 1986), 168; interview with Jean Nepote.

Nepote had a relatively simple management task because the Headquarters staff was small and the bulk of the work done was of a routine character. Nepote could be in full command and it was possible for him to know virtually everything about the policy and administration of the organization. Policy could be determined by him with the assistance of one or two close advisors.[3] The financial resources of the organization were small, which permitted a simple system of budgeting, accounting, and management of reserves.[4] Representation of Interpol—mainly with the French government, the governments of the countries in which General Assemblies took place, the United Nations, and the Council of Europe—was in his hands, although deputies attended some meetings on his behalf.

Many changes took place during Nepote's term of office—the organizing of regional conferences, the establishment of a Drugs Subdivision in Headquarters in 1972, the setting up of a sub-regional office in Bangkok, the introduction of seminars and training programmes—but the organization remained small enough for policy-making and management to remain in the hands of the Secretary General. Until 1987 the organization was in three divisions: the Police Division, which managed liaison with the NCBs, and maintained criminal records, case files, and *modus operandi* files; the Studies and Research Division, which analysed crime and law-enforcement subjects of interest to the membership and which published a monthly journal and special studies;[5] and the Administration Division, which maintained the global tele-communications system and dealt with housekeeping matters. These divisions still exist, but a fourth division (the Technical Support Division) was added in 1987, composed of two subdivisions detached from the Administration Division—telecommunications and criminal documentation (see fig. 4.1) These divisions are divided into a number of subdivisions and units, which are reorganized from time to time.

In the late 1970s, reservations about the management of Interpol were expressed by police officers with experience in

---

[3] Interview with Jean-Jacques Marc, 12 Jan. 1987.

[4] The extremely conservative management of reserves caused complaints in the last phase of Jean Nepote's term of office. As Michael Fooner kindly puts it, ' . . . Interpol investments are made with a greater concern for security than for a high rate of interest' (M. Fooner, *Interpol: The Inside Story of the International Crime Fighting Organization* (Chicago, 1973), 8.

[5] For example, studies have been made on hostage taking, drug trafficking, typewriter identification, international fraud, immigration law, and offenders.

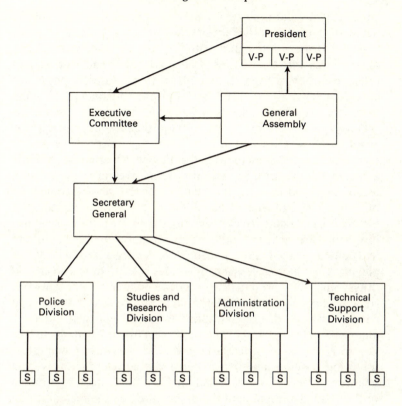

V-P   Vice-President
S   Subdivisions and specialized units

FIG. 4.1. Global organization of Interpol, 1988

progressive law-enforcement agencies where the new information
technology and modern management methods had already been
introduced. Carl Persson, the most active of Interpol's Presidents,
was among those who saw the need for change in financial
management and in reviewing the methods of Interpol to make it
more effective against drug trafficking and organized crime. His
presidency of Interpol, which overlapped the end of Nepote's
tenure of office and the beginning of André Bossard's, marked a
watershed. Persson's innovative and forward-looking attitudes
persuaded the US law-enforcement community to take Interpol
more seriously and may have been the key factor in keeping the
United States in Interpol. In addition to Persson's attitudes, new

circumstances and pressures made a change in the nature of the Secretary General's office inevitable.

André Bossard attempted, with only partial success, a strategy of continuity with the policies of his predecessor and his tenure of office came to a premature end in 1985. After a period of considerable difficulty, and the growing discontent of some members, his health broke down and he took early retirement. His achievements were by no means negligible—he steered the negotiations which led to the successful conclusion of the second Headquarters Agreement with the French government in 1982, commenced the process of introducing the new information technology, and initiated the planning of the new Headquarters building. The problems of his period of office were explained at the time by personality clashes, but structural factors were also involved. Headquarters staff was increasingly heterogeneous and less dominated by its French members. The organization itself was playing a marginal role in many crimes related to terrorism and drugs. Since these were putting pressure on national police forces, some leading members of Interpol were impatient with the alleged conservatism of the organization. Bossard's personal authority among the Headquarters staff was a shadow of Nepote's and he was to some extent isolated because the Executive Committee, following a well-established pattern, was not closely involved in management decisions. The final incident illustrated the problem of this: a management consultant appointed on the recommendation of Bossard produced an inadequate report and presented a large bill for his services. The subsequent enquiry by Carl Persson was highly critical of Bossard, but the Executive Committee had clearly failed to ask the right questions at an earlier stage.

Bossard's successor, Raymond Kendall, first appointed Acting Secretary General in 1985 and confirmed in office the following year, emerged from within the organization. Kendall's different background and personal style were well suited to the circumstances. He was the first non-French Secretary and this was important at the symbolic level as a step towards the maturing of Interpol as a genuinely international organization. As a French speaker, married to a French wife, he has a good understanding of the host country and, as former head of the Drugs Subdivision and head of the Police Division, he has long experience of Interpol. He is a former Scotland Yard Special Branch officer with operational experience, important for the standing of a Secretary General with serving police officers in the member countries.

The role of the Secretary General has changed because the Executive Committee, during and after the period of Bossard's departure, became heavily involved in management decisions. This reduced, at least for a time, the discretionary authority of the Secretary General, because the Executive Committee wished to define the parameters within which the Secretary General should act. This was particularly the case in the field of financial control and budgetary planning, an area of grumbling controversy since the late 1960s. The Executive Committee pressed on with the appointment of financial advisers and a budgeting specialist on the Headquarters staff, embarked on management auditing to improve efficiency, and even became involved in matters of considerable detail, such as the efficient use of space in the new building in Lyons. The budgetary planning and financial management systems, which the Executive Committee had been pressing for, came into effect in 1986–7. These allow members to be warned in advance of General Assemblies (where decisions have to be taken), of requests for new expenditures, and of the raising of subscriptions. They also allow the Secretary General to take a more distant role in financial management. Most of the routine financial decisions do not have to be referred to him and there is now extensive delegation of signature.

Routine personnel matters no longer need occupy the time of the Secretary General. The new personnel statute, approved by the 1987 General Assembly and implemented in July 1988, formalizes regulations for both permanent and seconded staff. Seconded staff in the past were in an uncertain situation and this involved the Secondary General in sometimes trivial special problems. The formalization of consultative and disciplinary procedures (the latter allow the right of appeal against the decision of the Secretary General to the ILO) helps to routinize personnel management and remove decisions from the Secretary General's desk. Senior appointments and difficult disciplinary cases remain his responsibility. In general, in financial and personnel matters, Interpol is taking on the normal characteristics of a large organization.

The management burden of the Secretary General could be reduced by two methods. The appointment of a deputy Secretary General presents the problem of finding an appropriate role for a deputy who is not already a head of one of the divisions of Interpol. At the time of writing there is a designated senior official who has the power to act in the relatively frequent absences of the

Secretary General. However, the appointment of a deputy before the expiry of the first term of office of Raymond Kendall in 1990 seems inevitable. The other method, the extension of the private office or *cabinet* of the Secretary General, is less problematic. Tasks which were previously done by the Secretary General with an assistant—digesting information from the divisions, preparing briefs, and writing statements or speeches—have now become too onerous and a properly staffed private office is essential. The main issue is whether the cabinet should be conceived on the French model of officials without tenure or on the British model of a permanent professional staff.

In order to be effective as a manager and as a shaper of policy within Interpol, the Secretary General must have a personal authority in the law-enforcement communities of the leading member countries. How this is done depends on circumstances. Jean Nepote had this authority because of his remarkable personal and diplomatic qualities. He was acquainted, often for many years, with leading police officers all over the world and was held in high esteem by them. He helped to educate senior and middle-ranking officers through conferences, seminars, and training courses. The role of educator has declined because these activities have become more professionalized. Other organizations have taken on some of the responsibility for training in international affairs and one of the most effective ways of educating police officers in the international dimension of policing is now through the activities of the NCBs or by sending Headquarter's officials to the national police training schools to conduct short courses.

In present circumstances, there are two new ways of securing the Secretary General's personal authority in the member countries. The first is the acquisition, with the consent of the national authorities, of a quasi-inspectorate role *vis-à-vis* the NCBs. Effective international co-operation through Interpol requires the adoption of best practices by all the leading members and adequate practices by the others. A significant advisory/inspection role by the Secretary General is required (although it would be resisted in some places) and it would provide a continuing basis for his authority in the member countries. The second is the effective use of the media and public relations. Receiving politicians and influential visitors is now routinely done and they are professionally briefed. The Secretary General is active in attending important international meetings, paying visits to ministers, and making speeches. Relations with Press and broadcasting were cautious until Raymond Kendall came into office, and systematically obtaining media attention has not yet entered the habits of the organization.

The role of the Secretary General is difficult and demanding but it is one with a considerable potential for development. Whether it can be developed depends to a degree on the personal qualities of the Secretary General, and his survival in office for a sufficiently long period to establish the necessary personal links. More crucially, it depends on the degree to which governments and national law-enforcement agencies regard Interpol as the central and most valuable instrument of international co-operation. The present climate of uncertainty affecting Interpol is unlikely to end until the move to the new Headquarters in Lyons (1989) is complete, until the new technology is in place and working properly, and until the expectations of the membership and the performance of the organization have reached a new equilibrium.

The NCBs

The NCBs' main function is to act as a link between the police forces in a country and the outside world.[6] This is done primarily through the Interpol telecommunications system. Just under half the membership (72) participate in the Interpol radio network; the remaining centres are reached by telex or cable. There is a constant upgrading of this network: recently the European countries have begun to encrypt their systems for greater security, an automatic message switching system has been introduced at the Saint-Cloud Headquarters, and a satellite communications system is under consideration. The organization of these bureaux and their location within the national police hierarchies has been entirely a matter for national police forces. Although there are now moves to impose conditions on new members in terms of facilities at the disposal of the NCBs, no two NCBs are exactly the same because of the wide variation in the structure of police forces. Many police forces have been strongly influenced by the British, French, and German police traditions, but there are differences even in those cases where police organizations are influenced by the same model.

Some NCBs play an important role in the national police forces.

[6] This section is based on interviews with the chiefs of Interpol NCBs or members of their staff in West Germany (Wiesbaden), France, the United Kingdom, the United States, Spain, The Netherlands, Austria, and Sweden.

Interpol Wiesbaden, the West German NCB, and the Bundes-kriminalamt (BKA) the criminal intelligence and co-ordinating office for the Federal Republic, are constitutionally identical. A similar, but not identical, situation exists in Austria. In the Netherlands and Sweden, which both have national and not federal police organizations, the central criminal investigation departments are also the NCBs. In Washington, the NCB is capable of playing a central co-ordinating role for international police relations because all the agencies with an interest in international police co-operation (FBI, Secret Service, DEA, Customs, US Marshalls, Immigration and Naturalization Service, (INS) as well as others with a lesser interest) have liaison officers in the NCB. At the moment, however, these agencies jealously guard their own overseas representation.

The French and the British NCBs are roughly comparable in terms of size and facilities, and there have been similar attitudes within them about the limited value of multilateral co-operation through Interpol. In France, because of a highly centralized police system, a geographical location exposed to transfrontier criminal activity, and senior police officials closely associated with the revived ICPC from 1946, the NCB has a strong position in the hierarchy of the Police Nationale. This position has secure legal protection:[7] the NCB is the only French institution empowered to correspond on behalf of French government departments or police divisions with both Interpol and foreign police authorities. Apart from special arrangements such as border agreements and the Franco-American agreement on co-operation in drugs cases, all contacts between French and foreign police officers must have prior sanction by the NCB. The NCB in New Scotland Yard is constitutionally in a weaker position than those of the other west European countries because of the decentralization of police powers in the United Kingdom. The German and American NCBs are better staffed and equipped than either the British or the French. But the difference in the technical capacity of the NCBs in the industrialized countries is insignificant compared with the gulf which separates them from many countries in the developing world. This is one factor supporting the demand for regionaliza-tion within Interpol, based on the belief that countries with similar technical capacities and professionalism in police matters can more effectively co-operate on matters of common interest.

---

[7] Decree no. 75–431, 26 May 1975. The original legal basis of the NCB was two executive orders (*arrêtés*), 18 Dec. 1928, 11 Sept. 1929.

Whatever the differences in resources and the level of their participation in the communications system of Interpol, a feature which all NCBs have in common is their independence *vis-à-vis* the Saint-Cloud Headquarters of the organization. No NCB is bound by treaty or international convention to send information to other NCBs or to communicate with Headquarters. Any NCB can refuse to answer requests coming from another member or from Saint-Cloud. Article 3 of the Statutes forbidding involvement in religious, racial, or political cases is relatively easy to invoke as a justification for non-co-operation but obstructive members can simply remain silent. The Washington NCB is particularly concerned, partly because of Congressional interest, with 'follow-up' information about what has happened to cases in which it has been involved; it has proved almost impossible to extract this information from a wide range of countries.

The status and the development of the NCB is often an indication of the importance accorded to international co-operation by the country concerned. The most interesting, in this respect, is the Washington NCB, whose staffing, message traffic (from just over 30,000 to about 90,000 per annum), and number of cases dealt with (10,500 to 42,368) have all greatly increased between 1980 and 1986. By 1986 the Washington NCB had reached the same level of message traffic as the Paris NCB, an indication of the very low level of activity in the previous period. Since 1981 its chief, former Secret Service agent Richard Stiener, has made a considerable impact both on Interpol internationally and on the US law-enforcement community. When Stiener was appointed, the NCB came to be recognized as a separate entity in the Department of Justice under the direct authority of an assistant Attorney General and, in 1979, the Attorney General himself was designated as the permanent representative to Interpol.[8]

The development of the Washington NCB in the 1980s is a sharp contrast to the low level of activity and relative disinterest shown towards Interpol in the United States prior to 1980. The FBI joined the ICPC in 1947, but left in 1950, possibly because Hoover wanted to develop the Legat programme (FBI officers in US embassies). Congress may have raised objections to this programme if other means for international police communications

[8] By a memorandum of understanding between the Departments of Justice and Commerce, 18 Jan. 1977, the two departments established a dual authority over the NCB; this was amended in 1981 giving the Department of Justice a leading role and amended again in 1983 to ensure management and leadership continuity in the NCB.

existed. Whatever Hoover's motives were, for over two decades after 1950 there was no serious US commitment to Interpol. Until 1958 the Treasury maintained informal contact with Interpol but no dues were paid. In 1958 the Attorney General officially designated the Treasury as the US representative to Interpol and an NCB was set up in 1962. This only became operational in 1969, with a tiny staff of three members who dealt, in the early years, with about 300 cases per annum. The first bureau chief was a member of the Secret Service, which, after the FBI, is the most prestigious federal law-enforcement agency. Continued Secret Service support, partly based on rivalry with the FBI, was crucial to the survival of the Interpol connection and helped the Washington NCB to survive in the difficult years of the 1970s.[9]

The growing influence of the Washington NCB has been dependent on several factors.[10] US law-enforcement circles in the 1970s were increasingly concerned about the international dimension of organized crime, although they also tended to be highly critical of Interpol. The pro-law-enforcement environment of the Reagan administration supported Judge Webster's (Director of the FBI, 1980–7) insistence on close collaboration between federal law-enforcement agencies. This meant closer co-ordination of the international business of these agencies. The political and entrepreneurial skills of an energetic NCB chief, Richard Stiener, helped to establish the Washington NCB as an important presence in this improved co-ordination. Even a critical report on the Washington NCB by the General Accounting Office (GAO) in 1977 was effectively used by Stiener.[11] Congress requested this report under pressure from members of the Church of Scientology who alleged that US citizens' rights were being infringed by Interpol. Stiener capitalized on the GAO report by accepting its recommendations and making it a management tool. He also publicized the NCB on Capitol Hill by reassuring those concerned with civil rights, such as Congressman Don Edwards of California, that Interpol was above suspicion. His efforts were successful and

---

[9] For details of the Hoover incident, see above, ch. 2. For the history of the Washington NCB, see Fooner, *Interpol*, and *Hearing on US participation in Interpol*, Subcommittee of the Committee on Appropriations, United States Senate, Ninety-fourth Congress, First Session, 1975.

[10] Interview with Judge Lowell Jenson, the first Assistant Attorney General of the Reagan administration, 5 Mar. 1987.

[11] GAO, *United States Participation in Interpol, the International Criminal Police Organization*, Report ID–76–77 (27 Dec. 1976).

on the next occasion that the GAO inspected the NCB, in 1987, its impressions were entirely favourable.

The achievements of the Washington NCB can be briefly summarized. It exploited its pivotal position in a criminal intelligence communications network—it links the on-line computerized systems of the Treasury Enforcement Computer System (TECS), the FBI's National Crime Information Center (NCIC), the INS computerized files, and to a lesser extent the DEA's El Paso Information Center (EPIC) to the international system of communication through Interpol. Its data processing and communications equipment is based on the best available technology, with a specialized Technology Management Unit to maintain it. Its unusual and innovative organizational features are supported by experienced senior management personnel. A strong policy advisory group, which includes the Assistant Secretary to the Treasury and the Assistant Attorney General, and an internal management group, which includes representatives of the leading federal law-enforcement agencies, help to maintain a high political–administrative profile.[12] It is now well known in US law-enforcement circles and, in time, could establish itself as the almost exclusive link between the 20,000 police agencies in the United States and the outside world. It has become influential in policy-making in the field of international co-operation both in the United States and in the global organization of Interpol.

Although the Washington NCB has undergone the most remarkable development in the last decade, other NCBs have come to play an important role. The strongest constitutional position for NCBs is to be legally identical with the central criminal investigation office in a national police force.[13] Everyday reality varies more than the statement of the constitutional position suggests. One crucial variable is the relationship between the specialized service dealing with Interpol business and the head of criminal investigation. In smaller countries, the head of the criminal intelligence department may come close to being the working head of the NCB. This is the case of Dr Robert Köck, chief of the Criminal Police Services and head of the Vienna NCB,

---

[12] Harmonious working relations between the Treasury Department (Customs, Alcohol, Tobacco and Firearms, and Secret Service) and the Department of Justice (FBI) are essential both for Interpol and for the general co-operation of federal law-enforcement efforts; this harmony has been achieved for at least part of the Reagan administration; interview with Frank Keating, Assistant Secretary to the Treasury, 20 Feb. 1987.

[13] *Bundesgesetzblatt für die Republik Österreich*, 59 (5 Aug. 1965).

and Mr Van Straten, head of the Central Criminal Intelligence Service and of the NCB in the Hague. But in West Germany, which is a larger country, the head of the BKA, Dr Böge, attends the General Assembly of Interpol and takes an interest in overall policy but the NCB chief Dr Schmidt-Nothen is in day-to-day control of Interpol and other international business. A similar situation prevails in Sweden. When the head of the NCB is in a relatively junior position or for other reasons is not close to the head of criminal investigation, the work of Interpol risks being treated as marginal.

The Austrian NCB is an important element in criminal policing for several reasons. These are partly historical and partly personal. The initiative for the ICPC came from Vienna and successful international initiatives are particularly prized in Austria. Dr Köck is the longest-serving NCB chief and his experience has given him a personal authority. Austria has contiguous land frontiers with seven other states and relatively open borders with all of them except Czechoslovakia. It is vulnerable to transfrontier criminality and in recent years has become a transit country for heroin from the Near and Far East, and cocaine from South America. The Vienna NCB is also a crucial link in police relations with Eastern Europe. The personal influence of Dr Köck brought Hungary back into Interpol in the early 1980s. Prior to Hungarian re-entry, an Austro-Hungarian treaty concerning mutual assistance on criminal matters had been negotiated in 1980.[14] Bulgarian and Romanian treaties were signed in 1988. In the absence of treaties, relations with these countries and others in Eastern Europe have been conducted on the basis of reciprocity. Occasionally political difficulties arise, for example, when the German Democratic Republic made dubious enquiries about 'missing persons' (suspected by the Austrians of being political dissidents), but in important criminal cases co-operation is regularly obtained. In Austria, investigating terrorist incidents is the responsibility of one of the four departments of the Central Office of the Criminal Police. Although not all anti-terrorist business is dealt with through Interpol channels, there is no communication blockage between the NCB and the department responsible for dealing with terrorist crimes. For all these reasons, Interpol–Vienna is an important police service and it operates in a supportive political environment.

Similar importance is given to the international dimension of

[14] *Bundesgesetzblatt für die Republik Österreich*, 154 (5 Sept. 1980).

criminal policing in the Netherlands. The Dutch situation with regard to anti-terrorist action is more complicated than the Austrian since the Ministries of Justice and Interior, and the Binnelandse Veiligheids Dienst (BVD), the security service, are all involved. However, the information which comes via the Trevi communications system to the Ministry of Justice is routinely circulated to the Criminal Intelligence Service so that the distinction between the Trevi and the Interpol networks is not as clear as it is in countries such as the United Kingdom. Headed by Van Straten, a perceptive and experienced official of high reputation both in the Netherlands and in the international law-enforcement community, the NCB works particularly closely with other NCB equivalents in north-west European countries. This is particularly important in the area of drug trafficking but less so in terrorism cases, since the Netherlands has been relatively less troubled by these than her larger neighbours. For geographical and practical reasons Van Straten is in favour of closer European regional co-operation, although remaining sceptical about how far this can go in the absence of criminal law harmonization in European countries.

The Swedish NCB has been important within the Swedish National Police since the foundation of the National Police in 1963. The first director of the police, Carl Persson, was convinced of the importance of international co-operation and immediately sent a police officer on detachment to Saint-Cloud. Persson became a pillar of the global organization, a member of working groups and the executive committee, and finally President of Interpol. Persson's commitment gave the international dimension of policing an interest and importance for young and ambitious police officers in Sweden which, until recently, has been relatively rare in other countries. Persson also pioneered the introduction (in Europe) of drug liaison officers posted to other countries and ensured that they reported to the Stockholm NCB. In this and other matters his thinking was in advance of most of his opposite numbers in Europe.

However, the BKA also has the reputation of being in the forefront of police techniques and in attitudes towards police co-operation. The law establishing the BKA gives prominence to the international role of the office and establishes it as the NCB for the Federal Republic.[15] The BKA has emerged as a powerful criminal

---

[15] *Gesetz Über die Einrichtung eines Bundeskriminalpolizieamtes (Bundes-kriminalamtes)*, 8 Mar. 1951 (amended). Article 1 states that the BKA has

intelligence service in a federal system whose constitution reserves police powers to the *Länder* (the states). Its political position is similar to that of US federal law-enforcement agencies, which continuously have to prove the value of their services to avoid marginalization and decline. The BKA is, therefore, inclined to extend its role when any reasonable opportunity arises. In the 1970s its resources increased after Baader-Meinhof, and successor terrorist groups, became a serious police problem. Terrorism also required transfrontier co-operation with other police forces and the BKA was eager and well prepared to co-operate. Although it perhaps relied, in the investigation of terrorist offences, too much on computerized data systems at the expense of traditional policing methods, its approach was considerably in advance of other national police forces. The very positive attitude towards international co-operation has led to a similar outlook within the BKA to that found in the Washington NCB. Some of the best-informed thinking about international police co-operation takes place in Wiesbaden. In supporting progressive policies within Interpol and sending very able police officers to Saint-Cloud, the NCB Wiesbaden has played an important role in reviving the organization.

The NCBs of the United Kingdom and France are of much the same size and, although they have not espoused modern technology as quickly as their American and German counterparts, they have a high reputation in the practical business of replying quickly to requests for case-related information. The Paris NCB with twenty-five officials in 1987 is slightly smaller than the London NCB with thirty-three, but the number of professional police officers in the former is larger. The police structure of the two countries is very different. In France, Interpol is part of the office of the national director of criminal investigation and it is possible to insist that most international contacts pass through the NCB.[16] The NCB in Scotland Yard has to rely mainly on voluntary co-operation because the Metropolitan Police have little direct control over the provincial police forces. Provincial chief constables may prefer to

responsibilities to counteract criminal activists who operate internationally and the same article established the BKA as the NCB for the Federal Republic of Germany.

[16] The National Director of the Police Judiciaire has attached to his office an International Relations Division which deals with Interpol work and other matters such as missions of French police officers abroad and foreign police officers in France, extraditions, international investigations, and international conferences.

work through the London FBI representative on cases involving the United States, rather than through Interpol. In both countries, Interpol has been regarded as a source of low level technical–administrative co-operation for routine matters, occasionally useful in fields such as drugs and counterfeit money. Both NCBs regard close bilateral co-operation as essential in complex cases. They tend to use the global telecommunications system parsimoniously—in other words they do not use it like the Germans for gathering general information or the Italians, who circulate an abundance of information on the grounds that it may be of use to someone. They are workmanlike but not given to enthusiasm about international co-operation.

In police circles, there is often thought to be a north–south divide in Europe, with a different law-enforcement atmosphere prevailing in Italy and Spain. The Italians cause irritation in northern Europe because some messages from Rome are unnecessarily marked urgent and information is sent which seems to be of Italian interest only. Italian police officers are keen to travel on missions to other countries and occasionally turn up unannounced. Although some Italian police behaviour causes raised eyebrows among their colleagues in other countries, there is a clear Italian commitment to international co-operation. There is now a US–Italian police agreement and the Italian authorities have worked closely with US law-enforcement agencies on drugs and organized crime cases—the most celebrated recent examples are the so-called 'Pizza connection' cases which in 1987 resulted in convictions in US courts.[17] In the Spanish case, an important reassessment of international police co-operation has been part of three developments: changes of personnel in the 1980s at the top levels of the Policia Nacional, the police reform promulgated in an Organic Law of 1986, and Spanish membership of the European Community. A desire to integrate the police, for long regarded as a caste apart, in Spanish society has been accompanied by a willingness on the part of the impressively able leadership of the Policia Nacional to adapt to changes in international society.

One of the few survivors of the Franco period in a senior position in the Policia Nacional is Asterillos, the head of the Madrid NCB. He has been a member of the Executive Committee of Interpol and occupies a key position in the Spanish police hierarchy. Until recently virtually all foreign police relations passed through his hands, but there is now a tendency among

[17] *Washington Post*, 3 Mar. 1987.

senior Spanish policemen to regard the Interpol NCB as an administrative office; they consider that questions of policy concerning international police co-operation should be conducted through EPC—the Trevi Group. There is no doubt that the senior officials in the Spanish police regard as essential close international co-operation in the fight against Basque terrorism[18] and in drug law enforcement, especially since Spain has become one of the 'gateways of Europe' for the import of drugs.

The hierarchical importance of the NCBs, their political influence and the degree to which those involved in them have positive attitudes towards international police co-operation are important factors in the development of the Interpol system. They have often failed to exercise influence on governments because they have not wished to play a political role and have sought to keep 'politics' out of police co-operation. Unwillingness to exert pressure on government ministers has been regarded by senior members of Interpol, such as Carl Persson, as old-fashioned and dangerous for the organization. Since in the Netherlands, Belgium, West Germany, and Italy critics of Interpol have often been strong supporters of 'Europol', a specifically European criminal intelligence organization, there is undoubtedy substance in Persson's view. The NCBs are essential providers of information about Interpol and are a potentially important source of considered argument about how Interpol can and should be developed. Some NCBs, such as Washington, Wiesbaden, and Stockholm, have been successful in producing a new type of diplomat–policeman, sensitive to the practical and political problems of international police co-operation. The vastly increased volume of international police business helps these new-style police officers to promote change because the increase in international crime is compelling Ministries of the Interior and senior police officers to take greater notice of systems of co-operation.

The leading members of Interpol and the decision-making process

In the advanced industrial democracies, despite some well-publicized cases, awareness of the implications of international crime has not until recently extended beyond small circles of those professionally involved in law enforcement. In small countries,

---

[18] Interview with chief of anti-terrorist division, Spanish Policia Nacional, 15 July 1987.

such as Austria, Belgium, and Sweden, with close transfrontier relations with foreign police authorities, the awareness has been more widespread. These countries have produced the men, Schober, Louwage, and Persson, who were respectively responsible for launching the ICPC in 1923, re-establishing it in 1946, and helping to revive it in the 1980s. Although small countries can initiate change in the international system, they cannot exercise a continuing and major influence over a genuinely international organization. Interpol is no exception.

Austrian influence in the inter-war period predominated because the ICPC was not a genuine international organization—it was administered as part of the Vienna police department. In the post-1945 period, French influence, which started to erode in the late 1960s, was maintained because the ICPC–ICPO was not a mature international organization. French dominance was a historical accident because no other suitable host country was available in 1946: it was not the result of an act of political will by a French government or by senior French administrators. After its establishment in France, Interpol came to be valued in the French national police but no evidence exists to suggest that it was deliberately used as a means of spreading French police or political influence. The STCIP in the Ministry of the Interior was a much more obvious instrument to exert such influence.

The special French position lasted for over a quarter of a century because of lack of British and US interest, and the temporary weakness of the West German position. Although Sir Harold Jackson successfully posed his candidature for the Presidency of Interpol in 1960, apparently irritated by the French preponderance, British influence seemed to be in the direction of keeping the organization as low profile and informal as possible. The United States gave no evidence of having much interest in Interpol until the late 1970s. The Nazi regime destroyed the international reputation of the German police and, until the Dickkopf presidency (1968–72), the Germans did not play a major role. None the less, in the 1980s these four countries, followed by Canada and Japan, can be described as leading members of the organization. They all have important police traditions and they are leaders in adopting new police techniques. They have shown over a long period a willingness to help other countries in training policemen and advising on equipment; they were the first, along with Sweden, to begin the practice of seconding police officers to the Headquarters of Interpol; generally, they have aspired to play a role in international co-operation, although in the case of Britain a narrowly circumscribed one.

These countries, however, do not control the organization. There is no analogy either with Unesco, in which the United States, before it withdrew, paid approximately 30 per cent of the budget, or with the United Nations, where the major powers have permanent seats on the Security Council. The six richest countries have paid the same subscriptions for some years and the leading states do not have permanent seats on the Executive Committee. There has been no consistent drive by the leading six for influence on all matters and the lead on issues often comes from other countries. For example, as a matter of tactics, the United States takes a secondary role if another country wishes to press a policy line of which the US approves. This absence of ambition on the part of leading members to control the organization can, however, be interpreted in some periods as a lack of desire to develop the role and effectiveness of Interpol.

Representation by eminent individuals can raise the standing of other countries, at least for a time. Obvious examples are Florent Louwage, Inspector General of the Belgian police, who was President of the ICPC from 1946 to 1956—the longest term served by any President either of the ICPC or of Interpol. Similarly Carl Persson, who already had an international reputation in police circles because of his role in establishing the Swedish National Police in the 1960s, occupied the Presidency during the difficult years in the late 1970s and early 1980s, preceding the signature of the second Headquarters Agreement. After he retired from the Presidency, he was still called upon to play an important advisory role. Professional respect for individuals is therefore a factor in the exercise of influence.

There are no indications that the influence of the major countries has been used to exclude or diminish the role of others: on the contrary, there has been an evident desire to include as wide a cross-section of General Assembly members as possible in the business of the organization. Maximizing support, not marginalizing some members, has been the aim of Secretaries General and Executive Committees of Interpol. Executive Committee membership has been spread as widely as possible and there is an equitable geographical distribution between the continents. Recognition of geopolitical realities led to a strong Japanese presence in Interpol (the head of the Police Division of the organization has, since 1985, been Akira Kawada of Japan) and to the incorporation of the People's Republic of China. In 1985, one year after the contested election over the membership of the Republic of China, a Chinese representative was elected to the Executive Committee. Both China and Japan had genuine interests in international police co-operation but they were also pursuing a general policy of extending their influence in international organizations.

Although the leading members of the organization can readily be identified, decision-making processes in Interpol cannot be described in detail because of confidentiality in the conduct of business. The process of policy-making is a mixture of formal resolutions in the General Assemblies, Executive Committee decisions, and action by the General Secretariat. The types of decisions taken concern representation in the organization, its aims and purposes, the boundaries between Interpol and other international organizations, programmes of activity, and operational and management decisions in the Headquarters.

The acceptance of new members is the simplest policy issue which regularly comes before General Assemblies. Prior to 1956, an application to join had to come from the appropriate ministerial authority in the applicant country; although this rule was not included in the 1956 Statutes, applications are normally made through diplomatic channels. After 1956, the only major disagreement about an application was in 1984 over the People's Republic of China. Future disputes are unlikely: an application from the USSR would not pose a major problem although there would be political reservations. The credentials of the delegates to the General Assembly, however, could cause problems. The composition of delegations has been left to member countries. This has resulted in very different sizes of delegation depending on the location of the General Assembly, the relative wealth of the member countries (the poorer and smaller countries are sometimes unrepresented), and the number of police agencies in a country with active international interests. This inequality in the size of delegations has no implications for voting rights because each delegation has only one vote. But the political weight of numerically strong delegations is greater than the countries represented by one or two people. Recent attempts to bring some standardization into the composition of delegations has been resisted, by the British amongst others, and this is one of the matters which would have to be addressed in any revision of the Statutes of Interpol.

The most important type of representation decision is the election of officers—the President and Secretary General. After the long period of office of President Florent Louwage, who, by taking the initiative to revive the CIPC in 1946, virtually selected himself for the office, no President has served for more than the one term permitted by the 1956 Statutes. According to the Statutes, any delegate to the General Assembly may be elected President, but a successful candidate almost certainly has experience on the Executive Committee because a good working knowledge of the organization is essential. This requirement creates the opportunity of electing Presidents from a wide range of countries because the Executive Committee membership is based on a balanced representation of the continents. Only Belgium has had two Presidents since the Second World War and one of these, F. Fransson, served for only two years.

Most elections to the Presidency have neither political significance outside the organization nor any international relations impact. The way in which delegates vote is not recorded; no one is asked and no one volunteers explanations for votes in elections. Political pressures and prejudices almost certainly have some influence—it would be surprising if, in the 1985 election for the Presidency, representatives of Hungary, Romania, and Iran voted for Mr John Simpson, the Head of the US Secret Service.

Presidents have been elected because candidates come from a certain region and because their presence is useful inside the organization. The location of the General Assembly has some influence on successful candidates. The planning or the holding of a successful General Assembly helps a President to 'emerge', not always with desirable consequences. Jolly Bugarin, the Phillippines police chief, was elected at the 1980 Manilla General Assembly. This election was inconvenient for the organization because communication between Saint-Cloud and Manilla was difficult during a critical period in the negotiations for the second Headquarters Agreement. More important, the external reputation of Interpol was not well-served by the election of Marcos's police chief. The election of a Chilean to the Executive Committee at a time when the Pinochet regime was the subject of international opprobrium was a similar political error (although unconnected with the location of the General Assembly). In police circles, the disingenuous argument is made that the criminal police are not directly involved in political repression by dictatorships and these elections should not, therefore, be regarded as marks of approval for these regimes.

The election in 1985 for the Presidency set a precedent because it was regarded outside the organization as politically important. Coinciding with the appointment of Raymond Kendall as interim Secretary General (an appointment confirmed for a full term of office by the Assembly General in 1986), this was labelled as an 'Anglo-Saxon' takeover in the French Press, reflecting a sentiment held in French police circles. More important, the election confirmed the serious interest of the US federal government in Interpol. The presence of both President Reagan and Attorney General Meese at the 1985 Washington General Assembly symbolically expressed the US interest. The Americans were known to be impatient with the lack of dynamism, the slowness to adopt new techniques, and the lack of effective participation in anti-terrorist action by Interpol. Some participants in the election argue that the choice of John Simpson was not as 'political' as it appears, on the grounds that the American turn was due. Seven previous Presidents had been drawn from European countries but only one from either North or South America. But the consequence of the election of John Simpson is that the choice of President will, in future, have greater significance outside the organization and have greater practical importance inside it. This, in turn, will lead to greater competition to serve on the Executive Committee and a tendency for member countries to build electoral coalitions with a view to influencing the outcome of the elections for President.

The choice of Secretary General is subject to different considerations. The French Ministry of the Interior was the 'grand elector' for the first four Secretaries General after 1946.[19] The decisive role of the French Ministry of the Interior was inevitable as long as the clear expectation remained as stated in the 1946 and 1956 Statutes—that the Secretary General would be French. Eligible candidates had to be drawn from the police officers made available to Interpol by the French Ministry of the Interior. When the time came to elect a new Secretary General, a nomination was made by the director of the Police Nationale, after consultation with the Minister of the Interior. The official elections by the General Assembly were, therefore, ceremonial rather than decision-making occasions. Candidates emerged who may not have been to everybody's satisfaction but there was no public controversy.

---

[19] For example, it was reported at the 1951 Lisbon General Assembly that Secretary Ducloux had consulted the French Prime Minister (also Minister of the Interior) Henri Queuille, who had 'advised' the CIPC to choose Marcel Sicot; *International Criminal Police Review* (Aug.–Sept. 1951), 251.

This situation could not long survive the internationalization of Headquarters personnel. It came to an abrupt end in 1985 with the resignation of André Bossard, because there was no obvious French successor in the General Secretariat. Imposing a senior French police official without previous Interpol Headquarters experience would have been impolitic. The elections of the President in 1985 in Washington and of the Secretary General in 1986 in Belgrade were real decisions with a significant impact on the organization. These elections will almost certainly affect the nature of future elections: in particular, it is unlikely that subsequent Secretaries General will be chosen from members of the staff of the General Secretariat. But the public impression given by Interpol was that both were as uncontroversial as all the previous elections.

Decisions concerning the basic principles and aims of the organization have often seemed, at the time at which they were made, mainly of ritual or philosophic significance. Examples of such decisions have been the adoption of the UN Declaration of the Rights of Man as part of the objectives of the organization;[20] Article 2 of the 1956 Statutes defining the aims of the organization as establishing and developing all institutions capable of preventing and repressing common-law crimes; and Article 3 of the same Statutes forbidding involvement in cases of a political, religious, or racial nature. The respect for the laws of member states was also written into the Statutes; the principle of national sovereignty has been reaffirmed on many occasions since 1956. Proposals for statements of general principles emerged from drafts prepared in the General Secretariat and were adopted without difficulty. Some have policy implications and in certain circumstances they can be difficult to implement. The most banal question, raised by statements of principle accepted by Interpol, is whether disregard for human rights, as defined in the UN declaration, is compatible with membership of Interpol. This is not a question which members address because virtually all countries have infringed these rights: a similar question is posed and avoided by membership of the United Nations itself.

Restricting the activities of the organization to ordinary law crimes creates practical difficulties. The first problem is that the separation between criminal and civil law is not the same in all

[20] *International Criminal Police Review* (Oct. 1949) published the Universal Declaration of the Rights of Man of 10 Dec. 1948, in full, emphasizing in heavy type the parts of interest to the police.

member countries and in Islamic countries it does not exist. This is not especially troublesome because the main categories of serious crime are also considered crimes in these countries. However, the NCBs of Islamic law countries sometimes unwittingly communicate 'civil law' information through the Interpol network.[21] With the more formal data-protection rules operating since 1984, this should cease, because the categories of information which can be transmitted are more explicitly defined.

The main difficulty is the threshold between 'ordinary' criminality and political crime, particularly as governments have persistently attempted to treat politically motivated acts of violence as ordinary crimes. The ICPC, after the Second World War, decided that fugitives from a country where a regime had collapsed were political, falling outside the competence of the organization. For many years Interpol was therefore not involved in the search for Nazi war criminals. The arguments in favour of this policy were that if Interpol had been involved on previous occasions it would probably have been ineffective. Involvement would have set an awkward precedent;[22] it would have been more difficult to refuse the controversial Cuban demand in 1959 (referred to in Chapter 2) to locate former officials of the Battista regime. But the decision not to assist in the tracing of Nazi war criminals was almost certainly mistaken. Nazi crimes had no precedent, they had been condemned by an international tribunal as crimes against humanity, and they were publicly abhorred by the great majority of governments and public opinion throughout the world. Interpol would have lost nothing, and would probably have gained some reputation as a defender of human rights, by circulating information about Nazi war criminals. Instead, Interpol attracted suspicions that it harboured Nazi sympathizers.

A more important modification of the principle of non-involvement in political cases has been the reinterpretation of Article 3 of the 1956 Statutes as a result of pressures posed by international terrorism. Until the 1980s Interpol followed a very cautious policy on terrorism, although involvement in the security of civil aviation and in illegal traffic in arms had brought the

---

[21] This has particularly affected France, which has had notably close relations with the Muslim countries of North Africa.

[22] The borderline between political cases and criminal cases was always difficult but pressure to become involved in the former has been resisted. Secretary General Marcel Sicot writes, ' . . . in cases concerning the FLN and the "red hand", I advised the French authorities to deal directly with other countries and vice-versa' (M. Sicot, *A la Barre de l'Interpol* (Paris, 1961), 33).

organization into terrorist-related cases. The turning point came in a resolution on 'Violent Crime Commonly Known as Terrorism' passed by the 1984 Luxemburg General Assembly. This resolution was based on the principle of 'preponderance' enunciated by the 1951 General Assembly—actions had to have a preponderant political, religious, or racial character to fall under Article 3. Terrorist acts always involve common-law offences such as murder, violence against individuals, theft, and the destruction of property. The 1984 resolution stressed the impossibility of giving a precise definition of a predominantly criminal rather than political, religious, or racial matter; a case-by-case approach had to be adopted. The change of policy was necessary to help Interpol to react positively to other international systems of communication established to combat terrorism and to avoid a marginal role in an area of policing which major governments took very seriously.[23]

Boundary problems with other international organizations

Anti-terroism raised a question of the boundary between Interpol and other international organizations, particularly the Trevi Group in Europe. This question had been previously raised in relations with the United Nations and the Council of Europe, both having certain interests in law-enforcement issues. Both the United Nations and the Council of Europe provide a meeting place to discuss common approaches to problems and these discussions may eventually lead to international treaties and multilateral conventions. Some UN agencies, such as FAO, WHO, and Unido, do deliver services; however, for the most part, this is not the case for the activities of the UN which touch on areas of concern to Interpol—human rights, treatment of prisoners, and drugs. The main functions of the UN in these areas are to arrange discussions between governments and non-governmental organizations, to draft conventions, and to publish reports and statistics. However, there is an overlap between the UNDND and Interpol; the UNDND receives the same statistical reports as Interpol of drug seizures from the member countries, runs courses for drug law-enforcement officers, and organizes the regional and world conferences of HONLEA. Although Interpol is a recipient of funds through a parallel UN agency, the United Nations Fund for Drug Abuse Control (UNFDAC), it has not, at the moment, the

[23] See below, ch. 6, for a more extensive discussion of Interpol and Terrorism.

resources to take over these UNDND functions. There is a potential boundary conflict between the UNDND and Interpol but, unless Interpol acquires greater government and political support, the conflict is unlikely to develop.

Boundary problems occur when a permanent multilateral agency performs a role similar to that of Interpol. The first threat of this kind of competition was the joint proposal of Egypt, France, Mexico, and the United States to the seventh session of the UN Commission on Narcotic Drugs in 1952 for an international agency to combat the drugs trade. This was revived by the American proposal in 1971–2 to establish an international drugs commission involving countries in which substantial quantities of drugs were produced, distributed, or consumed. A specialized agency, according to American arguments, was the only effective way of controlling trafficking. Jean Nepote, then the Secretary General of Interpol, made some pointed criticisms of the proposal,[24] but the proposal was not completely buried and the Reagan administration hinted at reviving it. The Pompidou Group, founded on the initiative of the French president in 1973, grouping the countries of the Council of Europe to co-ordinate the fight against drug abuse, was an embryonic international drugs commission for Europe but this group did not develop an operational function. The Trevi Group has, however, developed an anti-terrorism communications network, and has started parallel systems of communication for 'undesirable individuals' (a blacklist of suspected terrorists) and information about explosives. The Trevi Group is also discussing methods of combating drug abuse, reinforcing external frontier controls, and co-operating to repress football hooliganism.[25] Not all the activities of the Trevi Group could take place within the framework of Interpol and, in the future, some kind of European police authority will be necessary. There are, however, difficult boundary problems with Interpol to be resolved.

The proposal for an international drugs commission and the establishment of the Pompidou Group and the Trevi Group show that governments of the advanced industrialized democracies are, at least intermittently, convinced of the need for closer law-enforcement co-operation. There is an ever-present temptation to

[24] Greilsamer, *Interpol*, 144–6.
[25] The range of Trevi group activities is contained in the press release, *Réunion des Ministères de la Justice et de l'Intérieur de la Communauté Européenne* (Bruxelles, 28 Apr. 1987).

establish new organizations rather than to strengthen existing arrangements for co-operation. Several factors contribute: politicians' ambitions to link their names to new achievements, ignorance of Interpol and negative judgements about the organization's effectiveness, and Interpol's lack of influence in national policy-making. The task of defending Interpol's unique role and contribution rests mainly with the Secretary General and the President of Interpol, aided by the more active NCBs; they have few resources with which to accomplish this task.

Internal policy issues

Interpol must make decisions concerning internal management, finance, and programmes of activity. These are broadly regarded as the domain of the Secretary General, although minor matters are delegated to subordinate officials, and major decisions and general policy have to be approved by the Executive Committee and the General Assembly. In common with all organizations, Interpol has experienced management problems. Personnel difficulties have been particularly severe in the 1980s because not all senior staff have been sufficiently adaptable in a period of rapid change. A persistent difficulty is that seconded staff have varying levels of professional competence and a less strong commitment to the organization than the permanent staff. Mutual confidence between the Secretary General, the President, and the Executive Committee can easily overcome these problems. This confidence has broken down on only one occasion—in the period when management problems were particularly difficult, immediately preceeding, and perhaps immediately after, André Bossard's early retirement in 1985. This period revealed limitations in existing practices and a certain managerial backwardness in Interpol compared with the police forces of its leading members.

The 1956 Statutes explicitly give the Secretary General the authority to propose to the General Assembly the programme of activities for the following year. This is done after consultation with the Executive Committee and other members of the organization. Interpol has now a very considerable range of activities covering matters such as conferences, training programmes, studies, working parties, and symposiums.[26] Many

---

[26] The programme of activities listed at the end of the 1985 Washington General Assembly was particularly ambitious; see *International Criminal Police Review* (Dec. 1985), 283–4.

activities are inherited from the past and some could not easily be jettisoned without causing offence. Decisions about the programme activities can have wider implications than is sometimes realized at the time: André Bossard considered that the early demands for regionalization in Interpol were the result, not of a genuine wish to decentralize the organization, but of the lack of a sufficient programme of activities at the regional level.[27] The vigilance and sensitivity to the needs of the membership on the part of the Secretary General is crucial to prevent the buildup of frustration about the lack of responsiveness of the organization.

There have been two persistent problems in financial management—the assessment and payment of dues, and the adoption of modern accounting and budgetary procedures. The system of assessing budgetary contributions prior to 1958 was a subscription based on population, which was unrelated either to the member's ability to pay or to its use of the Interpol system. The system adopted in 1958, on the proposal of Jean Nepote, contained four criteria: the per capita income of the population, the use made of and benefit derived from membership, the financial position of the state, and the size of its population. These are aggregated to calculate the number of budgetary units a member should pay. The members themselves choose their own level of subscription, although if they are uncertain the Secretary General can offer advice. Members are naturally reluctant to revise their subscriptions in an upward direction and are occasionally exhorted to do so by the President and Secretary General.

Failure of members to pay their subscriptions in time is a long-standing problem—the problem has become worse in recent years because of policies of public expenditure restraint in most countries. Even the United States was reported in 1971 to be three years behind in its subscriptions. A number of countries have had General Regulation 53 (since the end of 1985 GR 52) applied to them, suspending their right to vote for not paying subscriptions. The club-like atmosphere of Interpol has made the organization reluctant to apply this sanction. In addition, suspension has had little practical effect because Interpol has always been ready to communicate with non-members. This easy-going attitude is changing: in 1987 the Belgian former Vice-President of Interpol, Van Hove, was charged with examining the whole question of subscriptions. Several ideas have been floated—action by the

[27] Interview with André Bossard, 16 Nov. 1986.

Secretary General in the form of personal visits and special letters to defaulting countries, inclusion as a regular item on all regional conferences, the withholding of certain rights and services from defaulting countries, as well as positive moves such as encouraging rich countries to pay the contributions of poor countries as a form of aid. The issue is a serious one because at the end of 1987 the arrears were about seven million Swiss francs, equivalent to the total technical investment programme of Interpol for the ensuing five years.

In 1968 the first serious demand for an external audit was made by the United States and thereafter the Americans kept up pressure over this issue. At the General Assembly of 1986 (following a resolution of principle adopted in the previous year) the French *Cour des Comptes* was appointed to conduct an external audit of the organization's administrative and financial management for the three years beginning 1 January 1987. Part-time external financial advisers and a full-time budgeting specialist within the General Secretariat were appointed at the same time. Despite the lack of publicity about financial matters in the past and what one leading member called 'corner-shop' financial management, there is no suggestion of profligacy, let alone corruption, in the organization.

Interpol's own resources are limited; although Jean Nepote succeeded in increasing the money available to Interpol, he constantly complained that it was not enough. Carl Persson, the President of Interpol, made a strong statement about the low level of resources at the Panama General Assembly in 1978 and said that lack of money limited the effectiveness of Interpol in various ways. The present Secretary General has complained with even greater force in an interview given to the French daily newspaper *Libération* on the occasion of the 1986 Belgrade General Assembly,[28] and on other occasions. The lack of resources has had the effect of a greater than desirable reliance on staff seconded and paid for by national police forces and less effective criminal intelligence gathering in certain areas. For example, economic crime involving international financial transactions requires professional, and expensive, analytical expertise in order to follow up leads. The Financial and Economic Crime Unit was expanded after a decision of the Cannes General Assembly of 1983 by the creation of a financial investigations group, Financial Operations, Profits, and Assets of Crime (FOPAC), but it is small by

[28] *Libération*, 14 Oct. 1986.

comparison with the fraud squads of police authorities in major financial centres.

In terms of expenditure, much more is spent on the NCBs financed by national budgets than on the Headquarters services financed by subscriptions. Calculating how much is spent by national governments on the NCBs is an impossible task because the funding of them is usually hidden under broader budgetary headings—not even members of NCBs of industrialized countries are aware of exactly how much money is involved. How much should be spent depends on the role of the NCBs: if they are conceived merely as communications facilities, the resources required are strictly limited; if they are providers of international criminal intelligence, them their need for resources becomes very much greater.

The context of policy-making

Wide experience and good judgement are required to make the very different types of decisions described in this chapter. The competence of the Secretary General and his leading collaborators are therefore important in promoting the interests of the organization. But the standing of Interpol, like any other international organization, depends on factors outside its control—general social and economic conditions, unforeseen events, policies of major powers, and influential public opinion. Interpol is operating in a relatively favourable environment in that long-term economic, social, and technological trends support the development of closer international police co-operation. The policies of major countries (with the exception of the USSR) are usually supportive and, at worst, constitute benign neglect.

There is, however, an ever-present possibility that a major country will propose the establishment of a parallel, overlapping, or competing organization because Interpol does not have the support of influential public opinion. Whether or not this support emerges depends on governments' priorities in law enforcement, the prominence given to particular issues by the Press and television, and the direct impact on citizens within member states of the activities of the organization. Public opinion-poll data show a high degree of awareness of the European Community among the citizens of member states because governments have given very high priority to issues of economic management and have stressed that prosperity depends on a favourable external environment;

the Press and television have given much coverage to the Community, especially in times of crisis; and the public at large is aware that in matters such as food prices and harmonization of legislation the Community affects them directly. Interpol's situation is very different and, in the absence of opinion poll data, it can confidently be asserted that few people, outside the circles which take a direct interest in police matters, know anything about its role or even the location of its Headquarters. Some change in this is essential if Interpol is to increase its influence and resources.

5. Drugs and International Law Enforcement

THE limits to a state's sovereignty are the limits to its ability to make good a particular claim. The claim of the richest and most powerful state in the world, the United States, to control its own territory is undermined by its inability to stem the tide of illicit drug imports, despite the deployment of vast police, intelligence, and military resources. Realization of the limitation of the effectiveness of states in this domain has led to a desire for inter-state co-operation and the establishment of a complex system of international agencies and instruments. Interpol plays a part in this system, which also includes an array of regional and bilateral arrangements. But a solution to the drugs problem is not in sight because it has a protean form, changing over time: suppression of one form of traffic and one pattern of drug abuse leads to the emergence of others. How the problem is defined is crucial to the development of approaches to it. Expressed in the simplest way, the defining of the non-medical use of drugs as a criminal act has allowed the growth of the largest criminal enterprise ever seen. No government is, however, prepared to deprive the drug traffickers of their profits by decriminalization because of the medical and social problems which are likely to occur. However, repression by the police and the criminal law has not worked.

This chapter briefly examines how governments came to recognize drug trafficking as a worldwide problem, the dimensions of the problem, how governments respond to it, and the attempt to put in place a global system of control. Current developments in this system and the central, if limited, role of Interpol in it are then assessed. The United States is the largest market for drugs and has been most active in seeking international solutions to drug trafficking, but the European countries have experienced increasing drugs problems in the last decade and have, consequently, followed the US example.

Drug trafficking as a global problem

Both law and opinion about drug abuse have gone through remarkable changes. In the course of history, the non-medical use of drugs has been widely approved in many societies for religious and social purposes. With the exception of alcohol, this has not been the case in advanced industrial societies but the extensive use of drugs in medical practice has seemed to encourage their non-medical use. The intractable problem of drug abuse in the highly industrialized countries seems to have originated in the mass consumption of patent medicines with opiate bases in the nineteenth century. Drug dependence was noted at the time by the American medical profession; but it was not considered as dangerous as the consumption of alcohol and tobacco until the Civil War greatly exacerbated the problem. The synthesizing of morphine from an opium base at the end of the nineteenth century provoked a significant rise of anxiety in the United States about narcotic drug dependence. In 1908 Congress established the Opium Commission to consider the effects and remedies for drug abuse. Also in 1908, the Shanghai Convention outlawed the Asian opium trade, mainly as a result of American pressure, in the face of the indifference of the European powers. The 1909 Act of Congress known as 'An Act to Prohibit the Importation and Use of Opium for other than Medicinal Purposes' was the first regulation of opium in the United States. The United States has since led the way, both in domestic legislation and law enforcement, and in pressing for international action to control drug trafficking. The results achieved are not commensurate with the resources devoted to the problem.

American and European perspectives on the drugs problem, widely divergent during most of the nineteenth and the twentieth centuries, have come closer together in the past fifteen years. The opium trade in nineteenth-century Asia was an important political and commercial interest for France and Britain, whereas influential and official opinion in the United States regarded it as an immoral traffic. In the twentieth century, down to the 1960s, European countries with some exceptions regarded drug addiction as a marginal problem which could be managed, for the most part, by the medical services. The Americans, on the other hand, have been acutely aware of drug-taking epidemics exploited by criminal conspiracies; the various responses to these epidemics have been both repetitive and ineffective. Since the Harrison Narcotics Act of 1914 the American response to drug addiction has been primarily repressive and this has been supported by strongly held moral attitudes. Since the 1960s, however, European and American policies to control drug abuse have developed a similar mix of education, rehabilitation, and repression. On both sides of the Atlantic drug trafficking, once considered to be a local or a regional matter, is now recognized as a problem for the international community which can only be tackled effectively by internationally co-ordinated action. However, the attempt to repress the non-medical use of drugs by the use of the criminal law is occasionally questioned because it fails to control the supply of drugs and allows criminals to gain enormous profits. The validity of promoting the use, and abuse, of one powerful drug, alcohol, and outlawing the use of other, possibly milder, drugs is also questioned.

The size of the problem and governments' response

Estimates of an illegal or clandestine traffic are always of doubtful reliability, but, according to the best available figures, the scale of the international traffic in psychotropic and narcotic drugs has vastly increased in the last two decades. Since 1977 the increasing amount of drugs seized, the fall in 'street' prices of some drugs, and the increasing diversity of drugs available suggest that there has been a rapid growth of supply as traffickers have sought to cash in on an immensely profitable trade. In some cases the amount of drugs seized by law-enforcement agencies has risen enormously; for example, in the United States the amount of cocaine seized more than quintupled between 1981 and 1984 without having much effect on the street price.[1] The trend has continued—as much as two tons in a single consignment was seized by US Customs in August 1987 and in November of the same year a DEA-led operation at Fort Lauderdale in Florida seized a consignment of cocaine valued at half a billion dollars. Also in autumn 1987 a combined operation of UK Customs and Dutch police and customs led to the seizure in Rotterdam of Columbian cocaine valued at £50 million. In 1987 UK seizure of cocaine increased by four times over the 1986 figures and heroin seizures were up by one-third; the European 'record' for a single drug seizure is one ton of cocaine found by Spanish police at a deserted warehouse in Irun in May 1988. Heroin prices have declined in the United Kingdom in the 1980s and evidence from other European

---

[1] The authoritative source of US statistics is the Narcotics Intelligence Estimate (NIE) published annually by the National Narcotics Intelligence Consumers Committee (NNIC) established in 1978 to co-ordinate foreign and domestic intelligence.

countries suggests that drugs are readily available despite a large increase in the amount of the drug seized.

The United States remains the largest and most profitable market, according to DEA estimates, there are 2 million regular and 12 million intermittent users of cocaine. The law-enforcement situation deteriorated during 1987 with the price per kilo of cocaine dropping in Florida from $30,000 to $13,000. The total illicit drug market in the United States may involve as much as $130 billion. But all industrial countries are affected and some third-world countries have reported serious problems. In addition, the association of drugs with other forms of crime is now well established. In the United States drugs are involved in between 30 and 40 per cent of crimes of larceny, robbery, and burglary, and 20 and 30 per cent of assaults and murders.[2] The trend in all the advanced industrial societies is for drug-related crime to increase, and the effects go far beyond local law-enforcement problems. The international traffic has been estimated in 1987 by the UNDND at $300 billion—more than the combined external debt of Mexico, Brazil, and Argentina. This results in large illegal movement of funds—sufficient in size to threaten the integrity of the international banking system. It also means that legitimate businesses and banks are extensively used by international criminal conspiracies. There is also evidence that drugs have been used as an alternative currency in illegal arms trading and in financing terrorism.[3]

These sombre facts have resulted in a change in the law-enforcement atmosphere in Europe and North America. Since the early 1970s the problem of drug abuse has assumed a regular and prominent place on the political agenda. Since the 1970s the movement to decriminalize drug use has ceased to command wide support. However, some influential figures in the law-enforcement community have recently been casting doubt on conventional views on the effectiveness of present policies. Decriminalization and the licensed sale of drugs for non-medical use could destroy the wealth and power of the drug traffickers, but this argument is

---

[2] DEA figures; see US Department of Justice, *Annual Reports of the Attorney General*; DEA, *A Profile* (various edns.); DEA, *Intelligence Trends* (Quarterly); DEA, *Drugs of Abuse* (various edns.).

[3] J. Adams, *The Financing of Terror* (London, 1986), 265–89, *passim*. The evidence of the links between drug trafficking and terrorism mainly relates to Middle Eastern and third-world groups. Despite allegations of IRA and FLNC (Corsican nationalist) involvement in trafficking, nothing has been proven. Interview, the head of the 6th division of the French Police Judiciaire, responsible for anti-terrorist action, 10 Dec. 1986; see also *Le Monde*, 7–8 Aug. 1988.

not taken seriously by governments. In European countries, deviant drug cultures continue to exist and drug abuse has penetrated some privileged milieux, such as the financial community of the City of London, as well as some surprising ones, such as prisons, but governments are in broad agreement about how to tackle the problem.

In the Netherlands, long regarded as the Mecca for drug takers in Europe, permissive attitudes are in decline. Toleration of soft drugs still has supporters in the police—in 1987 Klaas Wiltung, a spokesman for the Dutch National Police, said that soft drugs were no more dangerous than alcohol and had little effect on the overall crime rate. But as a result of the burgeoning social, medical, and criminal problems associated with drug abuse, Dutch official and public opinion now generally takes a repressive view. After a 1987 meeting of the Pompidou Group, the Dutch Minister of Justice stated that there was now agreement among European governments on drug abuse. A similar change has taken place in Spain. In the post-Franco wave of libertarian sentiment, tolerance of soft drugs was widespread and the mayors of some large cities backed the cause of decriminalization. But Spain experienced the same problems as elsewhere and also acquired the reputation of being a major European gateway for the import of drugs. There has been a rapid improvement in Spanish police capacity to deal with drugs traffic, and, since April 1987, a major crack-down in the coastal regions, code-named 'Operation Springtime', has helped to correct the impression, in international police circles, of lack of determination in the pursuit of drug traffickers.

European policy-makers have accepted the American approach because of evidence of the grave consequences of drug addiction in terms of the destruction of individuals' health, family breakdown, crimes of violence, crimes against property, criminal conspiracies, and huge illicit profits. The long-term benefits of education and rehabilitation programmes are generally recognized, but emphasis is placed on attacking every link in the chain of drug trafficking— financing, manufacturing, growing, transporting, wholesaling, and retailing of drugs. International co-operation is regarded as essential in all these links, with the exception of retailing. Many third-world countries are now more aligned with the official views in the advanced industrialized democracies than they were in the 1960s. For some this change is recent and results from the increase in the demand for hard drugs among their own populations. For example, opium has been grown in the area of modern Pakistan from at least the early nineteenth century but no heroin addiction was reported there until the beginning of the 1980s. In 1987 official estimates put the number of addicts at over half a million.[4] Asian, African, and Latin American countries are reporting rapidly increasing problems associated with drug abuse and admitting their incapacity to deal with them.

At UN meetings to discuss drugs problems, deficiencies of police training, equipment, and organization in developing countries have been freely admitted by the countries concerned. In poorer and smaller countries, traffickers control whole regions with substantial support from local populations. Even in Brazil, a large and relatively rich country, drug traffickers control some of the poorer districts of the cities. Government ministers from the Turks and Caicos Islands and from Surinam have been convicted in US courts for drug-trafficking offences. Traffickers therefore influence the highest levels of some governments. Mr Ray Robinson, Prime Minister of Trinidad and Tobago, has stated that 'the power and complexity of the criminal drug network is such that it has penetrated the very fabric of our societies and threatens to corrupt our most sacred institutions'.[5] Violence is occasionally a more effective weapon than corruption in Columbia, Bolivia, and other countries. The association of drug trafficking with terrorism, political violence, corruption, and large-scale fraud has made the uncorrupted elements of governments of developing countries conclude that they must participate in a general international effort to repress the traffic. However, they tend to take the view that the demand for drugs in the rich countries remains the fundamental problem.

Despite the agreement, which cuts across ideological barriers, about the nature of the problem, it is a difficult task for the international community to devise and to implement effective policies to repress drug trafficking. The complex network of arrangements to combat trafficking already established at the global, regional, and bilateral levels has achieved some major coups but is clearly having only a marginal effect on the overall problem. Co-operation arrangements include both 'forum organizations', in which policy is discussed and some degree of harmonization of practice is achieved, and 'operational organizations', whose tasks are to pursue traffickers and to seize drugs and profits

---

[4] Figures presented to UN inter-governmental conference on drugs, Vienna 1987; *Le Monde*, 27 June 1987.   [5] *Financial Times*, 3 Sept. 1987.

from drugs. The distinction between these two types of organization is clear in principle but can be blurred in practice.

The international control system

The first attempt to introduce an international narcotics control system came just before the First World War with the signing of the 1912 Hague Convention.[6] After the First World War the system was expanded by the setting up of the International Narcotics Board and its integration into the League of Nations. In 1946 the UN Commission on Narcotic Drugs was established, with the UNDND as its executive arm. Under the authority of the General Assembly and ECOSOC, the Commission, with the help of the UNDND, was charged with drafting international conventions on drugs, providing a forum for exchange of information and co-ordination of national policies, acting as an agency to gather intelligence of drug trafficking, promoting research on drugs and drug abuse, and administering funds to assist aid programmes. Important landmarks in the work of the Commission and the UNDND were the drafting of the 1961 Single Convention on Narcotic Drugs and the 1971 Convention on Psychotropic Substances for drugs such as amphetamines, barbiturates, and LSD. The preparation of an important new single convention covering both types of drugs is now well advanced.[7] The UNDND keeps a register of national legislation in the drugs field with special reference to legislation introduced as a consequence of the international conventions. It also publishes brochures intended to be of practical help in combating drug abuse and trafficking.[8]

New patterns and increased prevalence of drug abuse in the 1960s stimulated further action by the UN General Assembly. In March 1971 it established UNFDAC to provide a means of supporting programmes too large to be financed from the regular UNDND budget. Money is provided on an annual basis by governments, non-governmental organizations, and private sources. It is well funded and ably led by Giuseppe di Gennaro, a professor of criminology and former head of the Italian State

[6] Interviews with Dr Ramos Galinos, director of UNDND, Bo Lewin (UNFDAC), Poulsen K. Bailey (UNDND), and Stephen Walsh (UNDND), 12 June 1987, greatly assisted in the preparation of this section.

[7] ECOSOC Commission on Narcotic Drugs, Report of the Secretary General, 2–11 February 1987, Draft Convention against Illicit Traffic in Narcotic and Psychotropic Substances, pp. 5–21, E/CN7/1987/2.

[8] See UNDND, *Publications Relating to International Drug Control* (Vienna, 1987).

Prosecution Service. The responsibilities of UNFDAC are wide—to combat illegal supply, traffic, and demand for drugs. It acts as banker, planner, and evaluator of projects, mainly in developing countries. It supports programmes for treatment and rehabilitation of addicts, education and information about drugs, drug research and the development of drug identification tests, laboratory training for chemists, and assistance for law-enforcement authorities. Depending on the issue, UNFDAC co-operates with other institutions in the UN family such as WHO, FAO, Unesco, ILO, and UNDND (and the narcotics laboratory under its control), as well as national agencies.

UNFDAC gives aid in the field of training law-enforcement officers—now usually done by sponsoring non-UN agencies to provide courses—in the provision to the developing countries of vehicles and telecommunications equipment and other materials to detect illicit drug cultivation and manufacture, and in assistance to monitor drug-trafficking routes. Since 1985 requests for aid are professionally vetted by, amongst others, an official with experience in both drug law enforcement and Interpol. Relatively modest amounts of money have been channelled to Interpol—notably $600,000 to finance a Caribbean telecommunications network to combat the transit of drugs through the area. UNFDAC also sponsors meetings for exchange of information about trends in drug abuse and techniques in drug-related police work. These serve the purpose of establishing personal contacts between police officers and public officials, which helps to ease difficulties in both bilateral and multilateral co-operation.

There are two areas in which the work of the United Nations comes close to police operations. The first is the Drugs Intelligence Unit of the UNDND, to which all member countries are supposed to report drug seizures; exactly the same information goes to Interpol, where it is analysed in a different way. Interpol could be the sole agent for collecting and analysing this information. UNDND also sponsors the HONLEA meetings. The oldest of these is the Far East Region, which has held thirteen meetings since 1972; the most recently established are for Africa and the Americas, both of which held their inaugural meetings in 1987. An inter-regional (world) meeting took place in Vienna in 1986 and a series of such meetings are planned. The UNDND is here involved in an activity in which Interpol has long specialized.

The question of duplication of effort occasionally surfaces. At the first inter-regional HONLEA a proposal was made for triennial meetings, but the opinion was also expressed that the law-enforcement community was already well served by frequent meetings held under the auspices of Interpol and the CCC, such as the European Drugs Conferences organized by Interpol, and the meetings of the Pompidou group. Although Interpol assists the UNDND in drawing up the agenda for the HONLEA meetings, joint sponsorship or even using Interpol as the organizing agency for the HONLEA meetings would be a more appropriate distribution of responsibilities. Interpol is the global organization with an operational role and therefore could be regarded either as the equal partner or as the leading agency in meetings on law enforcement. However, this would reduce UNDND responsibilities and governments would oppose it on the grounds that too much influence would be given to law-enforcement officers.

In Europe, a major political input is necessary to tidy up some of the overlaps between the Pompidou Group, the Trevi Group, the UNDND, and Interpol. In Asia, there is an equally complicated situation: in addition to the regional HONLEA, there are various forms of sub-regional co-ordination through the Interpol office in Bangkok, the Foreign Anti-Narcotics Community (FANC) in Thailand (an informal co-ordination group to pool intelligence and experience), the Colombo plan administration, the narcotics desk in ASEAN, and *ad hoc* co-ordination by the foreign drug liaison officers in the region. The ASEAN arrangements are the most highly developed sub-regional system. The narcotics desk of ASEAN was established in 1982 and in 1984 the six ASEAN countries adopted a common programme to counter drug trafficking and related criminal activity. An effort was made to harmonize legislation on matters such as the refusal of travel documents to convicted drug offenders and refusal of entry of offenders to the member countries. The death penalty was also introduced for serious drug offences. This was not controversial whilst the penalty was applied only to the nationals of these countries. However, in 1987, two Australians, one British born, were executed in Malaysia for offences relating to heroin, causing indignation in both Australia and Britain. Representatives of the ASEAN countries complained that there was a widespread belief in the highly industrialized democracies that Asian countries were lax about drug offences, but when they took strong action against foreigners, they were subject to racially prejudiced criticism.[9] In

---

[9] A British citizen was sentenced to death in 1988, see *Independent*, 19 Apr. 1988. Eight Asian countries have carried out the death penalty for drug offences;

addition to repressive measures, three ASEAN training centres have been created (for prevention in the Philippines, for treatment and rehabilitation in Malaysia, and for law enforcement in Thailand), and efforts in the field of education are planned.

Relationships between global, regional, sub-regional, and bilateral arrangements are obscure and constantly shifting. Difficulties arise between them for political reasons relating to sensitivities concerning state sovereignty and the varying strength of commitment on the part of governments to fight drug trafficking. The wide number of professions involved in this fight adds another layer of complexity. The expertise of many specialists is mobilized—in rural development, education and training, chemical, pharmaceutical, and psychological research, social policy, law, economics, political intelligence, and police. Specialists in these fields, and officials in agencies responsible for delivering services relating to them, differ in their interests and outlook. Differences in language, culture, and education are additional obstacles to international co-ordination. But there is often more goodwill at the international than at the national level, because most of those involved in international co-operation are interested to learn from the experience of other countries. In addition, the bureaucratic interests involved are not competing directly for government favours and resources. Despite this international goodwill, forum organizations, in particular, generate frustration. The conduct of business often seems to waste time—political posturing goes on when representatives from smaller and poorer states, for understandable reasons, want to gain publicity; the information communicated through the meetings of forum organizations can usually be obtained by other means, as and when required; and their activities often seem far removed from concrete problems.

Law-enforcement officers are particularly prone to treat the proceedings of forum organizations as 'talking shops' of little practical use. Police officers are faced with practical problems of arrest of persons and seizure of goods, which are of considerable technical and physical difficulty; these problems are seldom of much interest to the forum organizations. The work of some specialists in other fields is regarded with only mild interest in law-enforcement circles. Reports of rural-development experts showing that the opium poppy has been replaced in some areas by other

the death sentence can be imposed in twenty-three countries. The severity of sentences appears to have little impact on trafficking.

crops is an example. The police know that, when the supply is cut off from one source, another will emerge; if crop-based drugs are eradicated, traffickers will turn to the laboratory. Also, police regard educational programmes as important but unlikely to help them with their problems in the short term. The 'preventative' specialisms have not taken the law-enforcement function as seriously as the police think it deserves. However, the police regard one function of the forum organizations as vital and this is the preparation of satisfactory legal bases for the suppression of international drug trafficking. The law on extradition, seizure on the high seas, the definition of illegal substances, the confiscation of the assets of drug smugglers, the harmonization of penalties for drug offences are the most important of a long list of topics of great interest to the police. In this field, the international organizations, despite slowness and unsatisfactory compromises, are credited with important achievements. However, although multilateral agreements such as the UN conventions represent substantial progress, they are not regarded as adequate for combating the epidemic of drug abuse in the 1980s.

Those directly involved generally agree that co-operation between forum organizations and operational law-enforcement officers engaged in international co-operation is improved by personal contacts. There is some circulation of personnel: officials with Interpol or law-enforcement experience are found in UNFDAC or the UNDND; at the regional level, law-enforcement officers meet in the Interpol European Technical Co-operation Committee, in the Trevi group, and in the Pompidou group, as well as through bilateral co-operation. This helps to mitigate the effects of the four major difficulties of international drug control, which are as follows. First, the system is so complex that few people grasp how the various elements fit together. Second, law-enforcement agencies within countries do not co-operate effectively—relations between police and customs sometimes descend to the level of vitriolic rivalry. There is plenty of well-informed gossip about this difficulty in police circles but little systematic understanding of its causes. Third, operational co-operation depends crucially on personal relationships of trust and these can only be established by personal contact. Fourth, it is always difficult for busy law-enforcement officers to identify what is important and relevant in the mass of paper which is circulated to them and they therefore learn a great deal through conversation.

Current developments

On 14 December 1984 the UN General Assembly instructed ECOSOC to ask the Commission on Narcotic Drugs to prepare a new draft convention based on a broad consideration of the drugs problem and paying particular attention to aspects not included in the conventions of 1961 and 1971. After receiving reports on preliminary studies, the Commission recommended that fourteen elements should be included in the new convention. With the exception of the first element devoted to definitions, the other thirteen were primarily concerned with law enforcement. A specific method of investigation, controlled delivery, is mentioned; another element is the 'identification, tracing, freezing and forfeiture of proceeds of drug trafficking', which borders on the sensitive area of property rights.

When comments were requested from national governments, a great number of observations were received pointing out difficulties. Significant objections were made to Article 6, which included matters such as the circulation of information between national law-enforcement agencies and customs authorities, mutual assistance in enquiries and in improving training facilities, posting liaison officers, bilateral and regional co-operative agreements, and the organization of international seminars on law enforcement. The Swedish response doubted whether these matters were appropriate for an international convention; the United Kingdom suggested their exclusion from the convention and their incorporation in a strategy document; and Belgium proposed their removal from the text of the convention and appending them in an annex or conclusion. These countries considered that these provisions were of the nature of unenforceable recommendations.

Some developing countries had not signed the 1961 and 1971 conventions because of their concentration on the supply of, rather than the demand for, drugs: the more activist approach to law enforcement in the new draft convention could arouse their fears about possible infringement of national sovereignty. Reticences on the part of developing countries could lead to a fate similar to that of the International Convention on Mutual Assistance for the Prevention, Investigation and Repression of Customs Offences (the Nairobi Convention of June 1977), which had only received twenty-two signatures by May 1986. However, the process of negotiation sometimes creates an involvement and a commitment among the negotiating powers. The director of

UNFDAC, Giuseppe di Gennaro, in expressing his belief in the multilateral approach to the drugs problem, said: 'We create commitment, it is a chain reaction. We create a psychological feeling in countries who see others coming for help and do not want the finger pointed at them for holding back.'[10]

In June 1987, to preserve the momentum on multilateral co-operation and to mobilize political support for the draft convention, the UN Secretary General convened a ministerial conference in Vienna. Delegates from 138 countries attended this meeting, and, although there were conflicts (there was an unseemly struggle for the chairmanship of the conference), ideological divisions were absent. The conference approved a wide range of voluntary measures, listed under thirty-five targets and covering four main areas: prevention and reduction of demand for drugs; control of supply; suppression of trafficking; treatment and rehabilitation of addicts. The political declaration appended to these targets included a commitment to the strengthening of law enforcement. Agreement on the text of the new convention and its ratification will be a test of the seriousness of this commitment.

Interpol and international drug law enforcement

The only global system of co-operation with an operational role in the drugs field is Interpol.[11] The 1926 ICPC General Assembly recommended a series of measures to combat illegal traffic in drugs; the 1930 General Assembly called for the creation of an international drugs intelligence unit. Since that time, drug trafficking has been a regular item on General Assembly agendas. In 1955, a specialized drugs unit was set up and, in 1974, this was upgraded to a subdivision of the Police Division. The Drugs Subdivision, with about thirty staff from eighteen countries in 1987, is the largest of three subdivisions within the Police Division. There has been a small increase in personnel in recent years and a vast increase in its activities. Its tasks are to sift the messages and enquiries coming through the communications system, to send out notices and *modus operandi* reports to the NCBs, and to analyse the data collected from message traffic and from the international drug-seizures reporting system. Since drugs crime accounts for

---

[10] *Financial Times*, 27 June 1987.

[11] Interviews with head of Interpol Police Division, 24 Aug. 1987, and head of Interpol Drugs Subdivision, 28 Aug. 1987, greatly assisted the preparation of this section.

approximately 60 per cent of Interpol Headquarters executive activity, the Drugs Subdivision is the most active of the three in the Police Division.

The Subdivision is a relatively simple organization, with three sections: the office of the Head of the Subdivision, the Operations Group and the Intelligence Group. The office of the Head of the Subdivision is responsible for routine management, the assessment of the work of the Subdivision, and the development of strategy. The Operations Group is subdivided into six geographical regions and has an officer responsible for liaising with the countries in that region. This group monitors drug seizures, co-ordinates international enquiries, develops regional drug-trafficking assessments, and organizes working groups. Different regions use Interpol to differing extents: the European countries are the heaviest users and pay additional subscriptions, 7 per cent of normal subscriptions, under the Stupéfiants Europe Plan d'Action à Terme (SEPAT plan) initiated by Carl Persson in 1971.[12] The Operations Group attempts to locate drug traffickers by bringing together police officers from many countries to discuss in-depth analyses of traffickers or groups of traffickers. The Intelligence Group is subdivided according to subject-matter: cannabis, cocaine, heroin, psychotropics, special reports, and data processing. Its main activities are preparation and dissemination of intelligence reports, management of an international data bank (the Strategic Intelligence System (SIS)), publication of studies, and the co-ordination of inter-agency programmes. It circulates a *Weekly Intelligence Message*, a *Quarterly Enforcement and Statistical Review (QUEST)*, and two annual reports—*International Illicit Drug Traffic* and *National Statistics on Illicit Drug Traffic*.

The Subdivision also has a modest training function, limited in scope by the small resources at its disposal. It circulates training guides concerning specialized topics such as clandestine drug laboratories, and more general training syllabuses. National police training schools often prefer to use their own training materials but there is potential for expansion of the Interpol programmes. The experience of the CCC suggests that, when officers of national agencies help with the preparation of training programmes for international organizations, the lessons learned often feed back into national practices.[13]

---

[12] See R. Littas, 'The SEPAT Plan', *International Criminal Police Review* (1979), 101–4.

[13] Interview with W. Thompson, head of enforcement, CCC.

The General Assembly of Interpol sometimes instructs the General Secretariat to review the activity of member countries in the combating of certain forms of crime. In 1987 reviews were being conducted on the programme to counter heroin traffic in south-west Asia—South West Asia Programme (SWAP), on the strategic programme to counter the expanding traffic of cocaine in Europe—Programmed Action Cocaine Traffic Europe (PACTE), and on the drug precursor and essential chemical diversion programmes. These reviews of activity rely on co-operation from the national police forces and, as with other international organizations, this varies considerably. Interpol is in regular contact with thirteen other international organizations, including five within the UN family, active in drugs control discussions or in aid programmes, which also monitor national experiences. This contact started immediately after the Second World War when the ICPC sent a representative to the meeting of the UN Commission on Narcotic Drugs in December 1946. From the operational point of view the most important partner is the CCC. Good working relations exist between the two organizations, by contrast with the poor police–customs relations often found at the national level. The Enforcement Working Party and the Enforcement Committee of the CCC have gathered information on trends, smuggling techniques, and methods to prevent smuggling of these substances. The CCC has also organized seminars, courses, and workshops, sometimes in conjunction with Interpol, as, for example, the regular joint conference of customs and police for the Mediterranean basin and specialized joint conferences, such as the one held in Wiesbaden in December 1986 on 'The Division of Controlled Substances and Precursors'.

Most of Interpol's activity in the drugs field is routine circulation of case-related information. Users of the system have long complained that it is slow and they sometimes express doubts about the security of the communications network—in other words, they fear that sensitive information might get into the wrong hands. The Interpol communications system itself is no less secure than most national police communications systems; the encrypting system being introduced into its telecommunications network will make it more secure. The problem lies in what happens to sensitive information when it gets into national police systems. Another criticism is that the quality of Interpol drugs intelligence is less good than that of many national drug law-enforcement agencies: the relatively small number of staff in the

Drugs Subdivision makes this a plausible allegation. These complaints against Interpol help to explain why many drug law-enforcement officers prefer direct bilateral co-operation. Bilateral contacts are, in addition, necessary for co-ordination of surveillance for investigative techniques such as 'controlled delivery', and for investigation of particular complex cases.

The role of the United States

The United States played little part in Interpol before 1979 but nevertheless developed an important international network of law-enforcement relationships.[14] The United States has over twenty formal agreements with states for the direct exchange of information about drugs, and informal arrangements are even more numerous. These agreements and arrangements involve the DEA and also other agencies such as the FBI and US Customs. The activist role of the United States is such that the domestic legislation of other countries has been amended to allow for effective co-operation with the United States in the drugs field. [15] US law, however, makes greater claims to extra-territorial jurisdiction than the European countries.[16] American politicians also make extravagant calls for international co-operation; for example, Vice-President George Bush, on the campaign trail in New Jersey in May 1988, proposed an international drugs strike force to 'wipe out crops wherever they are grown and take out labs wherever they exist'. But there is an ambiguity about American policy in that, for broader political considerations, the United States has supported regimes which are either incapable or unwilling to take action against drug traffickers.

The DEA has the largest overseas presence of any law-enforcement agency and its example is influential both in the United States and elsewhere. According to the DEA organization

[14] Interviews in the DEA Office of International Programs, Washington, 26 Feb. 1987, and with the DEA representative in Paris, 26 May 1987, greatly assisted in the preparation of this section.

[15] An example is the UK Drugs Trafficking Offences Act (1986), which allowed an Anglo-American agreement to be signed on 9 Feb. 1988. The Act brought British practice in line with the United States in that it allows courts to freeze and confiscate the assets of drug traffickers; banks must also disclose information about accounts if they are suspected of involvement with drug trafficking. However, differences remain: when a US court attempted to reward Scotland Yard for its part in a drug seizure, the payment was blocked by the UK Treasury.

[16] See. S. S. Lewis, 'The Marijuana on the High Seas Act: Extending US Jurisdiction beyond International Limits', *Yale Journal of World Public Order*, 8 (1979), 359–83.

and functions manual, its first responsibility is the investigation and prosecution of major violators of drugs laws operating at the inter-state and international levels. Its narcotics intelligence system therefore involves co-operation with international as well as US federal, state, and local officials. The DEA's EPIC, staffed by officials from nine federal law-enforcement agencies, is the clearing house for drug law-enforcement information. In addition, the Special Field Intelligence Programs (SFIP) collect a variety of intelligence not available from conventional sources, often by using paid informers—a potential source of conflict with foreign police and judicial authorities. The SFIP has 'responsibility under the policy guidance of the Secretary of State and US Ambassadors, for all programs associated with drug law-enforcement counterparts in foreign countries; and liaison with the United Nations, Interpol, and other organizations on matters relating to inter-national narcotics control programs'. These international activities consume 10 per cent of the DEA's budget and occupy about 6 per cent of its personnel—excluding the headquarters staff engaged in international work and US-based investigators, involved in inter-national investigations. The DEA's training function includes training foreign officials at the Federal Law Enforcement Training Center (FLETC) at Glynco, Georgia, as well as special training packages or programmes sent, with or without instructors, to foreign countries. Fifteen African countries and nearly all Latin American countries have used these facilities.

In 1983 the FBI was given joint responsibility for narcotics investigations and the most senior officials of the DEA are FBI agents. But the DEA is always involved in major drugs investiga-tions in the United States and, outside US borders, in any investigation which has US connections, whereas this is not the case for the FBI. The expertise of the DEA is widely admired in the United States and in foreign law-enforcement circles; it has pioneered investigation techniques in controlled delivery and undercover operations. However, the activities of the DEA are controversial both within and outside the law-enforcement com-munity. It has been accused of concentrating too much on quick quantifiable results in terms of arrests, seizures of drugs, and confiscation of financial assets (these seizures are now so large that they cover much of the cost of the DEA);[17] the methods necessary to achieve these may not always be the most effective way of

---

[17] The figures are published each year in the appendix of the section on the DEA in US Department of Justice, *Annual Report of the Attorney General*.

tackling the roots of the problem. In addition, DEA agents are often involved, because of the great difficulties of obtaining evidence, in encouraging or allowing the commission of a crime, in order to gather evidence against suspects: this brings agents into dubious legal territory.[18]

The international operations of the DEA have also attracted criticisms. In a 1986 DEA operation, Operation Blastfurnace, the United States lent Bolivia 170 soldiers and an unknown number of DEA personnel to destroy coca crops. Some Latin Americans considered this as an infringement of Bolivian sovereignty and its effects were said to be short-lived. A drugs intelligence specialist said that, despite '180 days of 7 days a week work' by the joint US–Bolivian operation, 'everything is back where we started'.[19] Moreover, the pressure on Bolivia, initiated by the DEA, for legislative changes and a complete eradication of the coca crop led Bolivia's Foreign Minister to complain at the 1987 UN Conference in Vienna that this policy would lead to unmanageable guerrilla war. Coca is estimated to produce $450 million a year—roughly equal to Bolivia's legal exports.

Kidnapping prominent drug smugglers is another of the DEA's spectacular activities. In February 1987 Carlos Lehder Rivas, alleged to be one of the most successful and dangerous drug traffickers in the world, was arrested and flown out of Columbia on the same day. The Columbian authorities admitted that he could not be held even temporarily in a Columbian prison let alone brought to trial because of the violence which Rivas could organize. In Honduras, a country without an extradition treaty with the United States, the removal by the DEA in April 1988 of a prominent trafficker provoked anti-American riots. It is estimated that 35 per cent of the heroin on the US market comes from Mexico, where DEA officials have been attacked, tortured, and assassinated. In the last three years, the once fairly successful co-operation between US and Mexican law-enforcement officials has been deteriorating amid mutual recriminations.[20] The US law-enforcement community faces very serious tactical and strategic problems in attacking links in the chain of drug trafficking south of the Rio Grande. Spectacular operations do not affect the basic conditions prevailing in the Latin American drug-producing

---

[18] For a discussion of this problem see J. Q. Wilson, *The Investigators: Managing FBI and Narcotics Agents* (New York, 1978), esp. ch. 2.

[19] *Washington Post*, 6 Feb. 1987.

[20] CCC, *The Narcotics Problem* (Brussels, 1987); 'Anger Rises at Mexican Corruption in the Drugs War', *The Times*, 6 Oct. 1987.

countries, where judges, ministers, and journalists are intimidated and murdered, and police forces are usually poorly paid and inefficient.

DEA presence and actions in Latin America reassure American public and Congressional opinion that everything possible is being done to combat drug trafficking. They publicize the fight against drugs—less dramatic, even if more effective, activities do not make front-page newspaper stories or the main evening television news broadcasts. They signal to the international community that operational co-operation is urgently sought by the US authorities. The morale of drug law-enforcement officials is boosted by these operations because they overcome the frustration of knowing the identity of the organizers of a traffic without being able to take action against them. Direct intervention also increases the sense of insecurity of those involved in the traffic, if only temporarily.

The main costs of DEA intervention in Latin America are political. The overlap between law enforcement and US intelligence—the CIA, which has been instructed to use its intelligence sources in the struggle against drug trafficking—presents problems for inter-agency relations and for US relations with foreign countries. The US intelligence and law-enforcement agencies have a general obligation, not always respected, to support one another; this leads to suspicions that anti-narcotics activities serve as a cover for intelligence operations. The DEA is seen by leftist politicians in developing countries and by some neutral observers as a means of establishing an intelligence presence in politically fragile regions of the world. On the other hand, the massive resources and professionalism of the US law-enforcement agencies inevitably encourages relationships of inequality, even though in the short term their assistance is greatly valued. Effective police co-operation is based on partnership and mutual support; it is difficult to develop a continuing relationship if the participants are manifestly unequal and one side is made to feel the inferior. DEA operations suggest a relationship of political inequality or a neo-colonial domination by the United States over its southern neighbours. Foreign police intrusion in the United States of a similar kind is inconceivable. Indirect forms of aid—equipment, advice, and training—could be more effective in the long run. The DEA has a substantial commitment to these forms of aid and sees no contradiction between the two approaches.

Outside Latin America, DEA operations are of a more limited character. They include co-operation with foreign police officers in investigations, but the DEA usually plays an advisory or observer role. In some cases, the limits of this role seem to be stretched, with the consent of the local authorities. In the early 1970s the investigation of the so-called 'French connection' in Marseilles, and in the 1980s of drug trafficking involving US servicemen stationed in Germany have been examples. In addition, in European countries the DEA has a network of paid informers and conducts undercover operations. Although this is known to the host countries, it takes the DEA into legally dubious areas. The urgency of combating drug abuse is so widely accepted in the European countries that unorthodox methods are more readily accepted than is the case in other areas of policing.

European responses

The DEA example has been followed by the posting in other countries of drug liaison officers from Canada, Britain, Australia, New Zealand, France, Germany, Italy, Japan, Spain, the Netherlands, and the Scandinavian countries. They are stationed in some of the main transit points for drugs, such as Cyprus and Rotterdam, or to the main supplier countries, such as Bolivia, Columbia, Pakistan, and Thailand. Carl Persson, the head of the Swedish National Police, led the way in Europe when he dispatched a liaison officer to Bangkok in the early 1970s. He wished to put pressure on Interpol to open a sub-regional bureau in Thailand and to improve the quality of police intelligence about the supplies of raw opium from the Far East.[21] The Interpol Bangkok sub-regional bureau was subsequently established and liaison officers from the United States, Canada, Britain, France, Germany and Australia are now present in Thailand. These officers are members of FANC. Similar groups have been formed in Nicosia (Cyprus) and Islamabad (Pakistan); they are useful sources of support for liaison officers, who have often to report on large regions of the world and cannot do so unaided.

Some police forces none the less wish to extend the programme of liaison officers abroad and to give them new roles. The BKA is the most forward-looking with about thirty liaison officers in the field; it hopes to increase this number to fifty-five, covering all the major European countries in the near future. In 1987 France and Germany agreed to exchange liaison officers in the anti-terrorist field and, if concern about terrorism continues, this practice could

[21] Interview with Carl Persson, 2 June 1987.

be extended to other countries. There is some reluctance, in European capitals, to discuss the disposition of liaison officers because coherent policies have not yet been formulated and because sophisticated criminals may be helped by disclosure of information.

Discussions about the development of the liaison-officer system have taken place in the European Technical Co-operation Committee of Interpol and the Trevi Group. At their meeting of 20 October 1986, European Ministers of the Interior invited Trevi 3 to examine the scope for building on existing arrangements to create a co-ordinated network of drug liaison officers to monitor developments in producer countries. The Trevi working group took into account present commitments and future plans of the member states of the European Community as well as Interpol arrangements. In spring 1987 proposals for co-operation and rationalization were formulated, but it was recognized that appointing European drug liaison officers, representing the interests of all the European countries, was not possible in the short term for legal, financial, and linguistic reasons. The proposals envisaged liaison officers sending regular intelligence reports (written in the liaison officers' own languages) to all the Community countries. Liaison officers could also provide, on request, information to any member state. States could also circulate information about activities and personnel involved in combating international drug trafficking. The system of liaison with Interpol is not yet clear. The Scandinavian countries pool the reports of their liaison officers and these reports are circulated to the Scandinavian NCBs,[22] who forward them to Interpol Headquarters; this could become a standard practice unless a political decision was taken to exclude Interpol. Closer co-ordination of the drug liaison officers of the European Community countries may result in non-communication of information to Interpol. A Community communications system for drugs intelligence could be set up parallel to Interpol but this would not have the justification of the Trevi anti-terrorist communications system— namely that there are certain types of sensitive political intelligence inappropriate for ordinary police channels. It would damage the international law-enforcement effort because the Interpol central file on drug offences and drugs intelligence would be less comprehensive and less useful as a result.

[22] Interview, Stockholm NCB, 1 June 1987; head of Interpol Drugs Subdivision, 28 Aug. 1987.

Conclusion

Drug trafficking is a genuinely international activity: Asian, African, and Middle Eastern ethnic groups with well-established communities resident in western countries are active in the supply of drugs to Europe and to North America. The financing and logistics of this trade are organized by international conspiracies and successful police investigations are beyond the competence of national law-enforcement agencies. The scale and the nature of the problem pushed the United States into a well-resourced police presence in other countries; the pattern of posting drug officers overseas has been followed by all the large, highly industrialized democracies. Considerable diplomatic activity is generated by the drugs problem—Britain has had discussions or negotiations with some forty countries about trafficking and other advanced industrial countries have been at least as active. Interpol facilities for combating trafficking are well established and heavily used, and there are a number of recent proposals to strengthen this co-operation. The practical problems of developing the system of co-operation are, however, serious and unresolved: it is not yet possible to discern a coherent set of relationships between the bilateral, regional, and global systems of co-operation in the drugs field. The problem of drug abuse is crucial to the development of international law enforcement because effective action has high priority at the governmental level and there are fewer political complications in this field than in the struggle against international terrorism. There is relatively little difficulty in obtaining broad international agreement on principles: it is the methods of police co-operation which pose the intractable problems. At the 1988 meeting of the Group of Seven (G7)—the seven most highly industrialized countries (Canada, France, Italy, Japan, United Kingdom, United States, and West Germany) in Toronto, an American proposal for an international task force to deal with the production, financing, and distribution of drugs was accepted: this may have no more success than previous proposals for an international drugs commission but the issue is firmly established on the political agenda at the highest level. Any proposals must contend with the realism (or cynicism) of many drug law-enforcement officers who are convinced that improved co-operation makes only a marginal impact on drug abuse. Policies, laws, and attitudes all must change before the rising tide of trafficking can be contained.

6. The Terrorist Factor

PRESIDENT MITTERRAND, during a state visit to Madrid, said in a communiqué broadcast by Spanish Television on 10 March 1987: 'Since terrorism is international, investigation, prevention, repression, and sanctions should also be international.' Many such statements have been made in recent years. Terrorist acts, or, more precisely, perceptions of terrorism within governments, have given a new prominence to international police co-operation, and some common views have emerged.[1] Three particular convictions are widely held in western governments. First, terrorism has become genuinely international through informal links and mutual aid among terrorist groups, even though their aims may be highly specific and local; terrorists also increasingly engage in action far removed from their own countries. Second, citizens and their property cannot be adequately defended without international co-operation, especially when people travel, or their property is located outside the national boundaries. Third, public opinion in the highly industrialized democracies finds violence against innocent bystanders especially obnoxious and expects effective action to be taken against terrorists when this happens. There has been, and remains, uncertainty about the most effective form of international co-operation against terrorism; Interpol was considered of only marginal assistance until after the 1984 reinterpretation of its statutory exclusion from cases involving political, religious, or racial elements.

Violence in pursuit of political ends has been a common feature of human history. But in the 1970s and 1980s politicans have sometimes spoken of terrorism as a unique evil posing an important threat to global stability. Terrorists have therefore been successful in their first aim, which is to shock and alarm. In recent years they have been singularly unsuccessful in achieving their basic political aims. Terrorism unsupported by other forms of political and military action is almost certainly doomed to failure.

[1] The literature on international terrorism is now vast. The most recent bibliography lists 5,622 items: A. Lakos, *International Terrorism: A Bibliography* (Boulder, 1986). This chapter does not attempt to review the findings of this literature but is concerned with the general impact of terrorism on police co-operation. The only substantive specialist work on international counter-measures is N. Gal-Or, *International Cooperation to Suppress Terrorism* (London, 1985).

None the less, terrorist campaigns pose difficult problems for governments, and have sometimes absorbed a disproportionate amount of government attention. Professional law-enforcement officers have also been baffled by terrorist action but their response has been calmer than that of the politicians. Their main problem has been to produce the quick results expected of them by governments, and by public opinion.

In this chapter, different forms of terrorism are identified as an essential preliminary to a consideration of governments' policies. This is followed by a case study of France, a country which has faced a wide range of political and organizational problems in coping with terrorism. The attitudes of governments to multilateral co-operation are then discussed, followed by an account of the increasing importance of Interpol in counter-measures against terrorism.

Forms of terrorism

Defining terrorism is notoriously difficult. The distinction between terrorism on the one hand, and covert military operations on the other, depends on the 'legitimacy' of those who order them to be carried out. Legitimacy, in turn, depends on approval and consent. Terrorist acts—bombing, hijacking, assassination, and kidnapping—must, therefore, be placed in their political contexts. In popular estimation, successful rebellions involving terrorist violence become legitimate, and even glorious; sovereign states whose governments pursue unjust and oppressive policies may lose legitimacy. Attempts to classify terrorism according to the context of terrorist actions involve value judgements about which there is no general agreement. A commonly used classification, which reduces value judgements to a minimum, is 'state-sponsored' terrorism, 'popular' or national-liberation-movement terrorism, and 'radical-minority' terrorism. States may sponsor assassinations, kidnappings, and other acts of violence to further their foreign-policy objectives; national liberation movements use terrorist violence in association with political and economic pressure to achieve political independence; radical minorities may not have available to them any form of action other than terrorism to make an impact on national and international opinion.

A belief in the over-riding importance of state-sponsored terrorism led some to contend that the USSR was primarily responsible for the recrudescence of terrorism in the 1970s. But the KGB, unlike the CIA, has rarely been caught red-handed in covert operations and evidence for the 'Russian-plot' hypothesis is limited. Small arms delivered to countries friendly to the USSR have found their way to terrorist groups and some terrorists have been educated or trained in Soviet bloc countries. Guilt by association is used in the absence of direct evidence. The alleged involvement of the Bulgarian intelligence services in the 1981 attempted assassination of Pope John Paul II by Mehmet Ali Agca has been interpreted as Russian involvement because the Bulgarians are the 'most Russian' of the Eastern bloc countries. Evidence of Syrian involvement in promoting terrorist acts in western European countries (in 1986, London and West Berlin trials revealed Syrian complicity) was regarded as compromising the Soviet Union because Syria was, at the time, the closest ally of the USSR in the Arab world. The USSR is also alleged to benefit from terrorist activity because this activity undermines global stability and damages the interests of the highly industrialized non-Communist countries. However, the USSR itself is not immune from terrorist action and allowing the spread of terrorism could be against the Soviet Union's long-term interests. There have, moreover, been indications that the USSR is ready to offer western countries limited forms of co-operation in combating terrorists. Soviet help for national liberation movements is insufficient evidence to suggest a consistent support for terrorism to destabilize the highly industrialized democracies.

The involvement of the CIA in coups, attempted assassinations, and arming of subversive groups, fully documented in John Ranelagh's book *The Agency* and admitted by the Agency before Congressional hearings, is regarded by opponents of the US role in international affairs as, at least, connivance with terrorism. The CIA's tactics are regarded as legitimate by those who support the Agency's defined purpose of defending the United States and the 'free world' against Communist, and other forms of, subversion by the most effective means available.

The three countries most commonly regarded as directly sponsoring terrorism are Iran, Syria, and Libya. The evidence of this involvement is strong; Iran and Libya have made no attempt to hide their support for political violence. Syrian involvement may be a deliberate act of state policy or may result from an inability to control both its own security services and unruly groups in Syria and the Lebanon. Terrorist actions associated with these countries have caused serious problems for western governments, particularly for France. Middle Eastern terrorism combines elements of state-sponsored, national-liberation, and radical-minority terrorism; these types of terrorism call for different responses. Negotiations are possible with a state which sponsors terrorism, although that state may find its own terrorist clients difficult to control. Occasional truces can be reached with national liberation movements and radical minorities but those involved usually regard conflict as a fight to the finish; for them 'victory or death' is rarely an empty slogan. National liberation movements, based on large populations, which combine political action with terrorist tactics are notoriously difficult to defeat, as the struggles in Ireland, Indo-China, Algeria, and other countries amply demonstrate. Even where the liberation movements are supported by a minority of the population involved, as in Northern Ireland, the Spanish Basque provinces, and Corsica, police action alone is insufficient to defeat them. In the case of radical-minority terrorism, it is possible to contain, and eventually, defeat it by police action. France, West Germany, and Italy have gone a long way towards doing so, but at considerable cost in financial and manpower resources and, some would argue, in civil liberties too.[2]

Official reactions to terrorism

Governmental response to terrorism has varied according to circumstances, and to the national experience of political violence. Presidents Carter and Reagan have taken international terrorism very seriously. This is partly due to the American experience of political assassination, which has had important consequences in American political history. It is also based on an American conviction that the problem is growing in global significance. A State Department report published in 1987 claimed that 1985 was a record year with 782 incidents causing the deaths of 800 people, and injuring a further 1,200. Most of the victims were tourists, or innocent bystanders. Sixty per cent of the incidents either took place in the Middle East, or were instigated by groups from the Middle East; western Europe was the next region most affected by terrorist incidents. Also, small groups of lightly armed militants in

---

[2] The best up-to-date study of national counter-measures is Y. Alexander and J. Denton, *Governmental Responses to Terrorism* (Fairfax, 1987). A good bibliography may be found in W. Lacquer and Y. Alexander (eds.), *The Terrorism Reader* (New York, 1988).

third-world countries have been able to outrage American public opinion, blackmail the American government, influence American foreign policy, and undermine the political authority of Presidents Carter and Reagan. Concern over the fate of American citizens has led successive American administrations into what, with hindsight, can be regarded as grave errors of judgement. The taking of the hostages by revolutionary guards of the staff of the US embassy in Tehran, and the subsequent failure to secure their release was a contributory factor to the loss by the incumbent President Carter of the 1980 election campaign.

President Reagan's undertaking to follow a firmer and more consistent policy in regard to international terrorism was exposed as empty rhetoric during the June 1985 hijacking of the TWA airliner to Beirut—this resulted in the release of six hundred Lebanese prisoners by the Israelis, after American pressure. In this case, the Israelis performed an act for the Americans which they had consistently refused to do on their own account. President Reagan's inept attempt to strike a bargain with Iran for what looked like an 'arms for hostages' deal, together with other activities surrounding this incident, resulted in the partial collapse of the political authority of his Presidency. These extraordinary, and humiliating, events were less the result of the terrorist actions themselves than the pressure of public opinion which requires Presidents to save American lives. This pressure comes mainly from people with little knowledge of the complexities of Middle Eastern politics, and often no understanding of the limitations of American power. American authorities are therefore very pressing in their demands for better international co-operation.

The only western country close to the Israeli position of no negotiation with terrorists is the United Kingdom under the Thatcher government. The actions of the IRA/INLA, first in killing Airey Neave, Mrs Thatcher's close adviser, in 1979, then in attempting to assassinate her and her cabinet in the 1985 Brighton bombing, as well as various other outrages, have made the Thatcher government especially resolute. The UK government has also been helped by the policy of successive governments of the Irish Republic of no negotiation with the IRA; Ireland has some of the strongest anti-terrorist laws in Europe. Irish and British opinion has sometimes diverged, as, for example, in allowing the 1981 'hunger strikers' to starve to death in the Maze prison in Northern Ireland. Sharp differences of view over the quality of policing the Northern Ireland border have emerged, but both sides accept the necessity of police co-operation. This co-operation was strengthened by the 1985 Hillsborough Anglo-Irish agreement, which was followed by a series of studies in the intelligence, operational, and technical field carried out by the Royal Ulster Constabulary (RUC) and the Garda. Direct radio, telex, and personal contacts were established, but some difficulties in co-operation remain. The two police forces have different characteristics. The Garda was originally organized to police a largely rural society and, despite the smaller population of Northern Ireland, the RUC has more manpower and a larger budget than the Garda. By European standards, however, the police of the Irish Republic are neither under-resourced nor under-manned. Another difficulty is that both the British army and the Irish army are involved in border policing; the Irish government, Irish courts, and Irish opinion are sensitive to any hint of British military intrusion on Irish territory. Although there has been British pressure on this issue, it has not been possible to establish the same level of co-operation between the military as between the police forces.

The willingness of the Thatcher government to take a hard line, to break off diplomatic relations with Syria, Libya, and Iran, and to support American retaliatory raids against Libya and terrorist bases in the Lebanon, has not been followed by the other western European governments. The main reason for this reluctance is that France, West Germany, Italy, and Spain all have important political and economic interests in the Muslim and Arab worlds which they consider may be damaged by breaking off diplomatic relations. In addition, there is a widespread view in western chancelleries that the complex and intractable problems in the Middle East will not be assisted by the diplomatic isolation of the 'radical' powers in the region.

All the major, and most of the smaller, European countries have experienced terrorist actions, or the problem of suspected terrorists on their territory. They have reacted in a variety of ways, influenced by an ever-changing composite of factors; the anxiety of the public about 'security', conflicting interests between ministries (Justice, Interior, and Foreign Affairs) with different perspectives, conflicting judgements among ministers about strategy, and economic interests, are all part of the mix. Although the establishment of specialized anti-terrorist police units has been an almost universal response, anti-terrorist strategy has proved difficult to co-ordinate within countries as well as between countries. The Iranians have skilfully played on this difficulty of internal co-ordination, especially in relations with the United States and France. The first requirement is clear foreign-policy objectives as a framework within which police anti-terrorist tactics can be decided. Authoritative public statements about policy do not always resolve uncertainties because, in bitter and protracted conflicts, there are always suspicions of a hidden agenda. For example, in Northern Ireland there have been doubts that the stated objectives of the governments of the Republic of Ireland and the United Kingdom are their real objectives.

The case of France

All the political and police problems of counter-terrorism are illustrated by the French case. In the last two decades the French government has confronted state-sponsored, national-liberation-movement, and radical-minority terrorism. Uncertainty about policy objectives, a complex police system, and conflicting views on international co-operation have produced a confused record of response to terrorism. Since the great Revolution of 1789, there has been much politically motivated violence in domestic French politics; two general features of French political history in particular have influenced attitudes towards terrorism: a history of violent overthrow of regimes has resulted in a higher level of tolerance of violence than is found, for example, in the Scandinavian countries; political changes in France have often resulted in periods of exile for prominent political figures in France, which has created a strong sentiment in favour of the right of political asylum. These factors have complicated France's relations with her neighbours, particularly Spain and Italy. France did not ratify until 1987 the 1977 European Convention on the Suppression of Terrorism (Council of Europe), and the 1979 Dublin Agreement on the Application of the European Convention on Terrorism (European Community): both were based on a commitment either to extradite or to try suspected terrorists. The former obliged states not to treat certain acts such as attacks on diplomats, hijacking, and hostage-taking as political crimes. To obtain the ratification of these texts by the National Assembly, the government had to make a solemn declaration stating that the government would refuse extradition if it thought that the rights of a political exile were being infringed. In the 1980s France already had a tarnished reputation as the country most likely to cede to the demands of foreign terrorists and a refusal by France to ratify at this late date might have been interpreted as a willingness to give sanctuary to terrorists.

The Middle East policy of France in the 1980s has been particularly obscure and an important obstacle to effective counter-terrorist action. The French willingness to commit troops in the Lebanon, to supply arms to Iraq, and to normalize relations with Iran whilst retaining strong ties and sympathies with Israel has led to confusion about French priorities. France has had a higher incidence than any other western country of bombings, assassinations, and kidnappings associated with the Middle East; this is undoubtedly connected with the French role in the region. Actions by Lebanese terrorists in particular were an outcome of French policy and were brought to an end by a change in that policy. This link between foreign policy and anti-terrorist action is well understood in French law-enforcement circles but the Police Judiciaire are supposed to act as though this link does not exist.[3]

France has seemed, on occasion, to favour enthusiastically international co-operation against terrorism and, at other times, to be reticent and obstructive. Imaginative initiatives such as the proposal of President Giscard d'Estaing for an 'espace judiciaire européen'—a region in which particular crimes would be dealt with in identical ways—have been accompanied by an apparent unwillingness to co-operate in practical matters. Effectively withholding, until 1985, co-operation from the Spanish authorities on the Basque terrorism is an illustration. French opinion was, in general, sympathetic to the armed struggle of the Basque nationalist organization, ETA, against the Franco regime. After the restoration of democracy in Spain (1975–7), Basques who crossed the frontier continued to be regarded as *bona fide* political refugees because Basque dissidents risked ill-treatment and injustice by the Spanish police and courts, still influenced by Francoism. The Spanish government considered that political violence had lost its justification after the restoration of democratic institutions in Spain, and that ETA terrorism could destabilize Spanish democracy by encouraging the intervention of the Spanish army in politics. In the 1980s the Spanish socialist government led by Filipe Gonzales found it difficult to understand why the French socialist government of François Mitterrand did not accept this

---

[3] The author's understanding of this was greatly enhanced by interviews with the head of 6th division of the Police Judiciaire responsible for anti-terrorist action, 7 Nov. 10 Dec. 1986, and with L. Casamayor, author *inter alia* of *La Police* (Paris, 1973) and *Et pour finir le terrorisme* (Paris, 1983), 15 Dec. 1986.

simple argument and the Spaniards became deeply suspicious of French motives. However, under the second socialist Prime Minister, Laurent Fabius (1984–6), French policy changed, and administrative expulsions on the grounds of 'extreme urgency' were used instead of cumbersome extradition procedures through the courts. Expulsions were few to begin with but, from 1986, became a matter of routine under the right-wing Chirac government.

After 1978 there were suspicions that the Spanish police, in the absence of French co-operation, had assumed the right of pursuit of Basque terrorists on French territory through a shadowy organization, the Grupo Antiterroriste de Liberación (GAL). 'Off-duty' officers and mercenaries—former members of the Secret Army Organization (the last-ditch defenders of French Algeria), or people recruited from French criminal milieux—assassinated Basque activists on French territory. The full extent of this became public knowledge in 1987, during the hearings before a *juge d'instruction* concerning the attempted assassination of three men in a Bayonne bar, and in 1988 two Spanish police officers were arrested for involvement in the GAL. The French authorities could not prevent this spillover of violence from the Basque provinces without Spanish co-operation. A change in the French policy became inevitable, after France finally accepted Spanish entry to the European Community; by 1986–7 the reversal of the French position was complete—from July 1986 to October 1987 there were 130 expulsions following the procedure of 'absolute urgency' and the French authorities were expelling anyone either they or the Spanish authorities suspected of involvement in terrorism. However, the leaders of ETA, believed to be in France, were not apprehended and in 1988 the Spanish government was urging the French authorities to increase their efforts to locate them.

Bilateral relations with Italy have followed a parallel course; France was the country in which Italian fugitive terrorists sought refuge. These fugitives belonged to a variety of extreme left-wing groups with wide European connections. The Italian authorities could not provide evidence for criminal charges against many of the fugitives and the French courts were not prepared to extradite on grounds of alleged membership of an 'armed band'—the Red Brigades, or one of its offshoots. In official circles in Italy feelings ran high, and France was accused of providing a safe haven for violent criminals. As in relations with Spain, changes commenced under the Socialist government of President Mitterrand but accelerated in 1986 with the arrival of the right in government. Administrative expulsions on grounds of extreme urgency were used for the first time against suspected Italian terrorists by the Chirac government, although more sparingly than in the Spanish case, and the French courts began to change their view about charges brought on grounds of membership of an 'armed band'. The number of arrests increased in 1987, not without controversy, amidst protests from French civil rights groups.

By contrast, relations with West Germany have been more harmonious than with Spain and Italy. The close political relationship between the two countries provided a secure basis for anti-terrorist co-operation. The regular meeting of heads of government and senior ministers established by the 1963 Franco-German Treaty of Friendship was a good context for discussing terrorist problems. Franco-German police co-operation on terrorism commenced in earnest in the middle 1970s, after the slaying in Alsace of the German industrialist Hans-Martin Schleyer. Both West Germany and France have been troubled by Iranian, Lebanese, and Palestinian terrorism, although, in the middle 1980s, the French problems have been more severe. The West Germans were more afflicted by the radical minority terrorism of the Baader-Meinhof gang and its successors in the 1970s. In recent years, both countries have had radical minority problems: the contacts between the French *Action Directe* and the German Red Army Faction have stimulated police co-operation.

The French Minister of the Interior, Charles Pasqua, and the West German Minister of the Interior, Friedrich Zimmerman, signed an agreement on 8 April 1987 to develop police co-operation, but both sides refused to divulge the content of this agreement (*Le Monde*, 10 April 1987). Frequent personal contact, including the exchange of police liaison officers, and exchange of information are the limits of co-operation without changes in law and police organization; more substantial changes cannot be introduced without publicity. But continuing common problems of the French and West Germans—in autumn 1986 the Red Army Faction killed a senior official of the German foreign office and *Action Directe* assassinated the managing director of the Régie Renault—have kept anti-terrorist co-operation on the political agenda. But both countries had, by the beginning of 1988, made significant progress in controlling the incidence of Middle Eastern and radical-minority terrorism.

France has difficulty in maintaining its credentials as a reliable partner in other western capitals. A reputation of not solving notorious cases, such as the 1965 Ben Barka affair, has been compounded by giving way to terrorist demands to avoid further incidents. In 1986 a more determined policy was introduced by the right-wing Prime Minister Jacques Chirac. His Minister of Interior, Charles Pasqua, coined the memorable phrase 'terrorizing the terrorists'. However, by autumn 1986 the government was compromising. It refused to give approval for the overflight of American planes from Britain for a retaliatory raid on Tripoli, undertaken because of Libyan involvement in terrorism. It gave weak support to British diplomatic retaliation against Syria for the involvement of Syrian intelligence services in the attempt to blow up an El Al airliner flying from Heathrow (in a notorious interview in the *Washington Times*, Chirac implied that this might have been a plot by the Israeli intelligence services). Chirac publicly thanked Syria, along with Saudi Arabia, and Algeria for obtaining the release of two French hostages in Lebanon. Although Iranian involvement in the wave of bombings in Paris in the early autumn of 1986 was strongly suspected, Chirac engaged in a process of 'normalization' of relations with Iran, which included important financial concessions, in order to obtain the release of further hostages in the Lebanon. There was some evidence of French government pressure on the judicial process to obtain a light sentence on Georges Ibrahim Abdullah in order to stop bomb outrages in France and also to obtain release of French hostages. The French strategy was rewarded by the release of the last three hostages held in Lebanon, just before the second ballot of the Presidential elections of 1988.

French police organization is not particularly well suited to anti-terrorist action. Too many agencies are involved: the external security service—the Direction Générale de la Securité Extérieure (DGSE); the internal security service—DST; the general intelligence service of the police—the Renseignements Généraux (RG); the criminal investigation police—the Police Judiciaire; the specialist police anti-terrorist unit—the Service de Recherche d'Assistance, d'Intervention et de Dissuasion (RAID); and the Gendarmerie Nationale, with its specialized anti-terrorist squad—the Groupement d'Intervention de la Gendarmerie Nationale (GIGN); a co-ordinating committee for terrorism, Unité de Coordination pour la Lutte Anti-Terroriste (UCLAT) has been in place since 1984 to bring an element of order into this confused situation. In matters of international terrorism the DGSE, under the authority of the Ministry of Defence and not part of the police, is inevitably involved: it has two main roles—to collect information about threats to French security and, if necessary, to act directly against such threats. Its reputation in both roles is low.

The DGSE was reorganized and transferred from the Prime Minister's office to the Ministry of Defence in the middle 1960s as a result of a scandal—the involvement of its agents in the disappearance and presumed assassination of the Moroccan opposition leader, Ben Barka. Its accident-prone reputation was confirmed by the Greenpeace Affair—the sinking by DGSE agents of the *Rainbow Warrior* in Auckland harbour to prevent interference with French nuclear tests. The evidence about this bungled operation revealed technical incompetence as well as poor political judgement. Its ineffectiveness in the battle of wits between eastern and western intelligence services has allowed a rival agency, the DST, to establish a role in this field. For example, the expulsion of forty-seven Soviet diplomats from Paris in 1983 was alleged to be the result of information from a DST recruited informer in the USSR. The director of the DST, rather than the director of the DGSE, went to Damascus in September 1986 to make contact with Syrian intelligence after the wave of bombings in Paris aimed at the release of Georges Ibrahim Abdullah, the Lebanese terrorist, convicted for murder and attempted murder in France.

Within the Police Nationale, the RG is also engaged in anti-terrorist matters. The terms of reference of the RG are very wide—to report on the public, political, economic, and social life of the country. As well as using sources in the public domain, it conducts private surveys and it gathers intelligence on foreign groups in France, and French extremist groups. It had an important success in dismantling the Lyons branch of *Action Directe*. Both the DST and the RG use methods which are illegal or extra-legal—telephone tapping, electronic eavesdropping, pressure on foreigners in a vulnerable legal position to turn informer—which occasionally causes scandal. Yet a third directorate of the Police Nationale, the Police Judiciaire, acting under the authority of a *juge d'instruction*, is involved when criminal prosecution for terrorist offences is envisaged.

There is an added complication because officers of the Gendarmerie Nationale also act as criminal investigation police, and, although most of its functions are in the field of civil policing, the

Gendarmerie Nationale also has military and civil intelligence responsibilities. In principle the Police Nationale and the Gendarmerie Nationale should provide mutual assistance to one another but, in practice, suspicion and conflict between the two are common—public controversy between the two ministers responsible for these forces occasionally occurs. Relations were not improved by the establishment, in 1974, of the GIGN, a specialist anti-terrorist squad within the Gendarmerie Nationale. This group, which has aproximately six dozen members, was charged with the search for, and arrest of, persons involved in terrorist acts such as hijackings, hostage-taking, and bombings; it is trained for commando-type actions against terrorists. In 1982 the officer commanding the GIGN was given by President Mitterrand a mission of 'co-ordination, investigation, and action against terrorism' and in 1983 a GIGN group was made responsible for the protection of the President of the Republic. Before the official appointment of the members of this latter group, one of its officers mismanaged an operation against a suspected group of Irish terrorists in Vincennes and was subsequently charged with attempting to pervert the course of justice. Although the Irish had INLA connections, it was the members of the Gendarmerie Nationale who ended up in the dock; the legal sequels of this episode were still continuing in 1988. Some members of the Police Nationale suspected the Gendarmerie Nationale of attempting to take over the leadership of anti-terrorist action and were visibly pleased by this unfortunate incident.

To ensure the circulation of information between the various police, Gendarmerie Nationale, and intelligence agencies involved, UCLAT was set up in 1984 under the direction of an experienced and independently minded officer, François Le Mouël. In the 1970s he had been the first director of the 'anti-gang' brigade established because the fight against organized crime was also troubled by poor co-ordination between police services, and he had also been the head of the anti-narcotics team which broke up the 'French connection'. In 1987 he was replaced by Jacques Franquet, who had become one of the best-known policemen in France because of his role in combating terrorism in Corsica and his previous appointment as head of the Office Central pour la Répression du Trafic Illicite des Stupéfiants. It remained the case, however, that sometimes the intelligence agencies refuse to hand over to the Police Judiciaire information in their possession. Co-ordination is perhaps better than at any time in the last two decades but the quality of co-ordination can deteriorate rapidly as a result of political pressures.

French problems with terrorism are an extreme case of the difficulties encountered by all the advanced industrial democracies. Uncertainty about general policy objectives, the necessity of confronting various types of terrorism, a wish to respond flexibly to terrorist incidents, the conflicting demands of domestic and international opinion have created problems which have been compounded by police organization designed for quite different purposes.

Recent developments in multilateral action

Divergences of strategic and economic interests and differing political judgements make it difficult to get the necessary international consensus on which to base effective police co-operation. The highly industrialized democracies have demonstrated solidarity by holding numerous meetings. Frequent statements stressing the desirability of co-operation do not obscure the paucity of results achieved. As the Italian Minister of the Interior, Oscar Luigi Scalfaro, remarked: 'If co-operation between states was already normal practice, no one would feel the necessity of constantly referring to it.'[4]

For example, in May 1987, the representatives of G7 met in Paris with the current chairman and a representative of the future chairman of the Trevi Group. Charles Pasqua stated that the objective of the meeting was to discuss the general problems posed by international terrorism, not to take practical decisions, and that no one had proposed the creation of a new institution, a new bureaucracy, or a new system of combating terrorism. The plenary session of ministers avoided all possible sources of friction; the meetings of experts, parallel to the ministerial meeting, also stuck to generalities. Signor Scalfaro again demonstrated his skill in choosing words by saying that the achievement of the meeting was to draw the attention of chiefs of state and government (due to meet the following month in Venice) on the necessity of achieving something concrete.[5]

The question is whether these meetings are on a road that leads anywhere. With each new outbreak of terrorism the same objective has been stated—closer police co-operation. Leaders of

---

[4] *Le Monde*, Nov. 1986.   [5] Ibid. 30 May 1987.

all highly industrialized democracies affected by terrorism have put similar statements on record. They are partly intended to reassure public opinion that everything possible is done to prevent the murder of innocent bystanders. Limited measures are certainly practicable, such as those proposed at the Tokyo summit of G7 in May 1986—reinforcing controls of suspect diplomatic represent-atives, tighter immigration controls, and more rapid extradition procedures. More ambitious proposals have sometimes been made. At the June 1985 Trevi group meeting in Rome, the Italians proposed, with the discreet backing of the United States, an international anti-terrorist unit. Ideas concerning an international intelligence group, and an international anti-terrorist force have been floated in several quarters but, like the idea of a European jurisidiction and a European jail for terrorists to prevent individual states being subject to blackmail, these proposals are regarded as imaginative but impractical.

Politicians and senior police officers often differ about the best way forward. The police frequently believe that their main difficulties are legal—limits on use of surveillance techniques, inability to hold suspects for sufficient time, and the rights of silence for suspects. In December 1985, at a Council of Europe meeting, Dr Heinrich Böge, head of the BKA, made a plea to politicians to avoid further limiting police powers in the interests of effectively combating terrorism. But only a small minority of police officers would like to see a European or international agency for counter-terrorist action going beyond the rapid and secure communication of information. There are formidable legal, organizational, and technical obstacles facing any proposal for an international anti-terrorist agency. Raymond Kendall, the Secret-ary General of Interpol, has consistently argued, since he took office in 1985, that the legal and political obstacles to such an agency are insuperable. He has also expressed the view that 'creating new structures on a limited geographical basis is not necessarily conducive to achieving the best results'.[6] It would be an entirely new departure in international affairs if such an agency had powers to collect evidence, to conduct enquiries, and to make arrests. Unless the stability of states was obviously and directly threatened by terrorist action, national parliaments are unlikely to approve such an important infringement of sovereign rights. Even if they gave their approval, intrusion into national territories

[6] *The Times*, 22 Sept. 1986.

of an international police authority would provoke potentially serious political problems.

Co-operation on other fronts in the European Community has made some progress. The Trevi Group has set up an *ad hoc* group on the reinforcement of external frontier controls of the Community. Police officers have been expressing concern about any dismantling of national frontier controls—as, for example, in resolutions of the International Union of Police Federations (in which Seventeen European countries are represented), of the UK Association of Chief Police Officers, and of the UK Police Federation. On the other hand, some experienced police officers consider that the main requirement is reinforcement of the external frontiers of the European Community in conjunction with strengthened police-to-police co-operation between the Community countries.[7] Since terrorists are very rarely caught through border controls, other methods of apprehending them must be found. One method of improving efficiency in this area is well under way—the exchange of operational information and good personal contacts between the specialized anti-terrorist squads, such as the British SAS, the German Grenzschutzgruppe 9 (GSG9), and the French GIGN. This is supplemented by close liaison, through Trevi, with the American FBI.

Interpol and terrorism

The French Prime Minister, Jacques Chirac, is reported as saying, during a discussion on terrorism at the 1986 Tokyo G7 summit, that one should not reinvent Interpol, implying that the setting up of a new international anti-terrorist agency would be an unnecessary duplication. The request for, and communication of, routine police information relating to terrorist cases—the tracing of persons, enquiries about identity papers, and various kinds of material evidence such as stolen vehicles and firearms—can be done effectively through the Interpol communications system. After the 1985 Brighton bombing aimed at Mrs Thatcher and her cabinet colleagues, approximately one thousand enquiries were sent by the NCB in Scotland Yard to other countries, including Libya, with only a 1 per cent failure rate.[8] In June 1987 the GAO of the United States published an exhaustive report on the

---

[7] *Independent*, 29 Dec. 1987.

[8] Interviews with Raymond Kendall, 15 May 1987; head of London NCB, 6 June 1987.

handling of counter-terrorist cases by the Washington NCB since it began accepting them, in January 1985.[9] In the two-year period 119 counter-terrorist case files, based on messages from twenty foreign NCBs and twenty-two domestic law-enforcement agencies, were opened. The FBI, the Italian NCB, and the Spanish NCB were the most frequent initiators of enquiries. All terrorist requests were treated in the highest categories of 'urgent' and 'critical urgent', although in some cases there were long delays in getting information. Some users, in reply to GAO enquiries, expressed dissatisfaction with the service provided by the Washington NCB, but, since the NCB had handled terrorist cases for only two years, countries had not become accustomed to working through it. More recently, in July 1988, there was heavy message traffic through Interpol concerning the attack on the tourist vessel, the *City of Poros*, in Greek territorial waters, despite the tension between France and Greece over allegations that French citizens were involved.

Interpol is forbidden by Article 3 of its Constitution to intervene in cases of a political, religious, or racial character and thus, for many years, was regarded as an exclusion from cases of politically inspired terrorism. The 1960s revival of terrorist activity, particularly of hijacking aircraft of the highly industrialized democracies, caused a change in attitudes led by the Americans. American opinion reacted sharply when, in the 1960s, American airliners became the principal target of hijackers. American initiatives resulted in the 1970s Hague Convention for the Suppression of the Unlawful Seizure of Aircraft (establishing the principle that countries should either extradite or try offenders), in the 1971 Montreal Convention for the Suppression of Unlawful Acts against the Safety of Civil Aviation, and in getting an important resolution passed at the 1970 Brussels General Assembly of Interpol, accepting that the organization should circulate information on hijacking.

In the early 1970s Interpol seemed to be moving towards a policy of regarding hijacking and other acts of terrorism as ordinary criminal offences. Resolution 5 at the Vienna Assembly of 1971 concerning 'Unlawful Acts of International Concern' recommended the use of Interpol channels for offences involving letter bombs, terrorist murders, hostage-taking, and bombings. Indecisiveness on the part of the Executive Committee resulted in

[9] GAO *Counterterrorism—The Role of Interpol and the US National Central Bureau*, June 1987.

failure to issue guidelines to implement this recommendation, even though in 1976 the General Secretariat had presented draft guidelines to the Committee. Resolutions passed at the 1979 Nairobi General Assembly and at the 1982 Torremolinos General Assembly kept up pressure on the issue. However, despite the lack of a constitutional decision to involve the organization in terrorist cases and a set of official guidelines on this issue, the communications network was used to some extent in terrorist crimes. This was facilitated by other policy decisions in matters such as the circulation of information about firearms—for example, the gun used in the attempted assassination of Pope John Paul II was identified through Interpol channels. In an interview in 1985 Mr Raymond Kendall, then Acting Secretary General of Interpol, said that for many years Interpol had issued, every six months or so, separate lists of hijackers and other terrorists wanted by police. He said that the combined lists totalled about four hundred names and this went up to five hundred names after the 1984 Luxemburg General Assembly decided that the organization should deal with a range of terrorist offences.[10] Involvement of Interpol in circulating information on terrorism 'to the extent that this does not contravene its statutes' was recognized by a ministerial recommendation of the Council of Europe in 1982.[11]

The important turning-point came in a resolution on 'Violent Crime Commonly Known as Terrorism' passed by the 1984 Luxemburg General Assembly. This resolution was based on the principle of 'preponderance' enunciated as long ago as the 1951 General Assembly—actions had to have a preponderant political, religious, or racial character to fall under Article 3. The resolution stressed that it was impossible to give a precise definition of preponderance, and a case-by-case approach had to be adopted. Certain actions sometimes designated as crimes by national penal codes—membership of organizations, limitations on liberties of opinion or the Press, insults to public authorities, endangering the security of the state, desertion, spying, practice of a religion, proselytizing, belonging to a racial group—were confirmed as under the ban of Article 3. All actions committed in their official capacity by persons holding political office also come under Article 3, even after loss of office, and exile. However, political

[10] See TVI Staff 'Interpol's Response to Terrorism', *Terrorism, Violence, Insurgency Journal* (summer 1985), 11.

[11] Council of Europe, Recommendation R (83) 1 adopted by the Council of Ministers, 15 June 1982.

motivation was not a sufficient reason for invoking Article 3. The resolution stated that actions having no direct relationship with the country or the cause of the perpetrators could not be regarded as falling within Article 3; examples of such actions are killing policemen, or taking hostages outside the 'conflict zone'; also included are instances when bombs injure bystanders unconnected with the conflict.

These general indications require the exercise of judgement by the Secretary General and by the NCBs involved. The resolution states that, when a case involves Article 3, the Secretary General should engage in a process of consultation with the relevant NCB. The NCB may persevere with a request in a borderline case but maximum clarification should be given by the Secretary General when the request is circulated. When the Secretary General disagrees with the NCB, he can stop circulation of a request. When an NCB refuses to comply to a request because, in its judgement, it contravenes Article 3, the Secretary General informs the other NCBs; a refusal to extradite must also be communicated to the other NCBs. If there is a disagreement between two NCBs, the Secretary General must be informed. If one, or several, countries refuse co-operation, this does not mean that the request is automatically regarded as coming under Article 3. The diffusion of information aimed at preventing terrorist acts is covered by the same rules.

After this resolution was passed, an International Terrorist Unit headed by an FBI agent was set up in January 1986 within the General Secretariat.[12] The Unit drafted a guide on practical ways of improving anti-terrorist co-operation with the main objective of preventing terrorists exporting their activities. This draft was discussed by the fourth Interpol Symposium on International Terrorism held in May 1986 and the final version of the 'Guide for Combating International Terrorism' was approved by the 1986 Belgrade General Assembly. This manual sets out the ground rules for sharing terrorist-related information among the member countries.

Anti-terrorist operations depend to a great degree on good intelligence, which becomes worthless if it becomes available to terrorist organizations. Doubts have been expressed about the reliability of Interpol as an anti-terrorist instrument. The Headquarters staff of Interpol has representatives from over thirty

---

[12] Interview with head of Interpol Terrorist Unit, 15 May 1987.

countries, and some could be a security risk in terrorist matters. Some of the Interpol NCBs do not have a high reputation for the security of information. States which have been alleged to connive at and even to promote terrorism—Libya, Syria, and Iran—participate in Interpol. For these reasons, western governments, which have been the targets of international terrorism, have been cautious about using the Interpol communications network for terrorist cases.

But Interpol membership of Middle Eastern and third-world countries, whose passports and facilities terrorists are likely to use, has advantages. Interpol can claim successes as a result—such as establishing the identity of Carlos, whose exploits included taking the OPEC ministers hostage in Vienna. Even when requests are unlikely to produce results—as the September 1986 request of the French *juge d'instruction* for the arrest of two Iranians, Nasser Dairyaei and Mahmoud Sceryari, implicated in terrorist offences in France and West Germany—these serve to alert other countries to terrorist activity. It is too soon to reach a judgement about the usefulness of Interpol, but there is, as yet, no reason to suppose it is less effective than the Trevi network. But the deliberate absence of direct official contact between Interpol and intelligence services makes an arrangement like the Trevi group essential. There are also good relations between the FBI and Trevi—senior FBI officials meet the 'troika' of the past, present, and future chairmen of Trevi at regular intervals; *ad hoc* arrangements for co-operation with other counter-intelligence agencies can be easily established. Whatever institutional arrangements for counter-terrorist co-operation are established, informal contacts, such as those between the FBI and Trevi, will continue to be considered essential by governments.

Conclusion

A specialized international counter-terrorist agency would probably not improve the circulation of case-related information and may well increase the difficulties of co-ordination between agencies. Better use could be made of existing communications systems such as Interpol by police, often rightly cautious about passing on dubious tip-offs, and better systems of co-ordination could be established between police and intelligence services, sometimes notorious hoarders of information. Governments have responded to terrorism by setting up specialized anti-terrorist units and promoting a specialized international communications network through the Trevi Group; although these responses were inevitable, they have exacerbated the already severe difficulties of co-ordination and co-operation between police forces. Pressure from governments for results helps with these problems; from this point of view, declarations of ministers and heads of government, sometimes dismissed as political posturing, are not entirely without effect. The terrorist factor has certainly promoted the issue of international police co-operation on the political agenda, assisted the revival of Interpol, and raised the question of the desirability of a European police authority. However, conflicting political interests are more likely to disrupt police co-operation in counter-terrorism than in any other field of law breaking. French experience provides the most striking illustration of this, but other countries have shared, to a lesser degree, the same difficulties. Political issues are raised by all forms of crime control but combating terrorism has the highest political content; attempts by governments to treat terrorist actions as ordinary criminal offences are doomed to, at least partial, failure.

7. Bilateral Police Co-operation

THROUGHOUT modern European history there have been frequent international police contacts. In the mid-eighteenth century the legendary Lieutenant General of Police of Paris, Sartine, comte d'Alby, was consulted by the Pope, Maria Theresa of Austria, and Catherine the Great of Russia.[1] In the first half of the nineteenth century the Austrian police under Chancellor Metternich (1814–48) had an elaborate network of police spies with many international contacts, especially with other German states. The Tzarist secret police, the Okhrana, had a formidable international network down to the First World War. These international contacts were mainly concerned with state security and hunting down political opponents, although they were also concerned with fugitive criminals. Assistance was given to foreign police authorities but international rivalries and tensions made an institutionalized system almost impossible to achieve.

Tension and friction continue to characterize many international police relations. Individual policemen may establish good relations with one another but police forces often fail to do so. This is the case within countries and between countries: for example, the relations between the FBI under J. Edgar Hoover (1924–72) and other federal police agencies was competitive and hostile; there has been a persistent fight over territory between the Police Nationale and the Gendarmerie Nationale in France. Relations can be even worse between the police and other agencies with police powers which are not regarded as equals by regular police forces—such as customs services and intelligence services. Even when clear mutual benefit is gained from co-operation, different interests, priorities, methods, and expertise produce friction and misunderstanding. There are many police stories about what goes wrong which attribute blame to lack of professionalism and lack of goodwill; a basic cause is the genuine difficulty of bringing together two police systems.

Relations are usually good when kept at the level of consultation and sociability, but much care and attention is necessary when police forces have to work jointly. Very simple matters can cause

[1] D. E. Emerson, *Metternich and the Political Police: Security and Subversion in the Habsburg Monarchy* (The Hague, 1968), 6.

friction, such as the desire of the US Secret Service agents to carry guns when protecting the American President on visits to Britain, where police have traditionally been unarmed. The majority of police officers have neither the background not the disposition to engage in diplomatic niceties and can often be blunt about the deficiencies of others—police relations between Northern Ireland and the Republic of Ireland have suffered intermittently as a consequence of this.[2] But incidents are not solely the result of the outlook of police officers. As James Q. Wilson stresses in his study of the FBI and DEA, law-enforcement officers are well aware of the bureaucratic problems and have thought of many ways of dealing with them.[3] However, governments seldom consider carefully the implications of police co-operation on the occasions when they have seen the necessity of it. The appearance of some current forms of bilateral police co-operation, such as embassy attachés and treaty arrangements for frontier regions, is therefore more impressive than the reality of everyday practice. There is a bewildering variety of bilateral police contacts, and the quality of co-operation which they represent can only be established by detailed empirical study of particular cases.

The purpose of this chapter is to outline the general characteristics of bilateral agreements and the understandings on which they are based. What bilateral arrangements contain, where they are typically found, and the limited significance of formal bilateral agreements are then discussed. The need to co-operate in frontier regions is emphasized but so is the wish to avoid foreign police intrusion that is sometimes keenly felt in these regions. Finally, the most rapidly developing form of bilateral co-operation—the posting of police officers abroad 'on mission'—is analysed.

The nature of bilateral arrangements

Bilateral police co-operation has frequently been based on informal understandings between police forces in neighbouring countries. Although bilateral police treaties started to appear in the second half of the nineteenth century, they have considerably increased in number in the last twenty-five years. These agreements are to be found most frequently between countries with a strong

[2] See, for example, reports of RUC criticisms of the Garda, *The Times*, 9 Oct. 1986.
[3] J. Q. Wilson, *The Investigators: Managing FBI and Narcotics Agents* (New York, 1978).

sense of political community, such as West Germany and France since 1962, Benelux and the Nordic countries, or those with a common colonial past, such as West African countries. On troubled frontiers, as in Ireland and on the Pyrennees, there is often a pressing need for operational co-operation but, for political reasons, the necessary arrangements have only slowly come into being. The United States has pressed hardest for bilateral police agreements because of the criminal problems faced by US law-enforcement agencies: the FBI in its investigations of organized crime, the DEA in combating drugs trafficking, and the US Customs for many purposes have sometimes been so active in seeking information abroad that they seem to be conducting ordinary criminal investigations in other countries.

International conventions and treaties respect the principle of sovereignty; police co-operation is therefore officially limited to the exchange of information, the co-ordination of police operations on both sides of an international frontier, and the sending of police officers 'on mission' to act as advisers or observers or to collect information. The basic difficulty of formal treaty-based co-operation is that co-operating police forces are based in legal systems whose principles, structures, and procedures vary considerably. When the legal systems have common historical roots, such as those of the United States and Britain, or France and Italy, procedural and substantive legal rules are often similar. However, the very existence of different jurisdictions creates formidable difficulties because police cannot normally have direct access to suspects, witnesses, and evidence in another jurisdiction. Applying for extradition of persons and obtaining assistance in acquiring evidence can be technically difficult, protracted, and expensive. These are disincentives for police officers to pursue an investigation; sometimes they are even incentives for police officers to engage in informal enquiries, making telephone calls to trusted colleagues in other countries.

Since an increasing number of police officers, particularly in European countries, know one another, informal contacts may be expected to increase. These informal contacts often take place within the context of multilateral arrangements. For example, the staff of Interpol NCBs frequently communicate on a bilateral basis without reporting to or passing messages through Interpol Headquarters. Certain semi-official consultative groups such as the North West Europe Association of Air and Seaport Police and the Cross Channel Intelligence Conference seem to have, as their main purpose, the facilitating of bilateral contacts. These contacts usually concern the communication of intelligence and the initiation of observation rather than co-ordination of investigations.

The content of police agreements

Interpol has prepared a model agreement which shows that the scope of international police agreements is potentially very wide.[4] They can cover the exchange of general police information concerning matters such as traffic offences or accidents, missing or stolen property; the exchange of crime-prevention information about operating methods of criminals; the reporting of movements of people who are either suspected of criminal offences or in need of protection; the surveillance of suspected persons and vehicles; and the reporting of the transport of dangerous substances. Co-operation in criminal investigations may consist of exchanging information concerning persons who have committed or who are suspected of having committed an offence or providing evidence required to establish proof of an offence; forwarding articles connected with an offence; exchanging police investigation records (police reports, witnesses, statements, records of interrogrations); advising or participating in an enquiry; pursuing offenders from the territory of one state to that of another; and using police vehicles on the territory of another state. Agreements on such matters must include stipulations about which police forces or authorities are competent to participate in transfrontier co-operation and how this should take place; details covered should include such matters as arrangements for meetings, the means of communication, the role of the NCBs, the form of requests to enter the territory of the other state, the regulations concerning the use of vehicles and the carrying of firearms, the procedures to follow in the case of accidents, and the civil liabilities of police in foreign countries.

In practice, comprehensive police agreements do not exist, partly because they are difficult to negotiate and partly because there is rarely strong political pressure for them. Indeed, they can confront political reticence and opposition. Most are very limited in scope and police co-operation is often an appendix to extradition treaties, as for example in the Benelux treaty on extradition and mutual assistance in criminal matters ratified in

[4] Report No. 19 of the Secretary General to the 1975 Buenos Aires General Assembly of Interpol.

1964 or in the West Germany–Tunisia treaty of 1969 in which direct contact between the BKA and the Sûreté Nationale of Tunisia is permitted in urgent cases. A similar clause is written into the 1972 Swiss–Austrian treaty. When an agreement concerns only police matters, the intention sometimes seems as much to limit as to facilitate police contacts. The 1960 Belgium–West Germany agreement, for example, states that liaison takes the form of periodic meetings and messages between specified police authorities, but any activity which could be construed as the intrusion of the police force of one state on the territory of the other is forbidden. In practice, closer forms of co-operation have developed. On the Dutch–Belgian–German border near Maestricht (The Netherlands), Aachen (Germany), and Eupen (Belgium) very active police co-operation takes place, based not on an international treaty but on the internal regulations of the police forces involved.[5]

Some agreements are more flexible than those referred to in the previous paragraph. The 'French connection'—the traffic of opium from Turkey, refined into heroin in the Marseilles area, for re-export to the United States—resulted in the 1971 agreement between the United States and France. It has since been renewed at five-year intervals, and amended in 1986 to include Canada and Italy; it allows law-enforcement officials of one state to reside in the territory of another to act in an advisory and liaison capacity. Close co-operation between the Office Centrale pour la Repression du Trafic Illicite des Stupéfiants in the Direction Centrale de la Police Judiciaire and the Bureau of Narcotics and Dangerous Drugs (subsequently the DEA) was envisaged to combat drug trafficking. In the original 1971 agreement three officials from the Bureau of Narcotics were stationed in Paris and three more in Marseilles. Two officials of the Police Judiciaire were assigned to New York and provision was made for increasing their number, if necessary. Direct access to senior levels of the police by the seconded officials was guaranteed by the agreement. The American police stationed in France are accredited to participate with their French colleagues in investigations of common interest (Article 7*b*) and the officers of the Police Judiciaire in the United States were similarly accredited (Article 7*c*); this gave a general authority for operational co-operation. Marseilles has ceased to be an important international centre for refining heroin, but heroin

---

[5] Interview with the head of the Hague NCB, 8 May 1987. This arrangement has the acronym NEBEDEACPOL (the Dutch, Belgian, German police conference).

abuse has risen sharply in France. Consequently, DEA officials now participate in operations to assist their French colleagues as much as vice versa.[6] The significance of this agreement extends beyond the specific problem of the 'French connection' because it has been used as a model for other agreements involving DEA presence in other countries.

Drug law enforcement is a special case because of the international character of drug trafficking, unparalleled in other areas of criminal activity. However, close bilateral police co-operation on other matters is found in certain circumstances. These include geographical situations in which countries share a contiguous land frontier with heavy traffic across it, where there have been strong historic links between countries, and where there is evidence of persistent transnational criminal conspiracies. The degree of co-operation varies considerably and a common approach to problems is essential for good co-operation. The United States and Mexico, for example, share a land frontier across which there is intense traffic but differences in interests and outlook are a hindrance to effective police, drug law enforcement, customs, and immigration co-operation. Numerous reports and public statements attest to this and it is confirmed by the personal opinions of US law-enforcement officers.[7] The United States–Canada border, where transfrontier problems have been serious although not as intense as on the Rio Grande, presents a contrast: relations between the FBI and the Royal Canadian Mounted Police (RCMP) have been particularly good. The RCMP has on-line access to the FBI's criminal intelligence computer which is, as yet, a rare form of transfrontier police co-operation.

Historic links are of various kinds. In the former Habsburg territories of central Europe, there are residues of former connections. The political ties between Land Tyrol in Austria and the South Tyrol in Italy remain strong and police co-operation is good, except in political cases involving German-speaking South Tyrolese autonomists. Hungary is the only Eastern bloc country which is an active member of Interpol (Romania is a member but does not appear to use Interpol much): long association with Austria allowed the re-entry of Hungary to the organization to take place without difficulty.[8] Links between former imperial

---

[6] Interview with DEA representative in Paris, 26 May 1987.

[7] Immigration officers regard Mexican co-operation on nationals other than Mexicans as good, interview with the Chief of Enforcement, Immigration, and Naturalization Service, 19 Feb. 1987.

[8] Interview with head of Vienna NCB, 12 June 1987.

countries and colonies usually result in some form of police co-operation, whether of a multilateral kind, as in the Commonwealth Crime Bureau, or bilateral co-operation, as in police training. The French remain closer than the British to their former African colonies because of the smaller populations and the political vulnerability of Francophone sub-Saharan Africa. For geopolitical reasons, France has wished to retain political influence in Africa and, as a consequence, there has been French military, intelligence, and police presence in many of the ex-colonies.

In 1961, coinciding with de Gaulle's decolonization of sub-Saharan Africa and the final stages of the Algerian conflict leading to the independence of Algeria, the STCIP was set up in the Ministry of the Interior. Sensitive political and intelligence interests were involved and the text of the ministerial instruction establishing the STCIP remains confidential. The main functions of the STCIP are to provide training facilities, both in France and abroad, to offer advice on police techniques and equipment, and, in special cases, to provide operational support.[9] In the early days of the STCIP there was much informal co-operation but overseas activities of the STCIP are now covered by formal bilateral agreements.

Only about twelve cadets come to France for the full two-year period of training. More come for short courses in the main technical specialisms—public order, criminal police, frontier control, terrorism, and record-keeping. But the main demand, and the most cost effective, is for French instructors to go abroad: by 1987 STCIP instructors had trained more than 70,000 foreign police officers. Permanent STCIP offices have been established in twenty-five countries and, until 1981, these were, with the exception of Equador, all in Francophone African countries. Since 1981 a scattering of countries without any colonial connection with France have been added, notably Saudi Arabia, Bolivia, Mexico, and Indonesia (1982–5). Temporary missions have had an even greater geographical spread. For example, in 1986 temporary missions were charged with the installation of radio communications networks for Togo and Guinea, a plan for continuing police training in the Ivory Coast, airport security in Egypt, organization of police colloquia in Saudi Arabia, and participation in a selection committee for the United Nations.

---

[9] Interviews with *chef de cabinet* of the director of the STCIP, 17, 26 Jan. 1987; the author is also grateful for documentary information communicated by the STCIP.

The Institute International de Police (IIP), founded in 1976, is an influential dimension of the activities of the STCIP, because it brings senior police officers from a large number of countries to Paris for international colloquiums. The IIP holds an annual conference on a general theme—for example, Police, Public Order and the Rights of Man (1981), Technology and Methods for Combating Terrorism (1983), and Police and Technology (1986). The STCIP is therefore growing away from its neo-colonial origins, although lack of resources severely limit any further extensions of its programme.

French police organization is relatively easy to explain in broad outline and it has characteristics attractive to developing countries, including some aspects most criticized in France. A divided rather than a unified national police often seems essential in countries where those who control physical force are often tempted to seize political power. The distinction, perhaps now anachronistic in France, between the Gendarmerie Nationale, controlled by the Ministry of Defence, and the Police Nationale, controlled by the Ministry of the Interior, is therefore attractive. The organization of special corps for matters such as riot control, political intelligence, frontiers, and a criminal investigation police working under the authority of examining magistrates are also features which fit the circumstances of some of the developing countries. Although aspects of the British and American models of policing are influential in many less developed countries, they are often seen as too rooted in specific national histories to be easily exported. However, the role of the United Kingdom, as well as that of the United States and West Germany, in providing assistance in training in police techniques is as great as the French, because these countries have appropriate resources, facilities, and contacts.

The United Kingdom Police College at Bramshill and the FBI 'university' at Quantico in Virginia (and the training programmes of other federal law-enforcement agencies) provide similar kinds of services as the STCIP. These institutions have the advantage of the English language, which makes their courses and seminars accessible to a much larger population. Courses, seminars, and technical advice create personal links and bonds of understanding which are sometimes useful in fighting certain types of crime. For example, the DEA holds an annual International Drug Enforcement Conference (IDEC) for those police officers from South American countries who have been on DEA training courses. This maintains personal contacts with drug law-enforcement agencies in different countries and helps the overseas operations of the DEA. In August 1988 a large-scale international anti-drugs operation was reported as being mounted through the IDEC. Professional contacts, through international meetings and training programmes, have greatly increased since the 1960s. The practical case-related effects are hard to identify but an international learning process has widened perspectives for a profession which, with the partial exception of some police officers of the old imperial powers, used to be hermetically sealed by national frontiers.

Frontier regions

Bilateral police agreements for frontier regions are intended to facilitate criminal investigation and to prevent the flight of suspect persons. Multilateral agreements for frontier regions between neighbouring countries also exist but they are rare. An example is the Lagos agreement (1984) on criminal police matters between Benin, Ghana, Nigeria, and Togo. The main purpose of this agreement is to centralize police contacts in frontier regions through the Interpol NCBs. Also, a series of bilateral agreements can in effect produce multilateral understandings, as, for example, the police agreements between Belgium and her neighbours: with West Germany (1968), Luxemburg (1968), France (1970), and The Netherlands (1973). According to these agreements, the procedures and the rules which are followed within Belgium are the same—although the Dutch police have a very limited right to hot pursuit across the border (according to the Benelux treaty of 1962) which the other countries do not enjoy. Belgium imposes three conditions for the calling of a police alert at the request of its neighbours: a serious extraditable crime of a non-political kind must have been committed; precise information about the nature and circumstances of the crime must be supplied; and there must be a likelihood that the authors of the crime intend to cross the frontier (it is sufficient if the crime takes place within thirty kilometres of the frontier). These agreements assume that co-operative action will be taken, but no state is obliged to act: the principle of national sovereignty remains sacrosanct.

The Franco-German police agreement of 3 February 1977 covers 186 kilometres of frontier, the northern part of which is often called 'the green frontier'. This frontier is difficult to police and has heavy traffic across it. There are joint Franco-German customs and police posts; frontier controls have been reduced to a formality for European Community citizens and will be abolished, according to the terms of the 1985 Shengen agreement, between France, Germany, and Benelux. Long-established links had, since the 1950s, ensured a reasonable measure of police co-operation. The informality of the relationships sometimes meant that cross border information co-operation was not always communicated by police officers to their superiors and therefore criminal intelligence was not always used to the best effect. The 1977 agreement had as its first objective to bring some order into a somewhat anarchic system of relationships. Officially allowing direct contacts removed the need for informal and confidential co-operation.[10]

Although the first article of the agreement claimed to be 'completing' Interpol police co-operation, it represents a very modest advance. Article 2 delimits the territory which the agreement covers and Article 3 defines the kinds of crimes on which co-operation is envisaged (those which normally attract more than one year's imprisonment). Article 4 allows countries to refuse co-operation if it is against the national interest: 'If one of the contracting parties considers that the assistance is of a kind to affect adversely the sovereignty, the security, public order or other essential interests of the country, [the authorities] can refuse assistance or some part of the assistance requested or [they] can subject the assistance to certain conditions or obligations.' The agreement was further restricted by the assertion that existing extradition, mutual legal assistance, and customs agreements were not affected by its provisions.

On the positive side, police messages can be communicated directly to the relevant police authority on the other side of the frontier (Article 6) but these messages then have to be reported to the respective Interpol NCBs (Article 9). The responsible police officials should meet periodically to consult about measures to implement the agreement (Article 7). The competent authorities should give technical assistance to the other country when circumstances require this, but officials giving assistance are advisory and cannot have operational authority (Article 8). Nevertheless, Article 8 provides a tenuous basis for joint investigations in the case of complex transfrontier criminal offences. Visits and telephone conversations are to be supplemented by direct

[10] The Direction Régionale de la Police Judiciaire of Strasburg kindly arranged visits to Metz and Saarbrücken and interviews with Saarland police officials, 17 Mar. 1987.

radio links via the Mulhouse transmitter and the German police radio network. The meetings between senior officers have produced joint working parties on drug trafficking and the theft of works of art. But the limitations of the agreement are that police officers who cross the international frontier lose all police powers. They cannot be armed; they cannot remain in direct radio contact with headquarters. Incidents have occurred: in 1983 a German policeman unwittingly crossed the border in the boot of a car during a surveillance operation in a bogus kidnapping case and emerged to confront the conspirators with a gun in his hand. If shots had been exchanged it would have been difficult to avoid a serious diplomatic incident with complicated legal consequences.

There is more spillover of criminal activity from Germany into France on this frontier than the other way around, at least in part for linguistic reasons because German and Alemannic dialects are spoken in Alsace much more than French is spoken in the German Rhineland. The German police, therefore, more frequently than the French, tend to come up against the limits of police co-operation in this region. They more than the French, therefore, have pressed proposals for closer bilateral relations (and incidentally for closer police co-operation at the European level). The Germans have asked for the right of hot pursuit over the frontier, and even for French number plates if their vehicles have to cross into France. The French have generally refused these requests because of the implied infringement of the principle of sovereignty. However, at a Franco-German inter-governmental meeting on 3 and 4 November 1977, an agreement on frontier surveillance was drafted with particular reference to hot pursuit in the context of the fight against international terrorism. This allowed surveillance by the police officers of both countries on each other's territory but the activity was to be tightly controlled by liaison officers in the respective Ministries of the Interior. The French had previously been willing to have German police officers on their territory during the Hans-Martin Schleyer murder investigation, but any presence of German police on French territory reawakens historic memories of the German annexation of Alsace-Lorraine from 1870–1918 and from 1940–45.

In bilateral agreements, two stages of co-operation must be clearly distinguished: the stage of exchange of information and the stage of active investigation involving interviewing witnesses, impounding evidence, and making arrests. The first stage may be entirely in the hands of the police but judicial authorities are, in most jurisidictions, directly involved in the second stage. For example, the police are acting under the authority of the public prosecutor in Germany and the *juge d'instruction* in France. The point at which judicial authorities invervene may vary; the notion of urgency is given a wider interpretation in Germany than in France, which allows an investigation to remain for a longer period in police hands. Once the judicial authorities are involved, a police enquiry becomes either French or German, depending on the nationality of the people involved and the degree of interest which one or other country has in the case. Communications become judicial communications which, except in cases of urgency, go through diplomatic, not police, channels. In general, different legal procedures can cause misunderstandings and even sour relations between police of different countries: the reasons for delay or procedural difficulties are not always understood. The Interpol NCBs often play a useful role in informing police authorities within their own countries about the nature of these difficulties.

Police officers 'on mission'

The considerable increase in recent years of police on official missions in other countries indicates the growing importance of international co-operation in police work.[11] Statistics of official missions, sometimes kept by NCBs, are a somewhat misleading indicator of the growth of police contacts, because the purpose of these missions is so varied and the unofficial missions may, in some cases, be the hidden part of an iceberg. By no means all missions have an operational purpose; they frequently have a diplomatic, advisory, or educational objective rather than being part of a criminal investigation. Unofficial visits are sometimes made for the purpose of investigating crimes. Occasionally such visits are clandestine; Dutch police officers, behaving suspiciously whilst conducting surveillance on Belgian territory, have been arrested by Belgian police. In regions where there is a common language and a high level of social contact, unofficial missions often take place, but the frequency of these is impossible to assess.

[11] A restricted distribution report was prepared by Interpol on this subject, 'Missions abroad by Police Investigators', Report No. 16, Nice General Assembly, 1981, this is based on a questionnaire completed by NCBs and concentrates on short-term missions.

Posting police officers to other countries for extended tours of duty is now a regular part of European police activity and is even more extensively practised by the non-European highly industrialized countries. During and immediately after the Second World War, the United States pioneered the practice of law-enforcement officers (other than state security police) as embassy attachés with responsibilities for a range of police matters. The large number of law-enforcement agencies at the federal level in the United States led to the proliferation of overseas representation of law-enforcement officers—the FBI, the DEA, Customs, the Internal Revenue Service, the Secret Service, and the Immigration and Naturalization Service are represented in large embassies. This large US law-enforcement presence abroad is sometimes a sensitive matter in the host countries; moreover, the entrepreneurial and sometimes informal style of US law-enforcement officials can jar on European susceptibilities.

The FBI were first in the field, but the DEA, with over sixty permanent overseas offices in forty-three countries, has become the most prominent. The FBI maintains contacts with foreign police forces through thirteen Legats (legal attachés) in embassies. The Bureau would like to increase this number by adding Madrid and Lima to the list of embassies with a Legat, although the State Department, in common with other foreign offices, is not enthusiastic about law-enforcement officers in embassies (other than the Regional Security Officers, responsible for embassy security). The FBI puts considerable effort into the FBI Legat system, and into the recently upgraded Office of Liaison and International Affairs in the Washington Headquarters.[12] The case for maintaining the system is constantly updated, with an inspection of the system every eighteen months and a performance appraisal of each Legat every twelve months—necessary precautions if the FBI's budget is critically scrutinized in the Congress. In the 1980s, the Bureau's budget has not come under serious pressure since Judge Webster (1980–7) re-established the FBI's standing with Congress and its position as the premier federal law-enforcement agency. However, the case for the FBI's overseas representation is not particularly strong compared with that of the DEA and Customs. The strongest arguments contained in the FBI's annual submissions to the Congress to defend the Bureau's budget are the Legats' role in counter-intelligence

---

[12] Interviews with chief of the FBI's Office of Liaison and International Affairs, 10 Feb. 1987, and Assistant Director of the FBI, 6 Feb. 1987.

(although this is the most delicate area of its overseas responsibilities) and in involvement in cases of organized crime.

The Secret Service is charged with the protection of the President, Vice-President, ex-Presidents, and some other members of the executive branch, but this does not provide a convincing justification for permanent overseas representation. Indeed, when the President travels abroad, the overseas-based Secret Service agents tend to play a subordinate role because of the very size of the security operation.[13] Investigating currency counterfeiting gives the Secret Service an international role because the dollar remains the most commonly counterfeited currency and foreign police authorities need the expertise of the Secret Service. The Secret Service is also the lead agency in credit-card fraud and this also strengthens its international role. But the overseas presence of the Secret Service is spread thinly—the only large office is Paris covering ninety countries in Europe, Africa, and the Middle East with subordinate one-man offices in London and Milan. Latin America is covered from the Miami field office and the Far East from Honolulu. The Service wishes to extend its representation to Wiesbaden, Madrid, and North Africa, but for public-expenditure reasons these ambitions are unlikely to be achieved.

The international interests of the Secret Service are of long standing—the Paris office was opened in 1947 with the advent of the Marshall Plan and the coincidental surge in numbers of forged dollars in European countries. The high educational standards of Secret Servicemen and their closeness to the Presidency help to explain a keen interest in international affairs. Two out of the last three Interpol NCB chiefs in Washington have been Secret Service agents. The first US candidate for the Presidency of Interpol and the present President of Interpol are both Secret Service agents. The maintenance of an overseas role for the Secret Service is doubtless a matter of pride and a mark of status as well as of utility for the Secret Service.

The presence of FBI and Secret Service agents in embassies may be defended on several grounds. Personal contacts are made with officials in the leading law-enforcement and intelligence agencies; the presence of the FBI Legat in London allows the Bureau to get to know officials in the Home Office, the Inspectorate General of Constabulary, many of the Chief Constables, and the officially

---

[13] Interview with Special Agent in Charge of Paris office of the Secret Service, 8 June 1987, and John Simpson, director of the Secret Service and President of Interpol, 24 Feb. 1987.

non-existent intelligence services, MI5 and MI6. Attachés can gain considerable knowledge of the law-enforcement and criminal justice system of the country to which they are posted and this knowledge can help to overcome difficulties in following up difficult cases. The attachés, rather than Interpol, are frequently used to transmit information about sensitive or highly complex investigations; policemen tend to be more forthcoming and more co-operative when they get direct enquiries from law-enforcement officers whom they already know and trust. Also, under the Crime Control Act (1984), for certain forms of crime (assassination of diplomats, air piracy, crimes on the high seas, kidnapping, and taking Americans hostage) the US claims extraterritorial juris-diction. These claims cannot be sustained without the active support of other governments, and direct contact between law-enforcement officers can help to obtain this support.

The role of the FBI in counter-intelligence and in combating organized crime has international implications. The FBI must have direct contact with intelligence agencies of friendly countries, especially in the absence of good inter-agency co-operation with the CIA. Judge Webster's appointment in 1987, after six years as director of the FBI, to the directorship of the CIA may improve a traditionally poor relationship, but the FBI has privileged relations with many law-enforcement agencies in friendly countries which, it would argue, are worth preserving. Mafia-type criminal conspir-acies which extend their operations to several countries require that the FBI maintains close relations with criminal investigation departments overseas—there are two Italian officers permanently seconded to the FBI in Washington and there are regular visits to the FBI in Washington of senior police officers from other highly industrialized democracies.

The case for a large overseas presence of the DEA is based on the assumption that action in the source and transit countries can significantly reduce drug abuse in the United States. The DEA has not, until recently, been convinced of the usefulness of the Interpol communications network because of alleged lack of security, slowness, and lack of capacity of poor countries to use Interpol. The DEA prefers direct contact with drug law-enforce-ment officers to obtain information and co-operation, since this allows the DEA to establish which officers and agencies can be trusted. Corruption of police, judges, and public officials is inevitable in poor countries because of the huge amount of money involved; but this is also a problem in the United States. The main purpose of the DEA's sixty-plus overseas offices is to gather accurate information and intelligence in co-operation with the local authorities. To do this effectively, DEA agents must be in a position to judge which local authorities they can trust.

The DEA, as a single function agency, is particularly concerned to defend its territory against other US law-enforcement agencies. Relations between the FBI and DEA have much improved in recent years, since the FBI was given, in 1982, co-responsibility in the fight against narcotics; US Customs, and state and local police forces are also heavily involved in investigating drugs cases. Since the 1970s multi-agency 'task forces' have been established in the fight against crime and the DEA has lost sole control over important narcotics cases. In 1987 the DEA was participating in twenty-four multi-agency task forces in the United States. 'Money tracking', the most successful technique in locating the financial backers of drug purchase and distribution, has also made the DEA a partner with other agencies. Officials in other federal law-enforcement agencies tend to be sceptical about the more flamboyant overseas operations of the DEA, regarding them mainly as a way of impressing the US public. But the international role is important to the agency in defending its overall position and independence. Internationally its services are valued—it is used as an international intelligence network by the French and other police forces. It thus competes with Interpol, even though the head of the Drugs Subdivision of Interpol in 1987 was a DEA agent.

The international activities of US Customs are extensive but less controversial than those of the DEA.[14] In 1987 the service had about seventy officers in twelve embassies. Customs is the oldest federal law-enforcement agency (established by the second Act of Congress); it has wide search and seize powers for enforcing a large body of legislation—over 250 Acts of Congress. Customs co-operation does not fall completely within international police co-operation as many countries do not regard customs as a police function but as an administrative and revenue-collecting one. Assisting another country to collect customs duties and enforcing the financial legislation of another state is seldom in the national interest, but states sometimes have an interest in trading information about financial crime. The collection of duties is, however, only one aspect of the work of US Customs and other customs

---

[14] Interviews with head of US Customs, San Francisco, 5 Mar. 1987; head of enforcement, US Customs Washington, 11 Feb. 1987; US Customs representative Paris, 22 Apr. 1987.

services. Amongst the criminal activities investigated by US Customs are the trade in prohibited goods such as drugs and child pornography, cargo theft, insurance fraud, and counterfeit goods. Interpol is used by US and other customs services when necessary to help enquiries into these crimes. The final category of customs activity goes beyond normal policing—this is the protection of the strategic or foreign-policy interests of governments, such as the US prohibition of export of 'critical' technology, potentially useful for military purposes, to Soviet bloc countries. The NATO countries, subsequently joined by Japan, have co-operated since 1949 through COCOM to prevent the export of critical technology. It has proved difficult to prevent the re-export of US goods from third countries to Eastern Europe, but COCOM has helped to achieve a greater harmonization of western views on the issue. To promote good co-operation on all types of cases, US customs gives high priority to answering requests for assistance from other customs services: all enquiries must be answered within thirty days.

In the first category of co-operation, except for the exchange of general information and intelligence through the CCC[15] international co-operation is always bilateral. In the second category, customs services are very often acting in conjunction with other police agencies and revenue services. Customs services also use Interpol for criminal investigations; other multilateral networks are appearing, such as the Pacific basin computer-based intelligence system, established in 1984, which associates the richer countries of the Pacific rim and which logs the movement of ships and light planes to prevent smuggling of prohibited goods. The third category must be multilateral if it is to be effective, otherwise re-export of high technology countries would be impossible to prevent. It is, however, difficult to see how even multilateral co-operation can be effective in the medium or long term. In general, the scope for multilateral co-operation in the customs field is limited, except in customs unions such as the European Community. The work of the CCC is, none the less, useful if unspectacular. It has drawn up recommendations on such matters as mutual administrative assistance (1953), pooling of information concerning customs fraud (1975), and an international agreement (the Nairobi Convention) on mutual administrative assistance for

---

[15] The CCC publishes a bulletin (with restricted circulation) on case-related material and criminal intelligence, but for rapid communications customs officers must use the Interpol system or direct bilateral contact.

prevention, investigation, and repression of customs offences. Although the text of the Nairobi Convention was signed in 1977 and it came into force in 1980, very few countries have ratified the convention, showing the lack of interest, and even the veiled hostility, of many countries to this form of co-operation. The CCC has been strengthening its enforcement activities in recent years with the appointment of an assistant director for enforcement; an experienced US Customs official has been in the chair of its enforcement committee.

The US federal law-enforcement effort has been characterized in recent years by greater co-ordination of an apparently chaotic system where agencies have proliferated and have sometimes been aggressively competitive. This has been the result of Congressional pressure and of determined effort by senior officials of the executive branch. There are limits to successful co-ordination because the interests of the agencies conflict and the system stimulates competition between agencies for resources and for the leading role in investigating complex criminal conspiracies. At the moment, however, inter-agency friction is no longer a prominent feature of the overseas activities of the federal law-enforcement agencies. Also, these agencies participate increasingly in the existing multilateral systems of co-operation, and particularly in Interpol. There is a counter-tendency among officials of agencies to prefer bilateral co-operation rather than multilateral arrangements and this preference is voiced more cautiously at the political level by officials with a supervisory role over these agencies.[16] Improved strategic thinking and increasing rationalization of activities in the United States is apparent, but the federal government, like its partners among the highly industrialized democracies, has as yet no coherent set of practical objectives in police co-operation.

Conclusion

Bilateral police co-operation comprises arrangements which have grown piecemeal over the years. It has, however, some general features. Police co-operation in frontier regions has become common practice between neighbouring countries. In western Europe this co-operation is increasing considerably, with the implementation of agreements between France, West Germany,

---

[16] Interview with Frank Keating, Assistant Secretary to the Treasury, 20 Feb. 1987.

and Benelux to eliminate frontier controls and the 1992 introduction of the single market by the European Community. Some peripheral countries, such as Britain, Ireland, and Greece, will probably retain frontier controls as long as possible, but frontiers will become less important as effective instruments of policing.[17] Bilateral police agreements for special purposes—to combat organized crime, drug trafficking, and terrorism—have increased in number and *ad hoc* co-operation to combat particular criminal problems is now commonplace. The police dimension is often ignored in treaties concerning extradition and legal mutual assistance in criminal matters—this causes concern in police circles and has been the subject of several protests by Dr Böge of the BKA.

The appointment of police attachés in embassies is a well-established US practice. This has spread to other countries such as Canada, Japan, and Israel but the European countries have been relatively slow to follow the US example. The Europeans have drug liaison officers in drug-producing and transit countries but on a smaller scale, and with a lower profile than the DEA. There is, however, some police resistance to stationing law-enforcement officers in embassies, because the police do not want foreign ministries to control the law-enforcement agenda; conversely, there are prejudices among some diplomats about having police officers in their embassies. Moreover, there is some disquiet in European countries about the large US law-enforcement presence in embassies: the lack of any general international agreement on the form of representation is a factor assisting the maintenance of these tensions.

There is an untidy relationship between bilateral and multilateral forms of co-operation. It is rare that the relationship is clearly spelt out. In the case of the Franco-German agreement for the frontier regions, it is stated that bilateral communications should be reported to the NCBs. The FBI has a rule that, if communication on a case starts with the Legats or with Interpol, the same channel should be used throughout the case. Overseas drugs liaison officers of Scandinavian countries pool their information through the Interpol NCBs. Rules and practice, however, often diverge. The existence of two or more channels of co-operation is bound, on occasion, to cause difficulties because

[17] The British Home Secretary made clear the British intention to retain frontier controls at the meeting of the Trevi Group, 3 June 1988. The political and economic costs of this policy could outweigh the advantages.

enquiries which start bilaterally may eventually have multilateral implications and those which start multilaterally may have extremely sensitive bilateral dimensions. In general, bilateral arrangements fit easily with multilateral organizations because of the distance of most international organizations from case-related activity. The United Nations, the Council of Europe, the IDEC, and the IIP have no case-related activities, although delegates to meetings taking place under their auspices may discuss cases privately. Friction occurs, although this seldom breaks out into public conflict, between bilateral and multilateral systems when they are involved in the same area. This could be avoided if there were clear and internationally recognized rules governing bilateral relations but these are unlikely to be negotiated in the near future partly because the international system is changing so rapidly.

8. Models of International Police Co-operation

FOR those who adopt Marxist or structuralist interpretations of the police (referred to in Chapter 1), Interpol is an agent of state institutions of coercion; these institutions in turn are based on a system of socio-economic relations. Some Marxists argue that capital is increasingly internationalized and therefore the nation-state is becoming less important as an instrument of class rule: in these circumstances, a greater role for international policing would be expected. Although this conclusion is unexceptionable, the deterministic approach of Marxists and structuralists to the development of policing implies a rejection of the discussion of models in this chapter. Others may dismiss model building as a theoretical exercise, out of touch with practicalities.

The invention of models assumes that present arrangements can be consciously modified by policy decisions and that governments and the law-enforcement community have the potential to choose, within certain broad limits, between various arrangements for international police co-operation. Circumstances may dictate that there must be some system of police co-operation and that police functions, for the time being, cannot be internationalized. But whether there are any formal institutions of co-operation, whether these have some independence and autonomy, whether there are strong regional facilities for co-operation—such matters are essentially a matter of choice and are not determined by some inexorable social process. Well-founded choices are based, first, on an awareness of the options, and, second, on the ability to recognize the moment or moments at which choices must or can be made. This chapter is a contribution to the first. It commences with an assessment of pressures for change in Interpol, in order to show that a consideration of models of co-operation is relevant to policy-making. Two contrasting models—the 'centralized-state' model and the 'decentralized-state' model—are then presented. Modifications of these models and variations at the global and regional levels are analysed. The factors which influence preferences for one or another of these models form a conclusion to the chapter.

Reforming pressures

There are two organizational pressures for a serious review of international police co-operation, although neither is strong enough to result in the negotiation of multilateral treaties in the immediate future. These are, on the one hand, the growth of bilateral co-operation of the kind discussed in Chapter 7—direct police-force-to-police-force contacts, liaison officers, police officers on mission—and, on the other, the growing interest in multilateral co-operation on a regional basis. The former need not disrupt the established arrangements of Interpol, since bilateral arrangements bypassing multilateral Interpol channels have been a common and accepted practice. However, the increased scale of bilateral contacts creates the need for international agreements along the lines of the conventions governing diplomatic relations: these may take a long time to negotiate but would raise no serious difficulties. However, enhanced regional co-operation could cause severe problems for Interpol.

Calls for regionalization within Interpol have a long history. They were first made on behalf of South America. Chile complained in 1955 that Paris was a long way away and that a South American Interpol was necessary. In 1960 newly established African states began to feel that their policing problems differed from those of the highly industrialized world and Ghana proposed an African regional conference. This demand was quickly met by Interpol and, although the African Regional Conference of Interpol was the first established and has been successful, more ambitious ideas for an African crime-fighting organization have been proposed in the 1980s. Regional conferences within Interpol have now become commonplace—the American Regional Conference was established surprisingly late but all regions are now covered. There are regional telecommunications centres in Tokyo, Nairobi, Abidjan, and Buenos Aires to facilitate message traffic; in addition, a sub-regional office has been established in Bangkok, and a South American liaison office is being established in Buenos Aires.

However, despite the European preponderance in the utilization of the Interpol communications network and in the number of officials at Interpol Headquarters, pressure for regionalization has been most intense in Europe. The long-term factor towards greater European co-operation in police matters is the increasing political and economic co-operation in the European Community.

The agreement to establish the Trevi Group has been an important stimulus in thinking about regional co-operation.[1] This coincided with some dissatisfaction about the management of Interpol Headquarters, and the idea of a separate organization, 'Europol', gained some supporters. The proposal for Europol has been revived from time to time.[2] Within Interpol certain measures were taken in the 1970s—the establishment of a European Conference and the appointment of European drug liaison officers at Interpol Headquarters dealing with a restricted number of countries (the SEPAT plan)—and from the beginning of the 1980s modest but genuine moves towards a European regional structure have been made.

In 1981, at the eleventh meeting of the European Regional Conference, the German delegation proposed a European Regional Bureau. A working party was established to examine this proposal, which delegated its mandate to a smaller group—the Technical Committee for Co-operation in Europe (TCCE). This committee has met on a regular basis ever since, and, amongst other suggestions, proposed the establishment of a European secretariat within the Interpol General Secretariat. This was established in November 1986 but did not obtain a proper staff until the following year. Its role is to provide services for the TCCE and the European Regional Conference, and to act as liaison office between Europe and the other regions and between the General Secretariat and the European NCBs.[3] At the Interpol European Regional Conference of April 1988, the development of the European Secretariat was discussed in the light of the increased space available to Interpol Headquarters after the move from Saint-Cloud to Lyons. It was suggested that countries should post liaison officers to the European Secretariat and avoid the high cost of a general bilateral exchange of liaison officers. Also a modest degree of operational co-operation is under consideration;

---

[1] Some information about European proposals is given in J. Lodge, 'The European Community and Terrorism: Establishing the Principle of Extradite or Try', in J. Lodge (ed.), *Terrorism: A Challenge to the State* (Oxford, 1981); see also J. Lodge, 'The European Community and Terrorism', in J. Lodge (ed.), *The Threat of Terrorism* (Brighton, 1988).

[2] Recently in the Parliamentary Assembly of the Council of Europe, 17–25 Sept. 1986; see P. Stoffelin, 'Terrorism, Arms Trade, Europol', *Forum*, 3–4 (1986), 2–3. For a trenchant review of European criticisms of Interpol and the bases for the Europol proposal, see C. Fijnaut and R. H. Hermans (eds.), *Police Cooperation in Europe* (Lochem, 1987), 38–9.

[3] Interview with the secretary of the European Secretariat of Interpol, 22 May 1987.

this would allow European police forces on-line access to Interpol's file to establish whether an individual was wanted in another country. Even if these proposals are not taken up, the European Secretariat could provide a much needed over-view of the forms and the deficiencies of existing European arrangements.

The difficulties in the way of further regionalization are, in general, threefold. The first is resources: the question of who is going to pay has held up progress in Europe; there is virtually no possibility of significant savings within Interpol Headquarters to finance regionalization. The second is the great differences between regions, which means a standard form of regionalization in Interpol would not be suitable for all regions, and there could be difficult problems of drawing acceptable geographical boundaries between them. The third is that there is no provision for regionalization in the Statutes of Interpol and the difficulties of revising the Statutes have been discussed elsewhere.[4] A genuine devolution to regions would also necessitate the negotiation of headquarters agreements with host countries of the regional bureaux; this is a slow and difficult process, as the negotiation with Thailand (an agreement was finally signed in February 1987) and Argentina over the establishment of very small offices has shown.

Systematic speculation about reforms requires blueprints or models. Inventing models of international police co-operation encourages critical examination of existing arrangements and suggests possible improvements. New international agreements may be necessary to meet rapidly changing conditions and models can provide policy-makers with a range of options for these. Models also stimulate thinking about the extent to which legally sovereign states, as presently constituted, can allow pooling of services in law enforcement. There are two ideal types of models—centralized and decentralized—and a number of possible variants of them, although only two variants are discussed in this chapter.

The 'centralized-state' model

This model is based on strict adherence to the principle of sovereignty in its pure form. Respect for state sovereignty is recognized in the Statutes of Interpol (Article 3) but the relationship of sovereign states to the organization is not made

---

[4] See above, ch. 3.

clear in the statutes. This lack of precision may be contrasted with a hypothetical form of co-operation based on absolute respect for state sovereignty called a 'centralized-state' model (fig. 8.1). In this model, a global police communications and administrative facility (controlled through a general assembly and an executive committee and administered by a secretary general) is established by the states to disseminate messages and to provide administrative, research, and documentation services. Its activities are conducted according to codified rules; it has no power of independent action outside the policies approved by state representatives in the general assembly. It provides a means of communication between member states, a data-storage facility, and facilities for meetings, and it can be given a research and training role. All messages to and from the global communications facility pass through national offices set up by each of the member states. There is no obligation on the part of the national offices to ask for information or to answer enquiries which are transmitted through the global facility. National offices can communicate with one another without necessarily informing the global office. Centralized state authority could be further strengthened by making the national offices responsible for co-ordinating information between the various police forces within the state. This would follow the pattern of the Office of Liaison and International Affairs within the FBI, which is responsible for co-ordinating both the American field offices of the FBI and the overseas Legats of the Bureau. An even closer

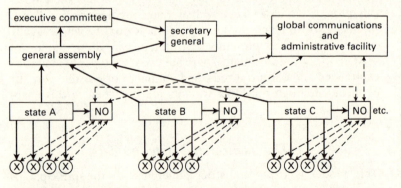

X   Police Authorities
NO   National Office
——→ Lines of representation and constitutional authority
--→ Lines of communication

FIG. 8.1. The centralized-state model

analogy is the BKA in West Germany, which is both the NCB and the co-ordinating office for the *Länder* police forces in important criminal investigations. This system gives the national offices greater scope for identifying cases with international implications and helps to curb any tendencies in the police forces of the country to establish direct contact with foreign police forces. The competence and organization of the national offices is entirely determined by the states but the scope of the national offices is narrowly circumscribed. For example, mutual legal assistance for criminal cases after charges have been brought is subject to bilateral agreements between states and is separate from the police co-operation system.

But the absolutist conception of state sovereignty is anachronistic in the field of policing, as it is in most areas of state activity. The model makes several unrealistic assumptions. Given the variety and speed of modern communications, it is difficult for a central office within each state to retain a monopoly of international police information. In addition, this monopoly requires a common understanding among states about the definition of police functions. In states where police functions are fragmented into a large number of authorities, national offices have great difficulty in dominating all external relations. In developing countries, these offices are often not in a position to supply the information which other police authorities need; in such circumstances, different means of acquiring information are developed—an example is drug-liaison officers from the advanced countries posted in developing countries. In this, as well as in other areas, small and poor states have difficulty in exercising their sovereign rights. In the advanced industrial democracies, where there is a high degree of mutual co-operation and interpenetration of social, professional, commercial, and industrial activities, police co-operation based on a single very simple system, which takes no account of this complexity, will be marginalized. Factors leading to the organizational flexibility and adaptability of national police systems also apply to international co-operative arrangements. For this reason, states are unlikely to agree to channel all communications through the national offices because of the necessity of establishing special arrangements in certain circumstances. The constitutional diversity of the states, the widely varying relationship between the police and the judicial authorities, and the different legal bases of police authority, make it difficult to envisage all states achieving the degree of centralization of police functions which the model implies. Finally, the denial of any independence to the general secretariat and to the global communications and administrative facility assumes a detailed control by the states over the international organization which is probably impossible to achieve.

These unrealistic assumptions do not mean that the official adoption of the centralized-state model as an ideal is entirely without merit or advantage. The clear identification of a single agency in all countries with sole responsibility for international co-operation and communications would help to limit the confusion in countries with either fragmented police systems or poorly disciplined police forces. The absence of any suspicion that police may be tempted to undermine the independence and the sovereignty of states might improve the flow of information. The clarity and transparence of a system based on the model would discredit arguments that international police co-operation allows the development of police conspiracies.

The 'decentralized-state' model

This model is at the other end of the spectrum to the one just described. Its main characteristic is that police forces in different countries are permitted to communicate directly with one another (see fig. 8.2). The informal and unofficial contacts between police across international frontiers which now take place would be allowed and, indeed, become standard practice by the adoption of the model. A semblance of a free market in police information develops; messages are sent to the police agency most appropriate for each case. The national offices still exist but their role is advising police forces about where to direct information and enquiries, acting as a post office for messages, and informing the global communications and administrative facility about arrangements in particular countries. The global facility would be useful for messages and enquiries requiring general dissemination. The national offices and the global facility supply advisory, technical, and administrative support services but neither control nor even are fully informed of the message traffic between police forces. The level and nature of the international police contacts are determined by the initiating police force; contacts depend on the nature of the investigation or the business in hand. The limits of co-operation between police forces could be defined by treaty: for example, operational co-operation beyond the simple exchange of information in accordance with national laws of data protection

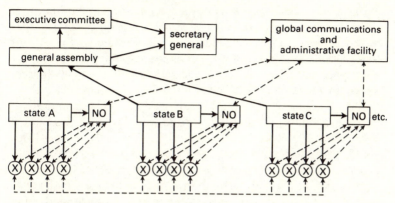

X   Police Authorities
NO   National Office
⟶   Lines of representation and constitutional authority
−−⟶ Lines of communication of police authority

FIG. 8.2. The decentralized-state model

and individual legal rights could be restricted or forbidden by international agreement. The secretary general and the executive committee are allowed freedom of action to make policy decisions regarding the global facility but this could not infringe the liberty of national offices and police forces to act independently.

The difficulties of adopting this model relate to both the sensitivities of states about their sovereignty and the practical considerations concerning the efficiency of a 'free market' in police information. The first implication is that state authority over the activities of police forces may be reduced and that the police may gain some autonomy of action in the international domain. As a last resort, the state could forbid or limit international communication of police information but this may be difficult to enforce and costly in terms of the loss of mutually beneficial services. Governments have become accustomed to the practice of various specialized ministries and public authorities exchanging information either with international agencies or with their counterparts in other countries. However, the exchange of police information is politically and legally a more delicate matter than, for example, exchange of economic information or statistics concerning pollution. In the present state of international relations it represents an erosion of sovereignty and control, unacceptable to virtually all the advanced industrialized democracies. However, it provides a model which is similar in some respects to that which exists within some federal systems such as the United States. If there is further political and economic integration in Europe, intra-European police relations may develop along the lines of these federal systems. Indeed, in Giscard d'Estaing's proposal for an 'espace judiciaire européen' the assumption was made that an act of terrorism should be regarded as a 'federal crime'.

The objections to the model are, however, not only political. An enormous number of police authorities would require near perfect information about where to direct information and enquiries. This could, in principle, be done through a computerized data bank, provided that police forces had the incentive to record the relevant information in it and keep this information up to date. Small police authorities with scarcely any international business and large police authorities with alternative sources of information may lack the incentive to do this. Allowing a free market would probably encourage the equivalent of cartels—relations of trust, common interests, similarity of backgrounds, and considerations of status could establish privileged relations between particular police forces to the exclusion of others. The tendency of all criminal investigators to wish to remain in control of the enquiry and to deal with people on an individual, and preferably face-to-face, basis would also encourage this cartelization. The widespread belief that not all police forces are equally trustworthy could lead to withholding information from 'unknown' police forces in case it got into the wrong hands.

On the other hand, the model could have advantages. There would no longer be clandestine or informal contacts between police, since all contacts would be 'official'. The model embodies a recognition that modern technology makes direct communication easy and that it is difficult to control and discipline communication flows by an authoritative set of rules. Lines of communication could be opened up, as and when required. Police forces would have to become more aware of the international environment and this could make them more effective in combating certain forms of crime. There would be a greater sense of immediacy and urgency if information was communicated directly from police force to police force. In frontier areas such as El Paso, Vancouver, Basel, Geneva, and Trieste, where there is a great deal of contact and a lot of movement across the frontiers, transfrontier police and intelligence systems could be freely set up. But these advantages could only be enjoyed if there was a considerable change in the nature of the international political system, increased mutual trust, and a high degree of harmonization of the criminal law of the states involved.

The intermediate models

Between the two ends of the spectrum, two intermediate models may be called 'qualified centralization' and 'qualified decentralization'. In the former, the national offices are normally in control of all communications between domestic police forces and the global communications and administrative facility, but in special circumstances police forces are permitted to communicate directly with one another. These special circumstances could be defined by states on a bilateral basis and could include criteria relating to urgency, geographical proximity, and categories of crime. These agreements would be based on the belief that the utility of information would quickly diminish if communication was delayed, particularly where two densely populated areas are separated by an international boundary with few or no frontier controls. Agreements could be more effectively monitored by the imposition of a rule that all communications between police forces must subsequently be reported to the national offices.

The application of this model would have the disadvantage of encouraging the proliferation of *ad hoc* bilateral arrangements based on a variety of law-enforcement and political considerations. This proliferation could undermine the position of the national offices and of multilateral co-operation through the global communications and administrative facility, to the point where they could become redundant. However, states have to initiate bilateral agreements and they are always slow to do so, unless problems of a particular political importance occur. For example, in the Franco-German frontier region, a bilateral police agreement had been needed since the Second World War but it required a major terrorist incident to negotiate the 1977 police agreement. The model has, however, important advantages because it avoids the rigidity of the centralized-state model, in which all states are treated as equal and independent. Special relationships to deal with particular problems are a practical necessity and the model allows for flexible arrangements without infringing the principle of state sovereignty.

The 'qualified decentralization' model allows direct communication between police forces but requires reporting of these communications to the national offices. The national offices would also have the right to intervene in important or unusual cases, to ensure that information was channelled in the right direction. The main disadvantage of the model is the high degree of uncertainty about the role of the national offices. Criteria could be established but inevitably some national offices would tend to be interventionist and others not. In highly decentralized police systems the national offices could be marginalized and have virtually no role. Once police forces become accustomed to direct communication with their counterparts in other states, effective intervention by the national offices could become more and more difficult, thus raising fears about erosion of state authority. The model has the advantage of allowing a diversity of practice without challenging the principle of state sovereignty. Those states sensitive about sovereignty rights could monitor closely the external relations of their police forces, whilst those states taking a more relaxed view could leave the external relations of their police forces relatively uncontrolled. The disadvantages of the pure form of decentralization—imperfect information among police forces and the growth of cartel-like police arrangements—would to some extent be mitigated by the active role permitted to the national offices.

Global and regional levels

Two additional variations can be built into these basic models. The first is to introduce different forms of global organization. The second is to insert a regional level between the global level and the states.

There are three basic types of status for the global organization. The weakest form is that of a 'voluntary' organization, in which the source of all authority is the member states; the states make their national offices their delegates to the general assemblies, and domestic police forces co-operate voluntarily with the national offices. The national offices co-operate by sending information to the global communications and administrative facility but are not obliged to do so. The organization of the national states and their relationship with the global facility, which is supported by voluntary contributions by the states, are strictly matters for the states. This type of organization cannot exist in its pure form for any length of time because regular co-operation and payment of contributions create expectations which have the force of obligations. In addition, the global facility acquires expertise and, therefore, authority to speak, through the secretary general, on problems of international co-operation, and its views will influence the membership.

Another status for the global organization is one in which the members agree to abide by certain rules contained in a constitution of the organization. This may be called an 'approved constitution' model. The constitutional rules may be sanctioned by customary practice or national legislation or treaty. They may include requirements to supply information, to respond to enquiries, to give financial support, to participate in meetings, and to supply personnel, although failure to meet these requirements cannot be penalized except by exclusion from the organization. The final type of status is a 'treaty-based' organization with autonomous rule-making powers. The states would undertake, by the treaty, to implement rules concerning matters such as the procedures of the global organization, the modes of operation of the national offices, and data-protection procedures.

An important preliminary in considering the second variation in the basic models is the geographical delimitation of the regions. Boundaries of regions may be drawn to coincide with conventional geographical entities such as continents, or to group countries with a common historical, cultural, or political heritage, or to define functions and groups of states according to criteria such as the intensity of message traffic between them. The first solution, to use the conventional geographical boundaries, seems the least controversial. They cause few problems in Africa, North and South America, and Europe, assuming the continuing absence of most East European countries from multilateral police co-operation. Asia and Australasia with the Pacific Islands cause real difficulty because the former is too large (the Far East and the Middle East would require separate regions and a Middle Eastern region poses the problem of associating the Arabs with the Israelis) and the latter is too small in terms of population. The second solution would have the most appeal in certain regions such as the countries of the European Community and the Arabic-speaking countries which have a common religious, cultural, and political heritage. The third solution is the most defensible in managerial terms but it would create a dominant north Atlantic region. This may not be helpful in combating certain forms of crime: for example, in the field of drug trafficking it would establish a division between supplier, transit, and consumer countries.

The weakest form of regional organization is the establishment of regional secretariats either within the headquarters of the global facility or directly dependent on it, with regional meetings of members usually held during the annual general assembly. Regional conferences of members would only have power of recommendation to the general assembly of members. A stronger form of regional organization is deconcentration of functions or delegation of powers of regional bureaux and conferences. The staff of bureaux would be appointed by the secretary general and together with the conferences would be responsible for adapting the policies laid down by the centre to regional needs and problems. The essential feature of a deconcentrated system is that neither the conferences nor the officials of the regional bureaux have their own resources—these are provided by the centre and by members assuming responsibility for their own expenses.

A genuinely devolved system, effectively a federation of regions or, in the extreme case, a confederation, is the strongest form of regionalization; both policy and administration would be regionalized. In a devolved system, the officials of the regional bureaux are appointed, or their appointments approved, by the regional conferences. Communications are based on a regional tele-communications system and the global system would be used only for inter-regional business. Regional conferences have authority to make policy for the region and regional officials act as intermediaries between the national central bureaux and the global organization. The regional conferences set the financial contributions of the members and the global organization is financed by grants from the regions. The global facility could, in the last resort, be abolished altogether. In this case, the regions would communicate criminal intelligence directly with one another and consult on matters of common interest.

The main drawback of regionalization is that it creates a situation in which the stronger and more effective police systems may be less likely to assist the weak, to appreciate their problems, and to channel various forms of aid in their direction. This would encourage the migration of international criminals and the funds derived from international crime towards the weaker regions. It is also likely that the efficiency of global communications would also suffer.

The choice of options

Each of the possible forms of global and regional organization presents different technical and management problems requiring different solutions. The more extreme forms would not find favour amongst law-enforcement officers, but the choice between them is essentially political. The relative cost of the different solutions enters the political equation although the true cost of each solution is difficult to calculate. The direct cost—the publicly declared contributions by states—of supporting the various kinds of regional and global organizations is the important factor for governments. Law-enforcement officers are more concerned to calculate how costly different forms of co-operation are in terms of the time of senior police officers consumed and the numbers of officers who have to be seconded to maintain the system.

More general factors must be taken into account—these relate to political values and to judgements about political feasibility. There are a range of general positions on these factors. Those who see a weakening of the sovereign authority of states as an important contribution to global and regional stability would choose a treaty-based global organization with effective rule-making powers, and the strongest form of regionalization compatible with such an organization. This is the least feasible of the options because the states are unlikely to negotiate away sovereign rights in the field of policing unless they have an overwhelming, and at the present time unforeseeable, motive for doing so. The second best alternative for those wishing to diminish the states' claims to sovereignty is a relatively informal global organization with a strong regional level. But strong regional co-operation without some treaty basis and some harmonization of criminal law is difficult to envisage. A federal element at the regional level in criminal law enforcement is, at the moment, an unacceptable challenge to state authority involving the possiblity of foreign police intrusion into the territory of states. Those concerned with civil liberties would be inclined to regard any strengthening of international police co-operation, even if subject to rules about data protection and the legal rights of individuals, as a possible erosion of the accountability of the police to courts and constitutionally established political authorities. Fears of an international police conspiracy or mafia with possible authoritarian political implications would be raised.

Defenders of civil liberties have no ideal form of international police organization. They consider that vigilance by civil liberties organizations and liberal political groups is the only way of preventing abuse of police power—in their view, the professionalization of the police, however organized, threatens the liberty of the individual. Civil libertarians would tend to favour a treaty embodying strict controls on police activity, an independent commission to supervise the content of messages going through any international communications system, and strong governmental representation (as opposed to police representation) in the general assembly of the international police organization. By contrast, those who give priority to the maintenance of state sovereignty have a clear choice. They would prefer a voluntary form of global organization, weak regional structures, national central bureaux which have complete discretion about whether to co-operate in a particular enquiry.

In comparing these models with present practices in international police co-operation, it is clear that the 'centralized-state' model represents contemporary arrangements more closely than the others. There are, however, some important divergences between the model and present arrangements (see fig. 8.3). In the first place, the 1956 Statutes are unclear whether the states *per se* are members of ICPO–Interpol, although Article 45 of the 1956 Statutes stipulates that members represent states. The Constitution is not well worded and, for most purposes, it is assumed that police forces are the members. Also, all police co-operation is emphatically not channelled through the NCBs. Diplomatic channels and direct contacts are extensively used. But, the practical implications of the doctrine of state sovereignty in the contemporary world are far from clear. State sovereignty undoubtedly exists as a legal principle, but in the field of law enforcement, as in other fields, adherence to the principle is not the same as having the political power to exercise sovereign rights. There are many examples of states explicitly or implicitly limiting their own sovereignty. For example, the United Kingdom has not integrated the European Convention on Human Rights, to which it is a signatory in international law, into its domestic law. Nevertheless, although it has the power to do so, it does not ignore the recommendations of the European Commission of Human Rights and the judgments of the European Court of Human Rights. Ignoring these recommendations and judgments would bring odium on to the heads of British authorities and damage the reputation of British Justice.

By constrast, countries sometimes refuse to co-operate with other countries when they are merely exercising options which are generally regarded as their inalienable right. A country without the death penalty may refuse to extradite if a person runs the risk of the death sentence in the country to which he or she is being

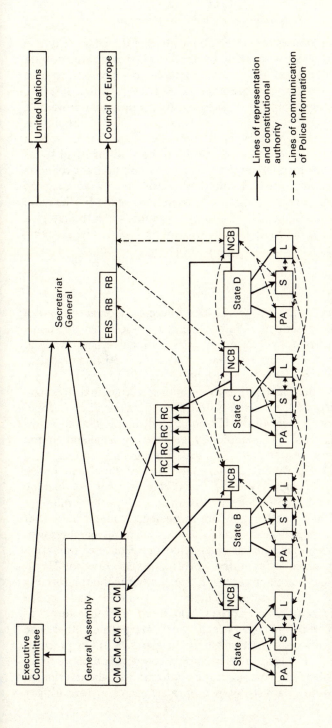

FIG. 8.3. ICPO-Interpol relations with states and international organizations (simplified)

CM Continental Meetings held as part of General Assemblies

RC Regional Conferences

PA Police Authorities

S Specialized Police

L Liaison Officers or police attachés in embassies

ERS European Regional Secretariat

RB Regional Bureau

⟶ Lines of representation and constitutional authority

---- Lines of communication of Police Information

returned or if doubts are raised about whether the person charged will get a fair trial. In the field of police co-operation, the criteria for non-co-operation are less clear but, for co-operation to take place on a regular basis, relations of trust are essential. If police malpractice or corruption is suspected by the police authorities of one country about the police of another, full co-operation is unlikely and even minimal co-operation may be withheld. In both mutual legal aid and police co-operation the sovereignty of states is expressed in practice by ignoring or refusing to grant requests coming from other states. Limitations on sovereignty are accepted when a requesting state agrees to conditions made by the state from whom assistance is sought. For example, a state may give assurances that the death penalty will not be applied when seeking the extradition of persons accused of criminal offences.

Conclusion

The situation in the real world therefore corresponds to none of the models described. Political and historical developments seldom converge to produce tidy organizational structures based on clear principles. The essential features of the existing organization are that the global organization, ICPO–Interpol, has no treaty basis but is recognized as an inter-governmental organization explicitly by the United Nations, by the Council of Europe, (the host government of the Headquarters), by the United States through the 1983 Presidential Order, and by Thailand in the Headquarters' Agreement for the sub-regional bureau, and implicitly by the other member states which allow their police forces to participate. According to its Statutes it has rule-making authority but it is entirely up to each member how these rules are interpreted and whether they are respected. A long tradition of practice has created a respect for them among those members who accept international rules of good behaviour. Police co-operation often takes place without the participation of Interpol Head-quarters: NCBs communicate with one another without informing Headquarters, an increasing number of countries have police liaison officers stationed abroad, and there are other forms of bilateral police co-operation which ignore Interpol altogether. The result is a very messy organization chart (fig. 8.3). In practice, police officers engaged in international co-operation concentrate on the business of communicating information about criminal matters and on relatively short-term activities. They are usually too busy and too much concerned with achieving practical results to devote time to reflecting on the general global arrangements.

Most improvements in international police co-operation have been incremented through adapting to often unpredictable changes in circumstances. The General Secretariat of Interpol is uniquely well placed to consider plans for a more orderly and rational system; the former Secretary General, Jean Nepote, used to do this by keeping in his desk a set of goals for the organization. The rapid change presently experienced by law-enforcement officers working in this field requires a fresh examination of the overall arrangement. The right way of initiating this examination and the effective form in which to negotiate general arrangements are not easy to prescribe.

9. Conclusion

INTERNATIONAL crime poses a major and increasing policy problem for the highly industrialized democracies. There is a growing awareness among governments of these countries of the actual and potential seriousness of the problem. Ministerial statements urging strengthened co-operation are common. Governments, such as the British, which have not in the past been very helpful in mutual assistance in criminal matters are modifying their positions. Douglas Hurd, British Home Secretary since 1985, has, in a series of policy statements and initiatives, shown a keen appreciation of the need for international co-operation. One of the significant indications of change in the British position is the modification of English extradition arrangements, contained in the Criminal Justice Act (1988). By the terms of this Act, it is intended that the simple procedure of endorsing the foreign warrant, without any examination of the merits of the prosecution's case, will eventually become uniform practice in relations with foreign states. Provision is made to dispense with the requirement of a *prima facie* case in respect of Council of Europe states, in the first instance, and with other states, if and when it is deemed appropriate.

However, parochial and nationalist reactions are strong in the areas of police and criminal justice. These are abundantly illustrated by the intemperate British responses to the failure of other jurisdictions to extradite 'obviously guilty' criminals or the inability of foreign police to repress drug trafficking and organized crime. Predominant British governmental, parliamentary, and Press opinion is usually agreed that it is up to other countries to put their house in order and foreign jurisidictions are deeply suspect. Civil servants with responsibilities for police and criminal justice are not likely to be an important pressure for change in these areas and they are likely to hold sceptical views about the limits of international co-operation. But the difficulties in formulating a programme for an improved international system are formidable. They stem from three sources: first, the very nature of the modern state; second, the frequently differing outlooks of police and governments on the problems; third, the unresolved question of how to organize appropriate institutions of co-operation.

The first difficulty, discussed in Chapter 1, is fundamental—the doctrine of sovereignty is still almost universally accepted in the field of criminal justice and crimininal law enforcement. Liberals and socialists, democrats and authoritarians hold the view that the authoritative source of criminal law is the state and the means of its enforcement should be exclusively controlled by the state. Though dissent from this view is voiced from time to time, the nature of the modern state seems inseparably linked with this consensus. The implications for crime control are serious— criminals can organize transnationally without encountering any major barrier, except perhaps the lack of a common language, but the obstacles in the way of international police co-operation are formidable and spring from the basic characteristics of the state system. The purpose of criminal investigations by the police is to bring criminals before *national* courts administering *national* laws. Although there has been a marginal erosion of absolute state sovereignty in criminal matters through developments flowing from the European Convention on Human Rights and claims for extra-territorial jurisidiction by states, criminal justice is, and is likely to remain for the foreseeable future, the almost exclusive preserve of the states. No inter-state agreement yet confers, on an international authority, police powers in criminal matters. Police co-operation must take place within the terms of agreements between states and conform to the domestic law of these states. This restricts the level of police co-operation to the exchange of information and of intelligence about criminal matters, and *ad hoc* co-ordination of police investigations. Integrated police operations are not possible until the theory and practice of state sovereignty changes.

In Europe, attitudes towards sovereignty and the territorial principle are undoubtedly changing, although British resistance to losing frontier controls for intra-European movement of people and goods with the introduction of the single market in 1992 shows that official as well as public opinion is moving more slowly in some countries than in others. At the global level, in the rich countries, as well as in many developing countries, it is becoming harder to defend absolute legal sovereignty and the full rigour of the territorial principle in terms of some abstract entity such as the crown, the race, or the revolution. The most widely accepted foundation for the independence and sovereignty of states is the now venerable principle of self-determination. This principle has become an accepted part of international law with the coming into force in 1976 of the International Human Rights Covenants. The doctrine of these Covenants is that peoples have the right to determine their own form of government; this implies that there is a contractual basis to the state based on consent. But this does not necessarily imply that the contract which binds self-governing communities together requires absolute territorial sovereignty. Peoples may freely consent to the erosion of sovereignty and this has been done in the European Community in the field of economic law. A similar step could be taken in the area of criminal investigation and criminal law if an obvious threat to the well-being of peoples is posed by the international activities of criminals. Willingness to pool sovereignty depends on the serious-ness of the perceived threat and belief in the effectiveness of the proposed arrangements. It also requires what might be called an international sense of community so that individuals consider their civic duties extend beyond the boundaries of their own states.

Some pooling of sovereignty would facilitate combined police operations but would not remove the practical problems encoun-tered in present forms of co-operation. Common law and Roman law traditions and, even more important, the legal traditions of Islam, China, and Japan create differences of outlook, some-times of a subtle nature, which hinder attempts of police and criminal lawyers to co-operate across international borders. Even if misunderstandings arising from these different legal traditions could be cleared up, the existence of separate jurisdic-tions in criminal matters will always pose problems in the transfer of information between them. At the present time messages about criminal activity communicated from one jurisdiction to another are of two kinds—they consist either of suspicions or of evidence. The first may be communicated directly from police to police or via Interpol; the second must be sent via diplomatic channels and verified, sometimes before it is transmitted, by a court of law. Similarly, warrants to arrest suspects must have legal authority in the jurisdiction where the suspect is found. In practice, the red notice of Interpol is regarded *de facto* as an international arrest notice in European countries other than (at the moment) the United Kingdom and the Republic of Ireland; in the United States judges issue warrants immediately on receipt of an Interpol red notice. The general understanding is that a request for extradition with supporting evidence will follow the red notice, without delay. Countries in which *habeas corpus* applies and courts must satisfy themselves by a direct examination of evidence tend to be slow in responding to requests for assistance in criminal matters and requests often fail. Speed in arresting suspects and acquiring evidence is often essential in criminal investigations and the present unsatisfactory state of extradition is a considerable advantage to the criminal operating internationally and an obstacle to international police co-operation. This is not a new problem—it was raised at the first conference on international police co-operation in Monaco in 1914.

The legal framework is crucial but it is not the only major difficulty. The professional and political interests directly involved in international police co-operation are numerous and form a kaleidoscopic pattern which works sometimes in favour and sometimes against more effective co-ordination in criminal matters. Police, lawyers, and governments have inevitably differing perspectives on the ways to improve the present arrangements for co-operation. Within these groups considerable divergences of view exist because these are influenced by different constitutional, legal, and police traditions. Police attitudes tend to vary according to the job that police officers are doing: police roles, police organization, and police training condition the outlook of police officers. Within countries criminal policing is overwhelmingly concerned with petty thieves, vandals, and violence by young males whose activities cause waves of insecurity in the large urban areas of the highly industrialized democracies. For most police officers, international crime may seem a marginal problem, although the trade in drugs has made them more aware of the impact of international criminal conspiracies.

Forms of police organization appropriate to dealing with local crime usually cannot cope adequately with international crime. But the pattern of what is local and what is international is fluid. The emergence of transfrontier football hooliganism has shown how problems, once considered exclusively local, can become international. However, in general, police forces engaged in a broad spectrum of crime control are not sufficiently aware of, and expert in, the problems of international crime; either specialized services, such as the Office of Liaison and International Affairs in the FBI, or an increased criminal intelligence, operational, and educational role for NCBs will be required in the future.

Police officers engaged in criminal investigation have two priorities in international co-operation: effectiveness and low cost in terms of time and resources. In the absence of these, a scapegoat for the failure of investigations is useful; Interpol has fulfilled this role from time to time. Police officers professionally engaged full-time in international co-operation have different outlooks, although there are often sharp divergences between law-enforcement officials at Interpol Headquarters and those who are serving as diplomatic attachés and as liaison officers. They have in common a concern with effectiveness of co-operation, particularly the speed with which accurate information is communicated. They are more continuously aware than domestic police officers or governments of the difficulties of eradicating international criminal conspiracies, of the obstacles to effective co-operation created by different national jurisdictions, and of the lack of mutual under-standing resulting from the different organization and methods of police forces in different countries. Co-operative action between police porces through Interpol often lacks the resources essential in areas such as financial fraud where the collection of criminal intelligence is a lengthy process requiring considerable financial expertise. However, in general, international law-enforcement officials see co-operation as being, for the most part, a technical matter which requires better agreements between states and more resources rather than an activity which has a high political content or, indeed, any political content. In order to keep co-operation at the police level, law-enforcement officials tend, at least in public, to minimize the political elements involved.

Awareness that governments may emphasize political and foreign-policy considerations in all forms of inter-state co-operation has led to a deeply entrenched opposition to greater government involvement in Interpol. This is partly because police officers do not think they carry much weight with governments. Many senior police officers consider that governments of the highly industrial-ized democracies are more easily influenced by lawyers than by the police; they point to the large number of agreements reached for co-operation between the legal systems of the national states by comparison with the very small number of agreements concerning police co-operation. Also law-enforcement officials are well aware that governments have been under pressure within the states to control and restrain the police in order to defend civil liberties. This creates a political constraint which makes it difficult even to raise the question of police autonomy in international co-operation.

Resource considerations often have more influence on govern-ment decisions than the pressures resulting from police attitudes or from the civil liberties lobby. Governments usually respond to demands for increased resources if these demands are supported either by electorally significant groups or by influential minorities. In the cases of drugs and terrorism, support has clearly emerged for more resources and for more effective international co-operation. At the regional level, in the European Community, governments share the judgement of the police that the virtual abolition of internal frontiers in 1992 will pose problems for law enforcement requiring greater police co-ordination. It is unclear whether these pressures will be felt consistently and continuously. Terrorism may wane or become a strictly local phenomenon; public attitudes towards the non-medical use of drugs may change or the system of drug control could cease to emphasize repression. Government interest in law enforcement relies to a degree on crude statistics of crime rates, on the occasional dramatic or horrifying incident, or on calculations about whether populist slogans about 'law and order' will mobilize electoral support. None of these elements is entirely predictable.

Lack of sound and defensible schemes for an improved system of co-operation is a major obstacle to progress. There is consensus, from which only the USSR and some of its allies are absent, about the need for a global system for exchange of information about criminal matters, for a forum in which criminal intelligence can be discussed and analysed, and for a means of co-ordination of transfrontier criminal investigations. These are the services which Interpol provides, but there has been much scepticism in influential police and official circles about the adequacy of the organization; this has not been balanced by any countervailing political support. The most frequent charges have been that the Headquarters of Interpol does not meet the highest professional standards, that the communications system is slow and uncertain, and that forms of co-operation are better adapted for tackling important types of international crime. However, critics of Interpol do not take sufficient note of the substantial changes which have occurred in the organization, especially in the last five years.

The criticism that Interpol, with 146 members, is too large for all but the most routine co-operation has some substance. Regional-ization has been introduced but works well only in the European region (with the possible exception of the ASEAN group). Whether regionalization will, or should, take place under the Interpol umbrella or outside it remains an open question. The establishment in the late 1970s of a secure communications network by the Trevi Group, before Interpol officially took cognizance of terrorism cases, was an indication that co-operative arrangements could, with relative ease, be set up outside the Interpol framework. This may be an augury, if further progress is made towards European unity. Some kind of European Community law-enforcement facility will be necessary, although enhanced bilateral police communications and co-operation may be the initial response to the single market in 1992. Interpol could be marginalized in the development of European police co-operation for three main reasons. First, aspiration to a distinctive political identity for the European Community will be a pressure to create a form of police co-operation exclusive to the Community. Second, there will be a reluctance to put increased resources into both Interpol and a European police agency. Third, the same senior police officers are likely to be involved in both forms of organization: since most of their business will be intra-European, there will be a tendency to concentrate on the specifically European form of co-operation. The risk may never materialize if the present effort to create an effective European regional entity within Interpol is successful and if it is recognized to be so by police forces and governments. However, strong Interpol regional organization in Europe could be a problem for the organization itself because the arrangements for Europe could differ substantially from those applicable to the rest of of world.

In many areas of the world strengthened bilateral police co-operation is a basic requirement. Sending messages via Interpol, attending occasional meetings to discuss criminal intelligence, and cementing personal relations at the annual General Assembly is not enough to cope with the police problems of densely populated and closely associated neighbouring countries. In these circumstances, direct police-to-police communications, face-to-face relations between police officers, and co-ordinated operations are increasingly important in crime control. The present network of bilateral relations is loosely organized and sometimes chaotic. Co-operation through diplomatic attachés has an impressive appearance but is of very varied effectiveness in dealing with case-related business. It is also asymmetrical—the United States probably has too many and the European countries far too few law-enforcement attachés. Apart from case-related work, especially in drugs and customs work, there is considerable value in having permanent liaison officers, with or without diplomatic status, posted abroad. The presence of a foreign police liaison officer who is personally known to the major law-enforcement agencies can greatly help mutual understanding. The *modus operandi* of foreign police forces are often misunderstood and some Press reporting is not helpful in this respect; police attachés can play a useful educational role.

Mutual comprehension between police forces of different countries is a necessary but not a sufficient condition for improved co-operation. A more transparent set of relationships is also required: the present practice of excessive discretion in bilateral relations is based on a probably unwarranted fear of political hostility. Important discussions have taken place to put some order into the use by European countries of drug liaison officers. A comprehensive appraisal of diplomatic attachés, anti-terrorist liaison officers, and their relationship with multilateral co-operation is necessary. A strengthened Interpol could undertake this task because the organization has a legitimacy based on a long and honourable, if often unrecognized, record of activity in international police co-operation. It is also the repository of scarce expertise in this co-operation.

International police co-operation confronts a difficult problem of legitimacy, analogous to the problem of legitimacy of policing within states. There is always public concern, bordering on suspicion, about the police. This is sometimes justified, because policing involves coercion, a degree of confidentiality or secrecy, and contact with criminals whose outlook values may be contagious. Police legitimacy in the domestic context is secured by scrupulous observance of the law and by wide public support for police action. In international institutions of police co-operation there is no precise equivalent of domestic law; police officers involved in these institutions have little contact with the public affected by these activities and therefore little opportunity of building up public support. But sources of legitimacy must be found in the observance of clear rules and public support, even at one remove, through national police forces and national governments.

Governments of the highly industrialized democracies tend to regard the police as an executive function which should be fairly tightly controlled. This view is widely shared outside government because recent and, indeed, contemporary history shows that uncontrolled and unacountable police forces can produce greater insecurity and oppression than ordinary criminality. It is imprudent and unrealistic to regard the police as invariably benign—they tend to reflect many of the characteristics of the host society. At the international level, the best practices of the most professional police forces should prevail. Public confidence in a strengthened Interpol would only be achieved if elements of political supervision, as well as the already established review for controlling data, are introduced. Both Interpol and other forms of co-operation should be authorized by treaty; what is expected of the police officers involved should be clearly set out. Publicity should be given to all the major forms of co-operative activity: the ready availability of information is the only sure foundation on which to build public trust.

A sound basis for progressive change exists in the well-established tradition of practical co-operation. International treaties on extradition, on mutual aid in legal matters, and for the suppression of certain types of crime support this tradition. Many criminal investigation departments consider routinely assisting colleagues in other countries engaged in enquiries as a matter of professional duty. Senior police officers in the highly industrialized democracies, and in many less developed countries, regard the resolutions passed by Interpol General Assemblies as serious undertakings to be respected, if at all possible. Countries wishing to maintain a reputation for international good behaviour would find it difficult to cease participating in Interpol and in other current forms of co-operation. Well-conceived improvements are possible although they require imaginative thinking and political support; both are in short supply.

BIBLIOGRAPHY

ADAMS, J., *The Financing of Terror* (London, 1986).

ALFORD, R. R., AND FRIEDLAND, R., *Powers of Theory: Capitalism, the State and Democracy* (Cambridge, 1985).

ALEXANDER, Y., AND DENTON, J., *Government Responses to Terrorism* (Fairfax, 1987).

AUBERT, J., AND PETIT, R., *La Police en France* (Paris, 1981).

BARROSO, C. G., *Interpol y el procedimento de extradicion* (Madrid, 1982).

BAYLEY, D. H., *Patterns of Policing: A Comparative International Analysis* (New Brunswick, 1985).

—— 'Police Function, Structure and Control in Western Europe: Comparative and Historical Studies', in N. Morris and M. Tonry (eds.), *Crime and Justice* (Chicago, 1979).

BIRNBAUM, P., *La Logique de l'État* (Paris, 1982).

BROGDEN, M., *The Police: Autonomy and Consent* (London, 1982).

BUNDESCRIMINALAMT, *Das Bundeskriminalamt: Seine Aufgaben und Funktionen im Federalistischen Sicherheitssystem der Bundesrepublik Deutschland* (Wiesbaden, n.d.).

—— *Das BKA in Zahlen* (Wiesbaden, n.d.).

—— *The Police in the Federal Republic of Germany* (Wiesbaden, n.d.).

BUNYAN, T., *The History and Practice of the Political Police in Britain* (London, 1976).

CARNOY, M., *The State and Political Theory* (Princeton, 1984).

CASAMAYOR, L., *La Police* (Paris, 1973).

—— *Et pour finir le terrorisme* (Paris, 1983).

CCC, *The Narcotics Problem* (Brussels, 1987).

—— *The Customs Cooperation Council: Its role in International Customs Enforcement* (Brussels, n.d.).

—— *Introducing the Nairobi Convention on Mutual Administrative Assistance for the Prevention, Investigation and Repression of Customs Offences* (Brussels, n.d.).

COLITRE, C. E., 'Interpol: The International Criminal Police Organization', *FBI Law Enforcement Bulletin*, 10/29 (1984), 1–7.

COUNCIL OF EUROPE, COMMITTEE ON CRIME PROBLEMS, *Activities in the Field of Crime Problems, 1956–1976* (Strasburg, 1977).

DEA, *A Profile* (various edns.).

—— *Drugs of Abuse* (various edns.).

—— *Intelligence Trends* (quarterly; restricted).

DICKERSON, G. R., 'The Customs Cooperation Council and International Customs Enforcement', *Police Chief* (Feb. 1975), 16–18.

DUNLEAVY, P., AND O'LEARY, B., *Theories of the State* (London, 1987).

ECOSOC COMMISSION ON NARCOTIC DRUGS, 'First Inter-regional Meeting of Heads of National Drug Law Enforcement Agencies (HONLEA) Vienna 28 July–1 August 1986', E/CN.7/1987/3.

—— Report of the Secretary General, E/CN.7/1987/2.

ELLIS, A., AND PISANI, R. L., 'The United States Treaties on Mutual Assistance in Criminal Matters: A Comparative Analysis', *International Lawyer*, 19/1 (1985), 189–223.

EMERSON, D. E., *Metternich and the Political Police: Security and Subversion in the Habsburg Monarchy* (The Hague, 1968).

EMSLEY, C., *Policing in its Context, 1750–1870* (London, 1983).

FIJNAUT, C., *Opdat de macht een toevlucht zig? Een historische studie van politieapparat als een politieke instelling* (Antwerp, 1979), 2 vols.

FIJNAUT, C., AND HERMANS, R. H., (eds.), *Police Cooperation in Europe* (Lochem, 1987).

FOONER, M., *Interpol: The Inside Story of the International Crime Fighting Organization* (Chicago, 1973).

—— *A Guide to Interpol* (US Department of Justice, National Institute of Justice, Research Department, Aug. 1985).

FOUCAULT, M., *Discipline and Punish* (London, 1977).

GAL-OR, N., *International Cooperation to Suppress Terrorism* (London, 1985).

GAO, *United States Participation in Interpol: The International Criminal Police Organization*, Report ID-76-77 (27 Dec. 1976).

—— *Counterterrorism—The Role of Interpol and the U.S. National Central Bureau* (1987).

GARRISON, O, G., *The Secret World of Interpol* (New York and London, 1976).

GIDDENS, A., *The Nation State and Violence* (Cambridge, 1985).

GOLDENBERG, A., 'La Commission Internationale de Police Criminelle' thesis (Paris, 1953).

GOTSCHLICK, G. D., 'Action by the Customs Cooperation Council to Combat Illicit Drug-Trafficking', *Bulletin on Narcotics*, 35 (Oct.–Dec. 1983), 77–81.

GREILSAMER, L., *Interpol: Le Siège du soupçon* (Paris, 1986).

GURR, T. R., AND KING, D. S., *The State and the City* (London, 1987).

ICPO–INTERPOL, *Interpol—Purpose, Structure, Activities* (various edns.).

IGNATIEFF, M., *A Just Measure of Pain* (London, 1979).

Interpol Dossier: A Special Freedom Report. Research File from Formation to 1975 (published by the Editors of Freedom, 1975).

JENSEN, R. B., 'The International Anti-Anarchist Conference of 1898 and the Origins of Interpol', *Journal of Contemporary History*, 16 (1981), 323–47.

KENNEY, W. S., 'Structures and Methods of International and Regional Cooperation in Penal Matters', *New York Law School Law Review*, 29/1 (1984), 39–99.

KRASNER, S. D., 'Sovereignty: An Institutional Perspective', *Comparative Political Studies*, 21/1 (1988), 66–94.

LACQUEUR, W., AND ALEXANDER, Y. (eds.), *The Terrorism Reader* (New York, 1988).

LAKOS, A., *International Terrorism: A Bibliography* (Boulder, 1986).

LARNAUDE, F., AND ROUX, J.-A. (eds.), *Premier Congrès de Police Judiciaire Internationale (Monaco 1914)—Actes du Congrès* (Paris, 1926).

LEAMY, W. J., 'International Cooperation through Interpol to Combat Illicit Drug Trafficking', *Bulletin on Narcotics*, 35 (Oct.–Dec. 1983), 55–60.

LEES, P. G., *Interpol* (New York, 1976).

LEWIN, A., 'Quelques souvenirs en marge de l'accord de siège entre le gouvernement français et l'Organisation Internationale de Police Criminelle', *International Criminal Police Review* (Apr. 1985), 49–56.

LEWIS, S. S., 'The Marijuana on the High Seas Act: Extending US Jurisdiction beyond International Limits', *Yale Journal of World Public Order*, 8 (1979), 359–83.

LITTAS, R., 'The SEPAT Plan', *International Criminal Police Review* (Apr. 1979), 101–4.

LODGE, J., The European Community and Terrorism: Establishing the Principle of Extradite or Try', in J. Lodge (ed.), *Terrorism: A Challenge to the State* (Oxford, 1981).

—— 'The European Community and Terrorism', in J. Lodge (ed.), *The Threat of Terrorism* (Brighton, 1988).

McCOY, A. W., *The Politics of Heroin in Southeast Asia* (New York, 1972).

MARABUTO, P., *La Collaboration policière internationale*, (Nice, 1935).

MAY, E., 'More than an International Post Office but less than the Myth', *Police Magazine* (May 1978), 49–56.

MELDAL-JOHNSEN, T., AND YOUNG, V., *The Interpol Connection: An Enquiry into the International Criminal Police Organization* (New York, 1979).

NAPOMBEJRA, B., 'L'Évolution de la Coopération internationale de police', thesis (Strasburg, 1975).

NATIONAL COMMISSION ON LAW ENFORCEMENT AND SOCIAL JUSTICE, *Interpol: Facts vs. Fallacies: A follow-up to the Investigation by the US General Accounting Office 1976* (Toronto, 1977).

NEPOTE, J., 'International Crime', *Police Journal* (Jan. 1967).

NOBLE, I., *International Crime Fighter* (New York and London, 1975).

PAIKIN, L., 'Problems of Obtaining Evidence in Foreign States for Use in Federal Criminal Prosecutions', *Columbia Journal of Transnational Law*, 3/2 (1984), 233–71.

PEZARD, A., 'L'Organisation Internationale de Police Criminelle', *Annuaire français de droit international* (1964).

POGGI, G., *The Development of the Modern State* (Stanford, 1978).

RANELAGH, J. *The Agency: The Rise and Decline of the CIA* (London, 1986).

SCHWITTERS, B., *Dossier Interpol* (Amsterdam, 1978).

SEAGLE, W., *The History of Law* (New York, 1946).

SICOT, M., *A la Barre de l'Interpol* (Paris, 1961).

SIMPSON, J. R., 'Interpol—Dedicated to Survival', *Police Chief* (June 1984), 31–4.

SLOMANSON, W. R., 'Civil Actions against Interpol—A Field Compass', *Temple Law Review* 57/3 (1984), 553–600.

SODERMAN, H., *A Policeman's Lot* (New York, 1956).

STOFFELIN, P., 'Terrorism, Arms Trade, Europol', *Forum*, 3–4 (1986), 2–3.

THOMPSON, E. P., *Writing by Candlelight* (London, 1980).

TULLET, T., *Inside Interpol* (London, 1963).

TVI STAFF, 'Interpol's Response to Terrorism', *Terrorism, Violence, Insurgency Journal* (summer 1985), 3–13.

UNDND, *Publications Relating to International Drug Control* (Vienna, 1987).

US DEPARTMENT OF JUSTICE, *Annual Reports of the Attorney General of the United States, The FBI's Mission* (Washington, n.d.).

—— *Interpol: Global Help in Fight against Drugs, Terrorists, Counterfeiters*, National Institute of Justice (Washington, 1985).

VALLEIX, C., 'Interpol', *Revue générale de droit international public*, 3 (1984); repr. in *International Criminal Police Review* (Apr. 1985), 90–107.

WIEDMER, J., *Interpol-Fälle. Falschgeld, Checkfäschung, Rauschgift. Ein Tatsachenbericht* (Berne, 1969).

WILKINSON, P., 'European Police Cooperation', in J. Roach and J. Thomaneck (eds.), *Police and Public Order in Europe* (Beckenham, 1985).

WILSON, J. Q., *The Investigators: Managing FBI and Narcotics Agents* (New York, 1978).

INDEX

Scandinavia:
  and drugs trafficking 125
  influence on co-operation 7–8
  see also Sweden
Sceryari, Mahmoud 146
Schengen agreement 24
Schleyer, Hans Martin 136,
  158
Schmidt-Nothen, Dr 86
Schober, Johann 39, 40, 91
Seagle, William 27 and n. 18
secretariats, regional 179–80
security services 1, 5–6
  see also CIA
self-determination 187–8
Senegal, police riots 18
SEPAT plan 118 and n. 12, 170
Shanghai Convention 106
Shengen agreement 157
Sicot, Marcel 43–4 and n. 13, 48,
  51, 53, 68, 75
Simpson, John 94, 95
Single Convention on Narcotic
  Drugs 111
social welfare 21
  international policing and 22
  treaties/convention on 23
Soderman, H. 40 and n. 8
Soviet Union:
  and co-operation 8
  and drug trafficking 50
  and information exchange 50,
    191
  and Interpol 50–1
  Okhrana 148
  responsibility for terrorism 128–9
Spaak, Paul-Henri 69
Spain:
  and drugs: amounts seized 107;
    attitude to abuse of 109;
    trafficking 90
  GAL 135
  Guardia Civil 6
  law enforcement reforms 89–90
  NCB 90
  police academy 5
  requests for assistance 21–2
  and terrorism 90, 132; and ETA
    134–5
  Trevi and 90

state sovereignty on law enforcement 182–4; model for 171 ff.,
  181–2; removing barriers to
  187 ff.
  decentralized-state difficulties,
    175
  infringements of 13–14
  limitations of 1, 105
  and police: behaviour of 4;
    monitoring external relations
    178
  theories and policing 15–17
  see also self-determination
STCIP:
  IIP conferences 155
  services 154
Steinberg v. *International Criminal
  Police Organization* 63
Stiener, Richard 83, 84
Surinam, drug problems in 110
surveillance 1
  electronic devices seminars 51
  on Franco-German border 158
  limits on techniques 141
  removal of frontiers and 30
  reporting agreement 151
SWAP 119
Sweden:
  and drugs convention 116
  and international crime 91
  and Interpol 65
  NCB 82, 86, 87
Syria:
  breaking relations with 132
  and terrorism 129–30

Taiwan, and Interpol 46
tax evasion/fraud 24, 27
TCCE 170
TECS 85
telecommunications 81
  Caribbean 112; funding 70
  encrypting system 119
  European use of 89
  participation in: inadequate 52;
    members 81
  seminars on 51
terrorism 27–8, 33, 127 ff.
  agreements: bilateral 134–6;
    Hillsborough 132